Life&Fable

A life story

Guislaine Vincent de Damas

LEAF BY LEAF

Published by Leaf by Leaf
an imprint of Cinnamon Press,
Lytchett House, 13 Freeland Park, Wareham Road, Poole, Dorset, BH16
6FA
www.cinnamonpress.com

The right of Guislaine Vincent Morland to be identified as author of this
work has been asserted by her in accordance with the Copyright, Designs and
Patent Act, 1988. © 2026 Guislaine Vincent Morland.
Print Edition ISBN 978-1-78864-866-0
British Library Cataloguing in Publication Data. A CIP record for this book
can be obtained from the British Library.

In the EU, we are fully compliant with GPSR (General Product Safety
Regulation). Our EU GPSR Authorised Representative, via Inpress Books, is
LOGOS EUROPE, 9 rue Nicolas Poussin, 17000, LA ROCHELLE, France
E-mail: Contact@logoseurope.eu

Designed and typeset in Adobe Garamond Pro by Cinnamon Press.
Cover Design Adam Craig from original artwork by Consuelo Child-Villiers,
photographed by Ekaterina Kuzminova. Author photo by Ekaterina
Kuzminova.

Cinnamon Press is represented by Inpress.

The quotation from *Civilization in Transition The Collected Works of C.G.
Jung Volume 10* is by permission of Harper Collins UK. Reproduced with
permission of the Licensor through PLSclear.

The poem on p.192 is by Stephen Crane, from *The Black Riders,* first
published in 1895, Copeland and Day.

CONTENTS

À PROPOS   11

Part One: New York, Belem, London, Paris, New York, Madrid, Andraitx, Strasbourg, 1944-1959

Red Lizard High-heeled Shoes   15

Talking About Cats   17

Ça S'appelle Jazz   19

Jazz, Encore   22

Unlocking A Secret   25

God Upside Down In Tarte Tatin   27

The Taste Of Capers   34

Butterfly Wings, Flutter   41

In Love With Spain   45

The Sound Of Tram Wheels   50

This Is Where I Live   57

Happiness Si Dios Quiere   62

What's It Like To Live In One Place For Years?   78

Conversation At The Dressing Table   82

Lolita Is A Spanish Name   85

The Taste Of Latin   87

Unter Der Linden   90

Under The Lamplight   96

Dancing In Circles   100

Routine Is A French Word For …   105

It's Rude To Stare At Ruins   114

Part Two: Paris, Maidenhead, New York, Quito,, Geneva, London 1960-1972

Kicking The Conkers   125

Learning To Steal   129

In Between Times   132

The World I See   135

The Full Catastrophe   153

When Life Walks In Looking Like An Englishman   166

Part Three: Two Marriages, Seventeen Changes of Address 1972—

Heads In Buckets   173

Grit In The Oyster   184

A Rose Is A Daisy Is A Rose   193

What Do You Do In A Convent?   201

The Agony Of Healing   212

Bitterness   216

The Upper Air, There The Labour Lies   221

Myth Lends A Hand   229

Echoes Across The Divide   232

The Thing About Trees   240

On The Road To Damascus   243

The Familiar Unknown   258

Endings   274

Christmas   285

Jung   289

No Name To Be A Witch Is Not A Willed Thing   292

Endnotes   301

Acknowledgements   302

If it is a truth that we create the world we live in, then here is a world as I have imagined and experienced it. Some names (mine included) and places are changed, and the chronology of things is uncertain.

One never knows, do one?

Fats Waller

To Family

to hear the song of the reed
let us turn homewards, friend
everything you have ever known
must be left behind
Rumi

"When we look at human history, we see only what happens on the surface....wars, dynasties, social upheavals, conquests and religions are but the superficial symptoms of a secret psychic attitude unknown even to the individual himself...The great events of world history are, at bottom, profoundly unimportant. In the last analysis the essential thing is the life of the individual. This alone makes history, here alone do the great transformations first take place. In our most private and most subjective lives, we are not only the passive witnesses of our age, and its sufferers, but also its makers. We make our own epoch"

C.G. Jung, *Civilization in Transition The Collected Works, Volume 10*

Life&Fable

À PROPOS

Looking through a turbulence of clouds and skies, and a canopy of swaying trees, down to a landscape where armies of men marching across wide plains, smashing the things that want to grow: The world is at war with itself. Books on a bedside table include *The Death of the Heart*, *A Handful of Dust*, the poetry of John Donne. Up in Harlem they sing *Black 'n Blue*, and *I Want A Little Sugar In My Bowl*, while downtown whitey sings *Happy Days Are Here Again*. D. H. Lawrence tells his sister that painting is a game, more of a game, and much more fun than writing—and it costs the soul far, far less. Piet Mondrian dies before finishing his masterpiece, *Victory Boogie Woogie*, a painting that feels exactly like Manhattan, but doesn't look anything like it. And then it is 1945 and the world takes to drink and drugs, and champagne in the shoes.

What else is there?

I am born a year ago.

Part One

1944-1959

New York Belem London Paris New York

Madrid Andraitx Strasbourg

Red Lizard High-heeled Shoes

New York, 1944

The young woman in my imaginings—soon to be my mother—crosses Park Avenue. Her red lizard high-heeled shoes (remembered, not imagined) make a nice sound, and her swollen belly is big with me inside. A small plaid suitcase with a fat leather handle is ready. My initials have been stamped on the front, same as my father's: L.V. de D., Jr. I am a boy, my mother thinks, so she is surprised when I am born a girl. What to do? Moïse Kisling, friend (perhaps lover), and fellow artist, has painted a portrait of my mother. He brings it to the hospital as his gift to her.

"Name her Loïse," he says. "Same initials as her father, and it sounds the same."

I will look upon this portrait for many years, all my life really, and always it will be this that I love—the art of it. It is my mother, recognisably so, yet also in the realm of goddess.

My mother-to-be is married to an olive-skinned Frenchman of unknown provenance who, at this very moment of my story, is flying an aeroplane somewhere over the Mediterranean. He is a handsome man who stands tall and makes her laugh and tells her stories about his grandfather—enfant trouvé, a foundling in the deserts of

Syria, whose silence about his origins will haunt the following three generations.

It is hot. This day is one of summer's hottest. There will be a hurricane next week that will breathe a heavy heat over the city. The red-shoed girl has just turned twenty-one. Her name is Ruth. But she never liked that name. By the time I get to know her, she has changed it to Thea, pronounced Téa, when we live in cities and countries that are not English-speaking.

Four years before me there came a boy, Stefan. He was born in France, in the south-west town of Bordeaux, delivered from our mother's womb during the bombardment of June 1940. Ruth, seventeen years old, had puerperal fever—a devastating disease potentially life-threatening to both mother and child. German troops entered the town and two days later, with hospital nuns bustling about in some urgency, the babe was wrapped up and carried out on his mother's back.

Ruth makes her way out of France, walking across the Pyrenees. Her (first) husband, a white Russian, is an apatride—without papers—whom she has married in a spirit of wartime camaraderie, not love. A French peasant hands over the young family to a Spanish peasant who, in turn, guides them on across Spain into Portugal. On the boat to New York City, by way of Argentina—the safest sea-route in those times—Ruth's husband, Szevolod, introduces her to a friend of his, Louis-Vincent de Damas. He laughingly announces that, of course, she is to be his wife.

"Mektoub," he says.

It is written.

Talking About Cats

My mother told me the scrap of a story en passant one day when we were in Spain. Or was it when we were driving down through France? We spent our lives in cars, leaving, arriving, leaving. She was shifting gears, down from fourth to third to second, about to overtake a very large lorry, when she began—she who never told stories. We'd been talking about cats as we would. We loved cats. And of my father, of something difficult and different about him when he returned from the war. I stared ahead as the story followed the road, fragments lodging themselves in the passing landscape, behind a tree, around a corner, as the story tucked itself away beneath the creases of my mind, forgotten, but waiting.

Years later, I write and begin to remember things, starting with the story she'd told me that day of the soldier and a panther. With only the bare bones of it left, I would ask my well-read husband, a friend or two, if they knew about the soldier who had been wounded in the deserts of North Africa, the soldier who had befriended a panther. Maybe it was written by Balzac? Taking place during a French campaign in Egypt? I summoned my mother's voice out of mnemonic storage, hearing her speak about *Illusions Perdues*, her voice sad. I looked for the story for years. Was it from a novel? A short story? Then, as it so often happens,

I found what I was looking for when looking for something else. There it was, a slim paperback, its very thin sky-blue spine almost out of sight between the hardbacks.

Standing in the doorway of our library, between two walls of bookcases, I read and I wept, wanting, oh so wanting, to understand a mountain range of things.

Balzac's short story, *Une Passion Dans Le Désert*, tells of the wounded soldier in the high deserts of Egypt during Bonaparte's campaign. Separated from his battalion, captured by Arabs, he escapes, wanders, finds shelter in a cave, which turns out to be the lair of a panther. Slowly, he befriends the beast, a female. She leads him to water. The days pass and his wounds heal. There is a bond, but one day, in play, a gesture is misinterpreted. The panther bares her teeth, she nips him in the thigh. Blinded by fear, he thrusts his dagger into her throat.

The last paragraph of the story describes not anger in the eyes of the panther, but only love and the question of his betrayal. As her body contorts in the agony of death, he sees the spirit leave her eyes… and his soul.

Ça S'appelle Jazz

New York, 1946

I'm two years old. Music drifts up the stairs into my room, echoes through the chambers of my ears, waves of colour dance in the air. I'm lying on my back, twirling my fingers and Daddy appears.

"You like it, ma Louloutte. Ça s'appelle jazz." He whistles a tune and sings a few words. "Cest si bon," he says and strokes my cheek the way he always does, then lifts me out of my cot.

I'm lying on my side, looking through the pink and white painted bars of the cot. There is a man on the other side of the window. The longer I look, the bigger he gets, big as a dragon. He lifts an arm, draws up and down watery lines and circles on the glass. It's raining. He doesn't say anything. My bottom lip trembles. There are shrieks and squeals and laughter and shoes on gravel from a school yard below. My left cheek is full of overnight-stored food. I stand, hold the rail. One leg over, toes of one naked foot between the bars cling on, other leg goes up, then down. Out of the room, across a short hallway, turn the knob of the door opposite mine with both hands, entering a darkness. Dots and dashes of light on the walls, on the rug, between the slats of blinds. Bumpy shapes under a white sheet, long hair the colour of fox on a pillow. Warmth, the smell of butter.

"Mmm, p'tit loup," one soft curly voice. Mummy. "Ma Loulou," another deeper, foresty voice. Daddy. He says good morning in English. "No nunch," I say, also in English, my daily assertion of preference concerning meals. This is our language. I know it as one language—I don't know it as made up of many. I don't know why other people I speak with don't understand me. I am lifted. The room goes round, the tops of things and furniture spin: a chest of drawers; a dressing table.

Scarves over the back of a chair swirl and fall behind like ribbons. Back across the hall and into my bedroom, down into my crib.

"Dodo, ma Loulette," my father says. There is a chair in the corner by the window. A dolly there—blue eyes, blonde curly hair, porcelain face and hands and feet. Either side of my dolly are two small bears, one brown, one black. I lie on my back, head sideways, looking at them. The man at the window is gone.

Years later, daydreaming at a red light, at the wheel of my car, something caught my eye. A man up high, seated on a plank against the side of a tall building, drawing circles on an office windowpane. I continued to watch, puzzled, uncertain, something tugging at a mental sleeve. Then, a balloon of memory popped. The light turned green and, laughing, I drove on singing to myself: "The dragon was a window cleaner, window cleaner. Who's afraid of the big bad wolf, big bad wolf?"

*

Like a star looked upon directly, the presence of a self blinks and blurs and melts in the blue-blackness of the night air. Little girl barefoot on a sandy beach, face up, body like the stem of a flower, so straight, vibrating, opening to a night sky, its lights, and a mother's bent face, crinkly with smile. Her upward stance, the open—petal by petal—look of the little girl as her mother says, "Choose your star." So she looks up and sees the very smallest star, tucked in the corner beside the Big Bear constellation.

"That's where I am going to live," the little girl says. So she climbs up onto the Bear's back and together they ride the dark hills of the sky.

The nightingale sang all night long.

Jazz, Encore

Manhattan, 1948

City on heat, skyline of cigarettes and ice cream cones. City of corridors and narrow skies. Grand Central Station, underground cathedral. Yellow taxis tiger-tail up and down Park Avenue. White river, black river flow on by...

A room. Summertime, nighttime, windows open. A party. Black man at the piano. White sock, brown leather moccasin thumping the floor. Right hand tiptoes up the ivories, hovers at the cliff edge, runs back down. Little black ants, alive alive-oh. The man at the piano winks at the tall, olive-skinned man with the amber eyes who stands centre stage. A woman enters the room. He kisses her hand, encircles her waist. Drink in hand does not spill.

"Let's make the world go round—war's over!" he says. He twirls the woman in the white dress, willowy folds of cloth billow and carrousel. She's imprinted, and he's gone.

My grandmother is seated on the sofa. Everybody calls her Maman. She is Daddy's mother, and to me she is Ninin.

"Bonsoir ma chérie," she says, because she is French. Her kisses leave damp spots on my cheeks and her arms make a necklace. I return her kisses, and her cheeks give way like little cushions. Her skin is cool, and she is round like a

Russian Baba dolly.

And there is my aunt, Tata Leïla—Ninin's daughter and my father's sister. That's the way it is in a family—one person is many people. Tata's hug is young, teasing, warm. Her skin is olivey and she smells of flowers. I like the way she plays with my hair, twirling, soothing.

"Mmm, c'est du bonbon, ça."

She murmurs a cooing sound, like the doves in Brazil because that is where she lives.

"*Vipers' Drag*," Tata says, "écoute, ma Poossinette." She says it's my favourite. I stop crying as soon as it plays.

Tata is seventeen, married to a colonel in the Brazilian air force and when they speak together their Brazilian language makes caresses and short, breathy, chewable parcels of air. Tata kisses me on the cheek, on the neck, lips sliding to where jawbone meets earlobe. I love that place.

"Donde esta mio Daddy?" I ask.

"Over there," she says, "Mira, aqui viene tu Papazinho, vamos bailar!"

Her arm curves through a foreverness of space. My eye follows the ruby-red arrows on the tips of her fingers. Her brother waves. Here he comes, it's Daddy! He tugs my left ear, a gold coin appears between thumb and forefinger. His name is Louis. In English I am Loïs, and sometimes my mother calls me Petit Loup. In French I am Loïse with an 'e' at the end, pronounced almost the same as Daddy's name.

Standing in the doorway, arriving a little late is a freckled girl of a woman. Her gaze seeks a way round the forms and faces of the figures in the room. She is shy, and wild. She picks up a drink, gives the bartender a heartrending smile and just as he begins to dream of spending his life with her, she walks away towards the windows at the far end of the room.

Someone calls: "Thea! Where have you been?" She dances, her movements singular, unpredictable, off the beat. Men watch, admire, but the dance is of her invention and—sensing an invisible but palpable presence of something other, untamed and fiercely private—they stay back.

My mother. A creature whose beauty, like that of the panther, is shy, alone, always on the move. I look for a memory of her in those times, but her form does not appear in my imagination until I am five or maybe six years old. The first memory is of freckled legs running by and her sweet voice talking about poor poor Desdemona, her husband so mean, while in the background Verdi's *Othello* plays. Only when I am eight will I see the 'all' of her. Yes, there she is! Waving from the roof of a long and low white airport building—her face, her beloved face, appears and shimmers like heat on the road which vanishes when you are near.

"We're going to live in London," she says on another day.

Taxis and aeroplanes.

The nightingale sings all night long.

Unlocking A Secret

It's with me in her belly and a different husband that Thea will change her name, write her first book, *Honeymoon in Hell*, and leave Stefan, her first-born, when four years old, in the care of a Benedictine orphanage in Boston. Such information remains locked in her body, what is called cellular memory—psyche/soma. She will never speak of it. It's in my writing of this book, now, that I stop mid-sentence… catch my breath… it comes to me as I'm counting on my fingers:

Stefan was four when left in the orphanage.

His date of birth: June 1940.

My date of birth, August 1944.

My father's jealous temperament, his violence when he discovers Thea has been unfaithful. Perhaps he was unable to accept another man's son.

My mother couldn't cope.

It all comes together—I see it, I imagine it. How being with child awakens her body's memory to giving birth at war. Bombs. Escape over the Pyrenees. The trauma, unspoken, without air, cannot heal. I am so sorry. For her, for me, for my brother, for us all. No more blame. Not interesting.

Stefan and I will meet when we are, respectively, nineteen and fifteen. We talk and tell stories, and learn about each other, and share meals, and go out dancing. We're attracted in a way that feels both familiar and forbidden. But soon the buzz between us levels out. Sometime later, when we are both in our fifties, I ask about the orphanage.

He remembers the nuns. "They were nice people."

He speaks without hesitation, without bitterness, though after a pause he adds that three years was a long time. His father had remarried, telling his new wife while on honeymoon that he had a son. Jean, Stefan's stepmother, is outraged—she had quite a temper, apparently. Breaking off the honeymoon, she takes off for Boston and whisks her stepson out of the convent. She has three children of her own and all are brought up together in one house, in one town. Stefan is not an angry man. He has the quickness, the almost fly-away lightness of our mother, and a nervous gut which has plagued him for years.

One day, in his sixties, an artistic streak burst out of him while staring out of a window at autumn leaves. He began to see as never before. He started to paint watercolours in the naïf way that evoked Thea's style. Stefan speaks of Thea as 'Mummy', and his stepmother as 'Mom'. When he smiles it's contagious, warm—you want to hug him, but you don't because you sense he'd be startled. He's growing a prize pumpkin, he told me the other day.

"My giardini," he says, and takes me down a secret path to a vegetable patch. He is proud of his tomatoes and carrots. There is a small plaque to his father, hidden between shrubs, nailed to a small boulder on the edge of the water.

"A secret," he says, his hand on a leafy branch, himself having been our mother's best kept secret.

"I love secrets."

God Upside Down In Tarte Tatin

London/Paris, 1949

One afternoon, home from school, my mother is doing up the buttons of my dark blue velvet dress, the one with the floppy lace collar. We are living together again.

"Your father is coming to visit," she says. "He's living in Paris now. Not far away like before."

Somersault in my tummy.

"He's coming to take you out," my mother continues. "You like the movies, don't you, Petit Loup?"

Yes, I remember afternoons with Daddy at the movies—people tap dancing, skedaddling through doorways, throwing hats up in the sky. I remember when Daddy held my hand and we skipped one foot on, one foot off, the pavement. I remember how Daddy whistled Sidney Bechet's *Petite Fleur*, and said my Mummy is his Fleur Bleue. I remember sitting on the bus and how he jiggled and neighed, "Hi-yo Silvaah!" and I'm all mixed up with longing and happiness.

"Probably somewhere smart for tea afterwards," my mother continues as she reaches the last button, doing up my coat. There is something odd in her voice, thick and sticky like a cobweb.

"Don't be late, will you, Loïs? School in the morning.

Tell your Daddy that you get tired. He's never tired so he won't think of it."

I am standing at the bottom of the stairs, coat on, waiting. I look up and see, as through a doll's house, the tiny landing at the top and an open doorway into my mother's study and there my father's trousered legs standing at her desk. There is a shuffling and rifling of papers. A drawer opens, a drawer closes.

He skips down the stairs singing, "It's just one of them things"—then we're outside, hand in hand, skipping, singing, "Oh just one of those sweet things." On the street corner he steps off the curb, sticks two fingers between his lips and whistles. A taxi swerves out of the traffic like a fish hooked on a line.

My father leans in the driver's window and, in his mock English gentleman's accent, says, "To the airport, old boy." He lifts me up and over the running board of the black taxi cab,

"H-opp, ma Loulou," he says. He has my passport in his hand, and says "Sssh," and makes a face, with a finger on his lips.

"Daddy is going to fly and you will be Daddy's co-pilot. We're going to Paris."

This is one of my father's favourite stories. He calls it, 'The rescue of my little girl'. Years later, someone refers to it as 'the kidnap'. It is a shock to hear the word as I'd never connected it to my memory of the story. Only then do I feel a thump in my chest and tears welling. I found a letter my mother wrote to my grandmother, her mother-in-law, dated soon after we'd settled in London. She writes of being concerned about my nervousness, how much I cry about nothing and asks that my father stay away a while until I am settled in our new home. Another letter, after the kidnap, talks about how I liked things to be tidy and how upset I would have been to be without toothbrush, clothes, books, and beloved teddy bear—the one thing that was always there throughout all of our travels.

It was just before she died that my grandmother gave me a box of such letters.

"You will understand, ma chérie." And I did. I asked my father not to tell that story anymore. With a pretend innocence he professed not to understand, but he never did tell the story of 'The rescue of my little girl' again.

I don't know where I am. Always moving, always movement. Rooms, places, houses, apartments, cities—their names change, but it's all the same somehow. Today it's my day out from Dupanloup, my new school. I've forgotten London, the name of my English school, the one in the mews next to my grandmother Moko's street, when Mummy and I started living together.

At Dupanloup, a convent school, a young novice says, "Je suis Soeur Elise."

I know I should curtsy. "Oui, Ma Soeur."

At night, uncoiffed, Soeur Elise lets me brush her long hair. The shape of her head imprints itself in my picture-mind with each movement of my hands, one brushing, one smoothing. I love this person. In the evenings, together we kneel, elbows on the bed. She talks about the soul. I must listen to how it moves between my bones, she says. Looking up, Soeur Elise talks to Le Bon Dieu who, she informs, is always there.

I look up at the ceiling.

In the mornings we walk down the long stone hall to the kitchen in silence. Only footsteps speak of our existence. I like hearing footsteps: "You-me you-me you-me," they say. In chapel, we draw the sign of the cross over our faces with drops of water on our fingertips. We prepare meals and eat together in silence, which makes the food taste better. In the afternoons we peel apples, plunge our hands deep in flour, clouds rising up into our nostrils. We make upside-down Tarte Tatin. I meet the Mother Superior, Ma Mère, and early in the mornings there is a priest whom I am to address as Père. Both are old and speak slowly and move quietly. The silence here is nice. I like it, like a person.

My father takes me out on a Sunday afternoon.

"Ho-ld on," he says. The car jumps ahead like a horse at the starting line. Click.

A man on the radio announces, "And he-re is BENNY Goodman with a STRING OF PEARLS!" We drive to the airport. This one is small, and there's a white plane poised on the ground like a stick insect.

Bits of Paris fill the two rings of a figure of eight. The line of the horizon tips up and tips down, drawing an X in the sky.

"Loop the loop. Hombre!" Daddy cries, and "laa-zy EIGHT!"

A whiteness of clouds billows past like sheets in our faces. We shoot upwards, and we're a rocket bursting through the air. My father is whistling bits of *Petite Fleur*. He tells me a story—he's always telling stories—this one about the desert and where we come from and the camel that saved his life during the war when he crashed his aeroplane, just like Le

Petit Prince. Our name 'Vincent' comes from the little boy in Damascus who was lost—a foundling with a medal of St Christopher around his neck.

"Like this, see? He was my Grandaddy. Your Great Grandaddy," he says and shows me a small gold disk on the chain around his neck.

Then, chanting in Spanish, "Arriba co-braaa!"

Paris upside down, cows on their backs, fields folding over la tour Eiffel, the tops of the Sacré-Coeur balloon in the sky. Tummy full of sea swells. I'm scared and can't speak. There's a wheeling and a tumbling roar in the eerie shells of my ears.

"Ho-ld on," my father croons and, like a bird folding its wings, the plane plummets to earth, then rises at the last moment, levels, and up into another grand loop, tilting back, back, back. I close my eyes and, when I open them again, we are high up and all around us is blue, only blue.

On another Sunday my father says, "We're going to Portugal, ma Louloutte, and then we're going to New York. You're going to be six years old, and you're going to live with your Daddy. Louis-Loïse. You came out of my tummy. Who needs Mummys?"

Soeur Elise gives me a small picture postcard. She bends down and whispers, "N'oublies pas Nôtre Dame de Paris, ma petite fleur jolie."

I take the picture of Mary and Child carved in milky stone and tuck it inside my missal, another present from Soeur Elise. I also have the picture book of *Les Fables de la Fontaine* which my French grandmother, Ninin, gave me. In one story Maître Corbeau and Maître Renard are in a conversation about not paying attention, and one of them steals a big piece of precious cheese when the other, falling for the foxy charm, opens his mouth and lets it go.

I remember Ninin's voice reading, "Maître Corbeau tenait en son bec un fromage…" and, "Attention, ma chérie, people don't mean what they say when they want what you have."

I know it's important because of the way she says it—it's in her tone of voice. Like a secret..

I collect things, faces, words, voices. I learn to hide my secrets between words and sentences the way fairytales do.

I remember my English grandmother who tells me that her nickname, Moko, is a name Stefan made up. She tells me of my half-brother who lives in America. He has red hair (the colour of fox), he is four years older than me, and his Papa is Russian. I like her voice. I want to rub my back against it. Mummy says that's why cows and sheep scratch against trees and fences. Their skin gets itchy and it makes them feel better. Moko's voice is soothing. I close my eyes and float on the back of the air like a dandelion thistle. Little clicks of teeth and an intake of breath punctuate Moko's speech.

"Up–" she begins, a little puff of air bouncing off the letter 'p'—"Up the faerie mountain, down the rushy glen." The soft feathery sounds of English speech draw a different landscape in my mind's mapping than the French, Spanish, Russian, Brazilian sound-shapes I know. Much white, much grey—different greys, so many greys—and a lot of green. Words meander and run into each other like watercolours. At the end of the poem, Moko's voice slows down to a hush.

"Beware of little men," she reads.

Moko sits at a dressing table facing an oval mirror framed in silver, her profile suspended in glass, pale as the moon. Long u-shaped hairpins make a light metallic noise as each drop into the oblong dish of cut glass, its silver top engraved with her initials. This object will appear one day on my mother's dressing table, and she will look happy-sad when she tells me that this used to belong to her mummy. One coil, a second coil, then an armful of quicksilver falls down her back. The sculpture of her face fills the mirror, hollowed cheeks, deep blue-eyed sockets, ancient shadows under the line of jawbone. Around her person there lingers a dry scent of powder, like pollen.

Taxis and aeroplanes.

The Taste Of Capers

Manhattan, 1950

This is the big room, with the big windows. This is where the black man plays the piano when Daddy has his friends around. The black man's name is Jo. He is Daddy's manservant and my minder when Daddy is out. We play games, we sing, and he puts the white enamel colander on his head and taps it with a wooden spoon and sings gospel songs like 'Operator Get Me Long Distance On The Line, I Want To Speak To A Friend Of Mine' and 'He Has The Whole World In His Hands'. He chases me out of the kitchen and across the hallway and into the bedroom. I sleep in my father's bed on the nineteenth floor on the corner of Park Avenue and 72nd Street.

I'm high up, so high I can see me in bed looking up at me. I'm looking down on the bronze-black skin of a man on all fours over her, that is over me. There's the twist of skin between his shoulder blades, the thick fold of it like the tiger's neck and shoulders at the zoo in Central Park. His thing is out, it brushes my lips, it's mottled-grey, darkish. The thing bucks, rears its head up and down the way horses do. This will lodge in memory—the odd little leaps, the sticky heat smell. It will lodge and it will squat patiently, for years, until finally it bursts out like the deep-sea diver who, having held his breath down in the depths for so long, breaks through the surface and roars for air. My vomit tastes bitter, like capers.

Another day. I am standing in the kitchen, my nose level with the counter, interested in a leather object, shiny brown, plump and soft. Inside, dollar notes. I take some and put them in my dressing gown pocket. My hands hold onto each side of the big armchair behind the piano. My feet don't touch the floor. Sounds are muffled. I know my father is shouting because his mouth is wide and I see down his throat. Pictures inside memory-time shake up and down like bits of snow inside a glass bubble: dollar notes; Park Avenue; Grand Central Station; red lizard high-heeled shoes; freckles and dappled shade.

"Voleuse!" My father says. I have stolen money from Jo's wallet. My bottom is wet, inside my legs too. I can't stop the warm flow. I am being dragged across the floor, bumping into things, the back of my dressing gown gathered in Daddy's hand like the scruff of the neck of a pussycat. Standing under the cold shower, I take off my pyjamas and dressing gown and leave them on the shower floor. I stand on tiptoe. I'm crying. I can't reach the high rail where the towel is.

There is a house by a lake, an island, and a little bridge. I don't know when or where this is. I don't know that a violence has happened in the family, a violence that I will be told about many years later.

One day I will ask my father, "Did you beat my mother?"

and he will say, "Yes, I did."

It was the time my mother had returned to New York, in another attempt to resolve her marriage to my father. On that day he'd sussed out that she was having an affair. It happened in the middle of a grand family lunch. Three generations seated outside at a long table covered in a white damask cloth. Tata Leïla described the scene where Louis grabbed Thea by her lovely hair, dragged her onto the lawn and beat her. She was taken to hospital. After that she left my father, America, and me. She would never set foot on American soil again. That is perhaps when, and why, I was sent to London. I don't know for sure, but memory stores these images until I am able to see behind them. They are gifts, potential insight therein, to be opened again and again. I will learn what the poets mean by there being a terrible truth in humanity—the violence and suffering within beauty and love.

Another moving image stilled from the same period shows my father standing on the shore, left arm outstretched, hand tight on a bow. A wide leather bracelet encircles his wrist. His right arm bends back, tendons and muscles expand rippling along the length of forearm and up to where the skin bulges. Thumb, forefinger and third finger hold an arrow just behind a sawn-off group of feathers of different colours. He pulls back, lets go. A quivering whistling mixes with the beat of wings as the arrow rips the air, skims the water, pierces the surface, and disappears. A snake erupts out of the water in a firework of muscle and spray. It falls back, slow. The arrow topples back and forth like a tiny mast.

I like to peer at the snakes at the bottom of the dry well behind the house. Insects are not to be trusted. A wasp has a way of appearing out of nowhere and gunning for you. It's the unpredictable quality of their presence and the potential for a vicious sting—even when you are good and sitting still. You don't know what their rules are. It's not safe around them. Animals have laws, an unspoken covenant: you be good to me and I will be good to you. I tell animals things, they listen. I see it in their eyes.

One day, the arrival of a big box with mewing inside from a marmalade kitten. A book and a note: 'I am Orlando, from London, with love from your Mama.' The kitten and I are one. He follows my feet in the bunny slippers, and we are attached by an invisible leash as we skedaddle out of my father's bedroom, into the bathroom, the sitting room, the kitchen.

Another day, the kitchen's swing doors flutter behind me, slamming onto Orlando's neck. Tiny strangled screams gurgle like water down a drain. I scream. Jo comes running and, seeing what he sees, he calls out "Mister Louee, Mister Louee."

I'm screaming "Daddy! Daddy!"

My father appears, looks down, says, "Oh shit," and walks out, returning with a small revolver in his right hand. He points it downwards. The orange and white stripes of the tiny body twist round one way, round the other way in wormy spirals. There's a loud crack like rocks exploding. My ears are ringing. Then silence. I pick up Orlando. The furry body lies in the palm of my hand like a glove, empty. Head, legs, tail, hang over the edges of my two cupped hands.

"Here," my father says, handing me a big square of silk, hand-rolled edges. "Wrap him up. It belongs to your mother. Poor puddytat."

He gives me a shoe box to carry to the park, "Allez, on y va. Château Central Park."

I look at the skyscrapers high up, castle tops, cigarettes and ice cream cones, Grand Central Station standing guard at the end of Park Avenue.

"Giddy up, Ma Louloutte," Daddy says. "Poor puddytat, he's going to his secret place and no one will know he's buried in Château Central Park except you and me."

My father whistles *Petite Fleur* and swings a spade, lent by the doorman, over his shoulder. At the big pond, we walk off the path and find a space behind bushes, and a hole is dug out. I open the box, unwrap Orlando (colour of fox), talk to him, wrap him up again with my words inside, close the box, drop it in the hole with all the taxis and aeroplanes. We cover him up with earth and walk away.

A table at El Morocco nightclub, by the dance floor. Palm trees made of paper. I'm sitting on a banquette covered in zebra stripes. A beat in the floor penetrates the soles of my patent leather shoes and rises up and through my legs.

Perona, Morocco's owner, joins us.

"Meet my buddy from the war," my father says, stroking my cheek.

He introduces me, "Mon cher, je te présente ma fille," then, at a change in the music, he lifts his head, sticks out his chin, and winks. "Here she comes."

A black lady in a shiny dark red dress weaves a lazy way past.

"Hey Mambo!" she sings. Pink petal tongue vibrates in the darkness of her throat, skin the colour of plums. Daddy waves his silk handkerchief and afterwards shows me how to shape it back in the little pocket of his suit jacket: open the handkerchief flat on your hand; gather it up from the middle with your other hand; hold it delicately, like a flower, sides flopping; then tuck in the ends and pluck and puff at the rounded part so that it sticks out just a little from the edges of the pocket. Or you can tuck it in the other way, rounded bit down, pulling up two ends but only just a little to make two points—never three. Edges of the silk handkerchief are hand-rolled, hand-sewn—never machine stitched.

Like the tam-tam through the forests and over the hills, music travels across time and people. It throbs under floorboards, through walls, slides under the door, rising high above rooflines, lifting spirits like smoke out of the chimney—connecting, reminding, disturbing, enchanting. Music takes the feet out of my shoes. I lean on the wisdom of songs: 'You're Not The Only Oyster In My Stew'; 'Don't Let It Bother You'; 'Life's So Sweet'; and, 'Another Day Over And Deeper In Debt'; 'St Peter Don't You Call me Coz I Can't Go', 'I Owe My Soul To The Company Store'. My father measures rhythm and tempo in the air, right hand semi-closed, rolling and rocking from the wrist. He walks through the door whistling *C'est Si Bon*, and *La Vie en Rose*. Like a nightingale he trills *Petite Fleur*. They are his songs, they are him. I dance, and we dance, at all times of the day. We dance without mercy. When the sun goes down we dance pour chasser la honte du jour—glasses are filled to chase the shame of the day away. We dance and we are the song, we are the singer, we are the sway of the canopy of trees, Daddy and I. We dance with the winds of the daemons until they are sated, and they slink back down into the night, and we are beautiful.

I live with Daddy maybe a week, maybe a month, maybe three months, when one day he tells me I am going to Brazil for Christmas with Tata.

"Your cousin Miguel is there. You'll go to school together."

Taxis and aeroplanes.

                                        The nightingale sang all night long.

Butterfly Wings, Flutter

Belem, Brazil, 1951

Miguel and I share a bedroom. Sometimes I wake up first and creep out across the hall and into bed with Tata. I go back to sleep beside the warmth of her body. When I next wake up she is still asleep, head under two baby pillows. She always does that. I wriggle up to sit on her sheeted bottom, soft and wobbly, and look out of the window. A fluttering like butterfly wings happens between my legs. Jungle noises: monkeys' wild, chittering, manic laughter; parrots' shrieks; thready whistles; the crackling of big, thick, heavy leaves. I am all these things.

The house stands on the edge of the village with its back to the jungle—white, porched and balconied. Narrow columns rise from ground level to an open gallery that runs the length of the second floor where the bedrooms are. We sit, legs swinging between the bannisters, hands up on the rail, noses between the bars. Below, the brown bare earth of the courtyard is fringed with grasses. Flowers are huge and red, petals hanging out in the heat like tongues. Palm trees stand at messy angles—some short and squat like pineapples, others tall and slim like giraffes, branches laden with bananas and coconuts and dates. Others, lean and rangy, look like old donkeys. The cicadas sing of the sun, and their song draws an arc from the morning to the end of day, and into the night.

A dirt track along the edge of the jungle leads in a straight line made of brown-red earth to a village zoo. It is edged by the Murumuru palms and the Samambaia ferns, and Cabelo de Nego, a frizzy and leafy succulent, tall as man. I love their names and say "hola Murumuru, Cabelo, Samambaia bella menina." Sometimes it can be so quiet you know everything is listening. When the leaves are rustling, though, I know where it is coming from—each tree has a sound that goes with its shape. A corral of huts and twiggy barricades combines the domesticated and the wild—hens and goats with backs like mountain ridges, a sleeping dog, and a fish tank which houses an electric eel. It stares and we stare back at the slithery grey-black of its body, at the flashes of red-green-blue enamelings in the eely eye. The head nods up and down from the mouth of a cave space, drawing an aura like the black headscarf on an old hag. Without warning, swift as thought, the eel disappears into its private gloom.

Miguel and I talk about fierce and frightening things. I want to understand, Miguel wants to know.

"Moi jouer con sand," he says. When I don't agree he says "Moi aime pas toi" in his mean voice. It works every time and I do a U-turn to get him back. It becomes our passport phrase and will keep working all the way into old age.

Miguel's father is a pilot in the Brazilian Air Force. A man in uniform, quiet, undemonstrative, with a certain stiffness and a silence that is sometimes empty, sometimes full. Now and then his face opens into a smile, long as a letterbox. His study is on the ground floor, looking out on the jungle forest. In his dark book-lined room there lives the household pet—a lady-serpent. Her home is a big round basket with a pointed hat at the side of the desk. The anaconda is young, growing longer and fatter every day, and she sleeps a lot, like Tata. If we count six steps, that is how long she is and one day, Tata says, she will grow as long as the Amazon river. One by one, her spirals match the basket's woven rushes—five so far, ten to go. We count them everyday. She whispers and hisses a sigh when night's darkness enters the house, and the salamanders run upside down on the ceiling or down the white-washed walls onto the stone floors.

When naughty, we are told to go to the study where Ana will keep an eye on us. We sit in the corner under the serpent's unblinking eye. I will be taken aback when, years later, I relate this memory to my psychoanalyst, far away in another climate, in London, and she exclaims, "How irresponsible. Dreadful." What to me was beautiful, funny, is now revealed as terrible, covered in darkness. Some years later still, I can look back and remember such scenes in their terrible beauty—but without blame. I cry because I love it so much.

The beach at Belem is as long and wide as the world. Waves high as mountains roll in long and slow, lazy as old walruses combing the sands, back and forth, with their foaming-white moustaches. The sky makes the eyes squint. Miguel races along the lacy edges of the sea.

"Viens jouer con sand," he says. Head down I collect the caracoles—the shells, their pink mother of pearl interiors spiralling round themselves like the centres of staircases. Every day is long and full and blue and hot. The little table under the window in the bedroom is declared mine—the treasures from the beach live there. Every day is the same: school in the mornings; nap after lunch; beach in the afternoons. Sometimes we climb up into the seaplane in our bathing suits and fly away.

Tatazinha—I love to say it, "Tata-djinn-ah"—twiddles strands of my hair. She strokes it and says it's blue-black, like the plumage of the Ara parrots in the jungle.

"Where is Mummy? Can I live with you forever Tata?" I ask.

Tata Leïla coos and murmurs in my ear and twiddles my hair.

One morning, when Miguel and I come back from the little school on the other side of the zoo, Tata says, "Louloutte. Your daddy's called. You're going to be with your mummy. She lives in Madrid now."

Tata is going to live in Geneva. She won't live in Brazil anymore. Miguel's Papazinho is gone. Miguel will join her later and I can come too, she says. For now, Miguel and I will go to Spain with signs around our necks, with a name and an address. We will live with Mummy, while Tata Leïla prepares her new home in Switzerland.

There are stones in my tummy, wheeling, typhooning.

In Love With Spain

Madrid, 1952

The aeroplane lands. The door opens, Miguel and I climb down the steep metal stairs to the tarmac. I feel Spain around me, earthy and warm like a person. And there she is—Mummy! From top to toe I see her, the all of her—legs and arms and face, and long hair (colour of fox).

"Donde?" Miguel asks, turning, searching.

"Look," I say and point, "là-bas, là-bas. Mira, ahí—on the roof of the white building, she's waving, see?"

My mother gestures wildly down at the ground below. Miguel and I hold hands and run.

"Monkey!"—that's me. "Monsieur Moustique!"—that's Miguel. Sometimes Miguelito, because he is so little and stick thin.

My mother bends over us both, kissing and hugging. A bracelet twines twice round her left arm just above the elbow. It has two red eyes and a pointy tail and it looks as if it has lived there forever.

"Dear Snake-y, d'you like him?" she asks, but doesn't wait for an answer. Her toenails are painted red and freckles cover her arms and legs the way I remember from before, always running by. Now I see how more freckles dance across her shoulders in starry constellations. The belt around her waist is black, wide, with a buckle of two gold teeth biting two gold holes.

"So much to say," she says, driving almost as fast as my father, but she has both hands on the wheel. She talks quickly, saying things like "How are you?" and "We're going to a corrida on Sunday" and "Wait till you see the bulls" and "It's your birthday, Monkey—eight next week! I'm taking you to the sea near France. Isn't Spain wonderful, don't you love it?"

Yes, I love it, instantly, immediately. The landscape of flame, the sounds of the guitar, the music, the dance, the language—all are the discovery of a joy that will last the rest of my life. We walk along the beaches at midnight. Miguel and I stay up as late as we like and we collect stars and put them in our pockets and we argue about which one is the best. He likes the big stars. I take the smallest star, the one next to the Big Bear, because it's safe there, too small for anyone to steal.

The apartment where we live in Madrid is on the top floor. The elevator doesn't work in summer, only when the rains come in the autumn months. My mother explains water is what makes it go up and down. Thea—she has asked that we call her by her first name—makes us remember the address by heart: Quatorze Calle Fernando Santo. Maria, the housekeeper, walks us to school, to the Lycée. I lead the way back and we zigzag home exploring different routes.

There is a balcony as big as a room. A parapet, and six squared columns make rectangular window spaces open to the streets below. Roofs and treetops stretch to the line of the Guadarrama mountains, where hermits and bandits live with eagles and wolves. It is the last wild place left in

Europe, my mother tells us. Swifts swoop past, whistling. Summer is as hot as an oven and we pant like dogs. I look up into my mother's eyes—they are so blue, like the sky. I am fascinated by her freckles, the way they crowd especially thick just under the collarbone, where they fall and rise as she breathes in and out. I want to touch, put my head there, count the freckles, learn them—they are me, they are mine, I want them.

Thea has many friends. Ali comes—I remember him from New York because he brought the box with Orlando inside. He looks a little like my father—dark hair, square build, but his skin, his smell, is wrong. He doesn't wear white socks and brown leather loafer moccasins. He doesn't skip down the pavement, one foot off, one foot on. He doesn't whistle *La Vie en Rose*. He talks about books and the people who write books, but not what's inside them. Walking down the street, he lifts me up and swings me over and back on his shoulders. Everything wobbles—I don't like being high up, it doesn't feel safe. For my birthday, Ali gives me a pink sleeveless dress, with zebra stripes on the edges of the arm holes and on the belt. I like the dress—I like the way it swings when I walk fast like Mummy.

And there is Alvaro. Not noisy like the others. He speaks English in a way that reminds me of Moko when she reads poetry, though his words have a different rhythm and punctuation—what grown-ups call an accent. It curves in the air. You close your eyes and can feel its shape. He asks real questions and listens and waits, even when it takes me a long time to find the answer. We stay with Alvaro's parents who have a house on the island of Mallorca, high in the hills of Valdemosa, with lemony trees and a view of the sea far away. We sit on the garden wall. Leaves rustle, hot and dry, crackling like fire. Lizards come and go, popping up their heads and diving down into the dark spaces between the stones, while crickets scratch their prickly legs. Alvaro tells me a secret.

"I love your mother very much. I will love her all my life." He is tall and his skin is a transparent tone of ivory when not tanned. He, too, is almost like my father. He will propose to my mother, and again ten years later, and again another ten years after that, and each time she will cry and say no.

Then there is Alfonso, who has a head as long as a horse's, and who talks, and laughs and talks more, and never sits down. He paces in and out from the balcony, and back in the drawing room, picks up an object, talks about it, puts it down, picks up my mother's guitar, plays *La Rumba des Launes*. I clap in the way Spanish people clap, and I stomp my feet in time and I dance.

And then Dennis, who is American, has red hair and says "Hi!" at the front door, upside down, standing on his hands, while ringing the doorbell with his big toe. My mother writes about them in her daily column for a Madrid newspaper, *Dia Y Noche*.

One day, my mother can't walk. We're halfway home to the apartment, when she must sit on a bench until she can get up again and slowly walk back to the Calle Santo Fernando. She is in pain. She says it is only a slipped disc, but the

Spanish doctors, thinking X-ray treatment is the new miracle cure apply the rays daily and burn her back. I will have the summer term at the Lycée, but then we have to leave Madrid and my mother will go to Paris without me. She explains that she will heal there with the help of doctors who know about radiation. She says she is broke and can't cope, so I am to go and live with her sister Agatha and brother-in-law Edred. I hear the words, or maybe I don't. All I remember is a blank-out, of not understanding, while at the same time it being so familiar: another break; another road; another country; another city.

This aunt and uncle live in Strasbourg.

"There will be visits, I promise," my mother says.

The Sound Of Tram Wheels

Strasbourg, 1952

"Where will I be going to school?"

We are approaching the outskirts of Strasbourg. My mother glances at the back of the envelope on which she has scribbled directions.

"Notre-Dame-de-Sion," she replies, changing gears, manoeuvring the car to a different traffic lane and indicating right.

"It's a convent school. Like Dupanloup in Paris. You remember Dupan, don't you Monkey, and Soeur Elise? You seemed to like her."

My mother turns into a long wide avenue with tram lines down the middle. It's the end of August and I have just turned nine years old. I think of Soeur Elise and apple tart— the Tarte Tatin we made together. I remember brushing her hair. Yes, I remember some schools: New York, the one on 60th Street that Tata always talks about; Belem, the village in Brazil where Tata Leïla lived; London—no, I don't remember London; yes, Dupanloup in Paris; yes, the Lycée in Madrid; and now there's going to be another school in Strasbourg, a convent day school, Notre-Dame-de-Sion.

*

Uncle Edred is podgy, he has pink cheeks, skin pale as sand and hair the colour of fox. He is covered in big freckles—not like Mummy's which are small and pretty. He wears brown suede lace-up shoes, woolly trousers and sweaters with holes in the elbow. He opens the car door on my side and puts out a hand.

"Hullo there, small person. I'm your Uncle Edred."

I look down at his shoes—no white socks, no moccasins, no dancing on pavements.

"Hullo," I say.

"Ee-dred," he repeats, "E for elephant, D for dog."

I look up at him. This could be interesting. Maybe.

He coaxes a little more. "Or you could call me 'Uncle E' if you like, that's small enough even for a mouse to say, don't you think?"

I know I am not much taller than Miguel, who is almost four years younger than me, but Uncle Edred doesn't know Miguel, does he? I reach out in my mind for Miguel to tell him about this strange man who has no eyebrows and whose skin is really quite pink. He speaks in a voice which frays at the end of sentences. Maybe he is laughing, maybe he isn't, I can never be sure. But 'Mouse' I am from now on. Uncle Edred does that—makes up a nickname that sticks to you whatever you do, like a paper joke stuck on your back. And he talks about animals as if they are part of a person, all in one bumpy package.

"There is at least one animal in there," he says now, poking my tummy. "I'd say three's more likely. Some people have whole herds scattered through them." I know what he means. I quite like this idea.

Uncle Edred glances over to Thea who is wrestling with the handle of the boot of the car, pulling out coats and bags and suitcases.

"Imagine that. Scattered, scatty!" he cackles, pleased with his own joke. "All over the place they go. Hullo, my dear," he says, embracing my mother, patting her bottom, taking hold of a bag—all in a chain of movements, oddly, but skilfully, linked.

"You do get around, don't you?" he says, chuckling and ha-ha-ing up and down a scale. Thea very briefly kisses both of Edred's cheeks, not responding to the joke. We enter the building and walk up to their first floor corner apartment where Uncle Edred introduces me to his wife.

"Darling, here she is, our Mouse."

He turns to where I stand in the doorway, waiting for my mother before I cross the threshold. "Loïs, this is your aunt Agatha."

I look at the lady who is my mother's sister. She doesn't look like my mother. I curtsy in the way Soeur Elise taught me to do.

"Hullo, Aunt Agatha."

We enter a wide hall. "And this is Albert," he says, looking down at a big black cat seated by the door like a doorstop. "Pleased to meet you, he is saying. There is another cat about, Victoria, who will appear in her own time. Women, you know."

Later, unpacking, we sort out our things. A trunk has been left in the room for the clothes my mother will leave behind, things she hasn't got room for in her apartment in Paris, where she now lives. I help fold a black dress with a red fringe, a pair of red lizard high heel shoes, castañets, a fan made of polished wood that makes a satisfying 'clack' when you slide it open, a long white satin dress covered in pearls made by the French couturier, Rochas.

Closing the lid, Thea remarks, "Mrs. Mouse—it suits you. Monkey, you do know that you are not their Mouse, don't you?" She sounds upset, even cross.

"Why am I a Mrs?" I ask, not knowing how to reply to her question. While I am beguiled by the title my mother awards my new nickname, I also sense the growing shape of a battle between my aunt and my mother regarding ownership of my person.

Thea answers my question. "Because Mrs. Mouse is a family person and one day she'll have a house of her own and she'll keep it very tidy." For a moment her statement makes me feel promoted, grown-up and we laugh and play our private 'Imagine' game about my husband-in-waiting. (I sense an unspoken but present parenthesis which makes it clear to me that I am not to be an artist or a writer, like her).

We sleep in the room called the Guest Room, which will later be my room. There are twin beds covered in matching quilts patterned with ivy. Curtains framing the two windows are green and white, where exotic birds fly about young men and women in eighteenth century dress. Thea sleeps in the bed by the window.

In the morning she says, "I'm off, Monkey. For now. You'll come and live in Paris with me soon." Opening the curtains she remarks, "This side is quiet, off the avenue. There's a tree, see? Hello tree. You'll look after my baby, won't you? Birdsong—listen!"

My mother's talk of trees and birdsong mixes up in my mind with her talk of Chekhov and Tolstoy and Balzac and Segovia and Antonio Bienvenida, her friend the bullfighter, and favourite repeated stories like *The Cat That Walked By*

Itself which begins, "Dearly Beloved." Mummy always looks up at me when she reads the 'beloved' part. I will think of all these things, holding on tight in case of the next move.

"If there's a tree outside your window," her voice in my head will remind me, "you are safe, Petit Loup. Home."

I have a small stone in the shape of a heart which I found in Spain. I keep it under my pillow. But for now, ignoring the tree, I ask, "We'll live in Paris?" repeating, "Pa-ris," and again in singsong French, "Paris, Paris."

"Yes, Petit Loup," my mother echoes, oblique, hesitating, then quickly, while packing her things, "Oh, who knows. Somewhere…," her voice trailing.

We hug goodbye, and she begins to cry. I stand in my dressing gown.

"Don't cry, Mummy. I'll be okay, there's a tree."

"A catalpa," Aunt Agatha says, appearing in the doorway, "and next Spring, Mouse, you'll see, it makes a long string bean. This is a fine specimen. At least eighty years old. The American variety, you know," and she recites, "*Catalpa Speciosa*."

Thea turns away, looking vague and above it all, the way she does when people go on and on about details, facts, numbers, dates, and Latin names. I feel odd, pulled between the safety of my aunt's world where things have names and numbers—solid and reliable as soldiers with name tags around their necks—and the free-for-all world of Thea, a world that is everywhere and nowhere, where things don't matter, 'not really-really' she will say, because things aren't real when you get down to it. It's all an illusion.

"You can't take anything with you," she says when she talks about Life and where you go when Life goes.

*

My aunt takes me by the hand, leads me back into the apartment. Edred carries Thea's suitcase and bundles her back out to the car. I watch from the corner of the dining room window. My mother's hands on the steering wheel, the gold snake with the ruby eyes tucked around her upper arm. She rolls down her car window, waves, honks the horn twice, and drives off. The small silver car is soon absorbed by the stream of traffic, like a little fish joining a school of bigger fish. A tram passes, stopping on the far corner of the avenue. People step off, down the steps of the middle door, and climb the steps at the front. Cars flow past. I continue to look out the window. Another tram passes, ringing its bell, and the metal wheels clang on their shiny steel tracks.

I turn to the bedroom and make up the two beds just like my mother would say a Mrs. Mouse must do—arrange the pillows and my two teddy bears, the porcelain doll, the leopard stretched out in its lazy position that belonged to Mummy when she was little. I stand in the doorway, taking in the new layout. A wide square hallway entrance, upright piano on one side, rectangular table on other side with a porcelain vase with a Chinese dragon that is very blue, a black telephone beside it, note paper and pencil. Drawing room on the left, dining room on the right. Large square hall. Kitchen. Aunt Agatha and Uncle E's bedroom, bathroom in between. I repeat all this in French out loud, with the address too, to make it more real, so that Ninin and Tata and Daddy will hear me.

"Je suis à Strasbourg, Appartement 2a, deuxième étage." Looking out of the window, I tell them about the big avenue, that I am nine years old (it was my birthday three weeks ago), that I don't have the telephone number as Mummy forgot. I will put it in the new notebook she gave me for my birthday in the Puerto in Mallorca, where we go in the summer.

Aunt Agatha appears out of the kitchen. She stands in the hallway facing me, eyes narrowed against the smoke of a cigarette stuck to a fuschia-coloured lip. I look at her, she looks back at me.

I ask, "Will you adopt me?"

This Is Where I Live

Strasbourg is a meeting place of three rivers: The Ill, the Bruche, and the Marne, which is really an arm of the great River Rhine. All flow, and meet, and intertwine through the town. Water runs and plays at every turn, throwing shadows on the walls. Willows bend over the rivers, paths follow their winding ways below the streets and under the bridges. Cobbled streets wind around and back on themselves, and out again, until you come to the main square where the cathedral sits with the implacable air of the Sphinx and the solidity of the Great Pyramid. The bells ring hollow and deep with cave resonance. Beyond the centre, where the narrow streets stretch out into wide avenues, the wheels of trams screech on their steel tracks.

Aunt Agatha and Uncle E are going to a concert. I'm left in charge.

My aunt says, "You are old enough to take care of yourself, Mouse. Almost ten years old now." She reminds me to keep the bedroom door open so I can hear if the telephone on the hall table rings, and the two cats can come and go. Albert and Victoria are named after the English queen and her German consort.

"Victoria was a bit dotty, you know," my uncle would

say, poking fun as he is wont to do at the feminine of the species. "He was rather a dear."

My aunt will reply that he is talking nonsense as usual, and that Albert and Victoria were remarkable people. It makes me laugh and feel fond.

After they are gone I go to my bedroom and sit on the end of the bed by the window. Victoria, tortoiseshell colour, pads across the threshold.

"Vicky puss, here Vicky." I pat my knee. "Here, pusscat."

The cat approaches, tail upright. I pick her up and, stretching my arms with all my might, throw the animal from me and upwards in the air, across the room. The cat falls on her side sliding along the polished floorboards into the wall. She twists, straightens up and, back on her legs, skedaddles out of the room.

Albert appears. He's panther-black, except for a white dot on his left ear. Larger than Vicky, his form full and round.

"Puss, dear pusscat." He comes up to me, purring. I love him more than Vicky. I pick him up, hurling him harder across the floor, my jaw clenched, teeth biting on my bottom lip which begins to bleed. Albert gets up more slowly, head nodding side to side.

Both cats pad back towards me.

"Oh, pusscats."

I pick them up as one complicated awkward parcel, squeeze them, once more hurl them away, hard, as far from me as I can. They fall, knotted and unknotting, scattering and skidding on the uncarpeted parts of the parquet floor. My bones are cold, like the railings I remember from the garden of my father's house in Paris. One of the cats makes a strange sound, a high question-like mewing. I'm scared, shaking, full of tremors. I feel like a ghost, not real.

The cats sit under the telephone table in the hallway. I tiptoe, sit on the floor beside them, stroke their tiny chins. I tell them I'm sorry. They move away, looking at me from under another table in the sitting room. I feel a little sick, my head is spinning. Returning to the bedroom, sitting cross-legged on the floor, arms in a hug, I rock myself back and forth, back and forth. The feeling-bad moment crumples in on itself, shrinking down and down and down into a little black speck of a thing. Albert pads back in the room, jumps on the other bed, tucks himself into a rectangle, paws under chin, tail round haunch, looks down, blinking, eyes slowly closing. I lie beside him and fall asleep.

Months later, we have moved to a big house with another catalpa tree. Uncle Edred teaches me to dance the Waltz. We stand, he counts. I am to nod and count with him.

"One, two, three… One, two, three… Now," he says, holding me very steady so I know when to follow, and we move and I count one, two, three, one, two, three in an exciting whisper. Round and round. I love to dance. It feels so free—to do and be anything I want, just me.

In the summer I bicycle to school. It isn't far. The new house is in a quiet residential part of town with lots of trees. My bicycle ride goes along a canal and over a little bridge. Albert waits for me on the first corner by the house. Every afternoon he's there, tucked round himself, neat as a finial on the gate post of the high white wall.

*

I'm listening to drops of rain on the leaves of the catalpa tree outside the house, staring at a window full of moon. This is Strasbourg. Thea lives in Paris, in a one-room apartment on the Boulevard St Germain. The window of her one-room apartment looks onto a cobbled courtyard. No plants, no tree. At night this is what I see in the window white as milk, lying in my bed.

"Hear the cuckoo?" Uncle E says one morning over the breakfast table, chewing his toast, "Spring is coming."

Windows are open, the breathy sounds of a car engine passing by, the cawings of a crow in the distance, the double bell of a tram, and from the other side of the kitchen door a clash of pots and pans.

Aunt Agatha lets out her high pitched sigh which means relief. "Ah, Monday. Madame Walter has arrived."

I think about the language of Aunt Agatha's sighs, Uncle Edred's little breathings. He likes to tease and has a way of chuckling when he tickles a person, even when they ask him to stop. And there are his inhalations at the beginning of a story, exhalations at the end of a story, about how a pause between words stretches the words, adding something that is not made of word. Or other times when words fall off their lines, words spoken fast, too fast to say anything that means anything.

I think about how silence can be wild, not private, penetrating, and ghostly. How the invisible thing has a way of haunting the visible thing, like a draft creeping up from under a door. You don't know it, but your legs feel it. Why am I frightened, all the time frightened? Courageuse, mais pas téméraire, my father said that day he took me up in his aeroplane. I think about jazz, the blues, the dancing, and getting away—skipping backwards like my father does, out the door we go with a carefree wave—see ya next time I meetcha—it's just just one of those things. I think about my mother, her softness, her freckles.

I remember the bird I once saw come down the chimney—how it flew around the room, wings whirling like cartwheels. I had called out for my grandmother, Ninin, who opened a window but the bird, not understanding the invitation continued its panicky movements and my grandmother and I sat and watched until the bird, exhausting itself, flew to the back of a chair and perched there, blinking. Quietly, a finger on her lips, Ninin took hold of my hand, and together, tiptoeing, we left the room.

Tonight I will put myself to sleep again with the make-believe when Daddy is driving, Mummy next to him, the car catches fire and they die, and I cry.

Happiness Si Dios Quiere

Puerto Andraitx, Mallorca,
Summers 1953 & 1954

The train from Strasbourg to Paris takes forever, and then I'm standing on the platform holding my suitcase. At the far end, my mother is waving, long and high and wide arches, with a scarf the colour of rainbows. I'm afraid my heart will explode with longing. The sea-wave of hair, the Ingrid Bergman face I stare at in magazines, the uncertain smile. I am running. The brown and black plaid suitcase, with initials the same as my father's, bangs against my legs. We're going to drive down to Spain, she tells me. Three days. To Barcelona. Then the ferry to Mallorca. On the way, we will spend a night at a friend's house, who is an artist. Her studio is above a barn. You climb up a ladder and there, in the studio, she does a quick pencil sketch portrait of me with long hair, looking so sad. Mummy and I talk about almost everything. She tells me a story about a panther and a soldier, and she cries about it. We don't talk about Uncle Edred and Aunt Agatha.

In the hotel bedroom a mosquito sings. I can't sleep. Strips of street light tremble through the shutter slats, making long-pointed stars around the hinges. My mother's breathing is barely audible. I listen for it. She sleeps on her side, her back panther-black against the sheets.

The night brings on the itch I can't talk about, where my uncle Edred's nightly tickling has left an imprint. I long for the touch of her skin. I can't move. I imagine it. Maybe if I move a little closer it will go away. The tickle maddens. I want to scream. Heat emanates from my mother's body and a little of her steam settles on the skin of my thighs. I inch closer. Has she stopped breathing? Is she awake? Can I ask? What can I tell her? Is it safe? I want to bite my mother, like the panther in the story, I love her so much. I move away, stretch my legs back into straight lines, hold myself stiff. Things ache. My right shoulder is squashed. My heart feels squeezed. The tickle runs up and down my spine, like a spider. I want to squash it.

We are up at dawn. The city is quiet and the air is fresh. Ahead, a whole day's sail. The ferry to Mallorca leaves at seven. Thea stands at the rail, an ice-blue chiffon scarf around her neck, fluttering wildly.

A slim, short man with wiry black hair comes up to us.

"Ola, Téa, hermosa. Que tal?"

As the two converse in Spanish, I listen. Picking up the gist of their speech, I am happy drifting on waves of the Spanish language. I have missed it. While my mother and the Spaniard in the black shirt (a bullfighter from Madrid, she tells me later) have a cortado, I go outside to read my new book, *Grimm's Fairy Tales*. It is a present from Uncle Edred. A group of red and white striped deck chairs are left on the small aft platform, their canvas cloths puffing out in the sea winds—they might get up and fly away. I find a sheltered corner and the afternoon is filled with the cries of seagulls. The sea lifts and the ferry rolls on the swells. Thea appears and we walk like drunks to the front of the ship. The wind rushes up our skirts. And then, rising above the horizon beyond the swells, an outline of Mallorca emerges.

We stand at the ship's rail. "There it is, Monkey. The puerto awaits us—Andraitx. See those mountains? It's right behind them." Thea's hand grips my hand, the way she grips the steering wheel.

The man who fights bulls drives us into town. The little grey car, with its yellow sidewings, was his car. He has come to Mallorca for a fiesta week, to fight Miura bulls. We drive past posters of the corrida on the walls of the town, his name at the top: Antoñio Bienvenida.

A blue white sky is a vast dome. The sun presses on our backs like a hand. A little breeze. Long leaves of palm trees crackle. The man and my mother exchange addresses, standing on a black and ochre-streaked marble floor, in the echoing lobby of a hotel.

"Hasta luego, guapa. Despuès la corrida." He adds, "Si Dios quiere." Then draws the sign of the cross and kisses his right-hand thumb looking straight into my mother's eyes.

Now we are together in the street, with bags and suitcases and the guitar—always the guitar—in its beaten up leather case. My mother is negotiating a taxi driver's fare. The cab is old, the paint patchy brown like the carapace of a beetle, and the engine rattles loudly. Inside it smells of feet and old shoe leather.

"Hey ho, and away we go," my mother sings. "To the puerto, owl and pussycat are we." She giggles. Recites a line from a favourite poem, "O catch me a falling star…" Sings a song of her own invention, "Where do the crocus go when there's a frost, where do the people go, when they are lost?"

The road is bumpy and white. "Olives! Hello trees." The air thickens with the muskiness of wild sage. Crickets hum. Thea rolls down her window, and hair blows across our cheeks in little whips. The drive begins along a plain, then enters hills that grow into mountains. We are high up, and the sea below slaps up against strange-shaped rocks. Boulders rise like monuments and little coves are lipped with froth. The road, made of grit and dust fine as talcum powder, turns inland once again, rising in one long swell. We drive through a forest of umbrella pines. There are whiffs of resin, like a lemony honey, and now a wide bay comes into view.

We arrive at the puerto as night falls. Our tongues, dry with dust, stick to our palates. The taxi drives down and along a quay, out of the village, round the bay, and back again. We can't find our address. No lights or street signs. Some doors have numbers and some do not. Shapes and darkness loom.

"Dear puerto," Thea sighs. There is peace in her voice, now she speaks slowly. "Isn't it magic, Monkey? I don't care where we sleep. We're safe, we're home."

Home is two rooms on the top floor of a cube-shaped house with a wide roof terrace. It sits halfway up the hill, overlooking the jetty and the lighthouse and the mountain across the bay. We sit on the roof like Indians—not doing, not saying, just there with the sky. The rooms are white, the balcony is white, the outdoor staircase that leads to the front door is white, and the soles of our feet are white. The parapet makes a wide shelf that we decorate with shells and starfish and tendrils of seaweed. There is no electricity, no running water—just a well in the middle of the house from where we draw water. The door is never locked and the key lies on the balcony amongst our sea mementoes.

When I stand in the sea, my legs are tickled by little fish, transparent shrimp kicking their tails. Sometimes a big fish cruises past. Thea sunbathes naked on the rooftop. I glance at my mother's naked body then turn away, a little shy, but pleased. I note the resemblance between my own and my mother's nipples—the same pale pink of the inside of seashells. Day by day our skin turns more and more brown. The Mallorcan sun imprints a thousand new freckles on our faces and we pad about barefoot like young leopards. Our bedrooms are separated by a small bathroom. I sleep well, not scared, no nightmares, no black dot, no itching. I read by candlelight for as long as I want.

The puerto's one bar and café belongs to Juan who begins every sentence with "Francamente." Chairs and tables fill the space outside the café entrance, leaving room for the evening paseo. There is no pavement. There is house and, when you step out of the house, there is earth. In the evenings, before the sun is down, we sit on Juan's terrace. Electricity comes on for three hours and, in the evenings, we go there to read our books. After eleven he brings candles.

I meet Taddeus—solid as a cupboard, round-faced with black gaps in his smile like a Halloween pumpkin. He smokes fat French cigarettes and speaks with a Greek accent.

"When August comes, I come to your birthday party," he says. I see his words. They have a way of appearing in my head, making a picture. There is the letter A for the month of August, my birthday month. The words wear shoes, the kind Uncle Edred and Aunt Agatha wear, and they tiptoe far away on the other side of the mountains. They say, "Soon you are coming home, home to us, but not yet."

In the evenings, just after sundown, a small fleet of fishing boats rounds the bay. The sea throbs with their engines, thumping in the eardrums like giant hearts. They approach the jetty, one by one, and dock, three of them. Nets of thick twisted rope, dark brown and heavy with sea-wetness, are thrown over the side and land with a hard slap. The nets are alive with fish, twisting and glinting like cutlery. One net, the ropes dry, is smaller and holds cartons of French and American cigarettes—Gitanes, Camel, Lucky Strike.

"Contraband," Taddeus says, pulling pesetas from his pocket.

"There must be a God somewhere," my mother says at the end of dinner one evening. We are on Juan's terrace. The fishing boats are moored, nets empty, spread out to dry on the quay like giant cobwebs.

"You feel it, don't you Baby. You're so wise. It is written, isn't it?"

That's what my father says. Mektoub. I say nothing.

The days turn the clock. We pay the hours no attention. We eat when the mood comes upon us. At table, under a tree, on a café terrace, out at sea in a little rowing boat, each holding an oar, floating about the waves. Our meals at Juan's café are paid for at the end of summer in the currency of my mother's paintings. Or we don't eat because we forget. My mother paints and I read or go fishing for shrimp in the rocks. We eat at noon or not at all or suddenly it is afternoon, and we have toast with the local apricot jam— breakfast at tea time.

Centipedes run across the shiny stone floors in straight lines like tiny trams. Big as my thumb, thick as fur (colour of fox), they run straight for the wall then veer off to run along the wall line. If they ever stop it is a hold-the-breath stop as if deep in thought—they are deciding where to shoot off next. And there are earwigs, smaller than the centipedes but none the less horrible. Shiny as beetles, they rush about off track skidding round corners, and I wonder if it's true that they get in your ears like my bad thoughts about Strasbourg.

Mummy never tells stories about herself, or about me when I was small, or about the people in her life. She talks about ideas and people in books. It's Daddy who tells me stories and talks about how I was when I was a little girl.

"Mamselle Chatterbox, and Miss TeeHee," he would say, and it is Daddy who tells me where we come from. The yellow packets of cigarettes with the camel and the palm trees and the pyramid make me think of one of his favourite stories. Where Daddy and Tata and I go back to the desert lands, to the great grandfather—my father's grandfather—and the time in the war when my father was a pilot, Lt. Vincent de Damas. I remember the part where he says he crashed in the desert of North Africa. He always says that's where he was born, in Algiers, and that he was saved by a camel. The camel kept him warm. He slept lying against its flank, and for two days he and the camel walked until an American military jeep appeared and Daddy got a ride. He tells me he feels bad whenever he thinks about the camel standing there on the side of the road, its ruminating face moving from side to side. He shows me how and I giggle. He didn't think to look back at the animal, to say goodbye, thank you for saving my life.

Wherever he lives, Daddy has camel objects and he always signs his letters with a drawing of the camel with two humps. Later in life, my father will call and leave me messages saying: "This is the Old Camel calling his daughter. He wants to know comment ça va." My brother Lionel says the camel story is made up, not true, but I don't care. It is our father's myth.

Daddy doesn't smoke. My mother smokes Gitanes, but at certain times of the day only, her cigarettes being of the pensive kind. She smokes the first cigarette with her cup of coffee after breakfast, which is late morning because she doesn't have breakfast until after she has finished writing, or painting. She smokes a cigarette after lunch, and then after dinner she might smoke two or three, each to do with a private punctuation, part of a conversation. The best cigarette is the one Thea smokes when she has finished with painting for the day. I can tell this by the way she holds the cigarette, stands back to stare at the canvas and concentrate, blowing smoke out into the air. No one is allowed to look until the painting is finished. I stand in the doorway. My eyes take everything in, everything I will need for later, when she has gone. There she is—my muse: paintbrush in one hand, cigarette in the other, facing her art, gazing at it, intent, narrowing her eyes. I imagine what it might be and something is fixed in the swirls of her cigarette smoke.

"Oh, Baby," she sighs, and for a moment her face darkens. "Life is strange." She murmurs about a falling star and child with mandrake root and that her father, who died last year, died too soon, before she could ask him the many things that start with 'why?' At dinner, pouring wine into my glass with a dash of water, she laughs, "Hey ho, life is magic. Vino para ti, Monkey. What the hell, life's too short."

Thea picks up her guitar, leaning over the stret, hair falling over her face, left hand with signet ring on little finger, strumming an idea for a song. A conversation begins—with the moment, with the music, with me. There is the warmth of presence around us, and the light of candles flickers against the blue night air.

We make up little Spanish phrases, using favourite words like 'francamente' and 'buenas', stretching the 'a' in the nasal way of the Mallorquins. We get skittish and flare a scarf as big as a cape, chanting 'Olé!' and daring the horns of life ahead of us. We talk about tomorrow, and death, and men, and the people we know, and the people she loves best, who live on the pages of books. Chekhov, always Chekhov. Or we speak in French, but she has a little accent and something of us is lost. We don't come from the same place anymore, we are apart. With Daddy there is no difference. We are the same whatever language we speak—English, French, Spanish, or the mix of all three. Or any of our other pretend-languages made of bits of Russian, Brazilian, German.

She speaks of Russia as the soul of Europe, and a little about the war, and of something broken that cannot be put back together. Then her face turns inward, "Oh, we'll never get to Moscow." This is a familiar refrain. I know what she is saying by the tone of her voice, though I don't know where it comes from until one day at the theatre I hear it spoken by actors on stage and I want to call out to them. "No! those words belong to me, give them back."

I learned to make my way along my mother's frontiers. I

learned how the line between my mother's country, and my own country, was not so much a border as a divide, growing wider as the years went by. What had happened in my mother's country, the fluctuations of its strange and unpredictable climate, accidents and fortunes unknown, could not be shared. That we were never able to live together until it was too late could not be spoken of. And I, too, learned to keep the goings on inside me, and my country, silent. This gap—of emptiness, not even an ocean—left us nothing to navigate with, nothing for us to get a hold on.

About once a fortnight we go to Palma on the old creaky bus with the ladder up its backside. We make a beeline for the American Library, a small house on a square where one large room is given over to bookshelves of light grey metal. The books—which smell of vanilla and salt—are covered in a linen cloth on which titles and authors' names are inscribed in handwritten black ink. A lined record book, with a red cover, lies on a desk. We sign, write in the date, and the titles of the books we borrow—usually four at a time. I choose according to the title. My mother chides me for not remembering the name of the writer. She loves the written word, the elegance of a sentence, the culture, style and poetic vision. The author of such stuff must be remembered. I love stories. For me, a book is an entrance—to a house, a room, a hearth where I sit, and then live. I find myself in books.

   We walk through the flower market and to the big square the main post office building. The floor is grey marble and the ceiling rises into a glass dome, making voices and footsteps echo and sound important. Thea stands in a queue of women. I go over to a bench by the main doors and look at my books, opening each one at random, reading a little, deciding which to start first, according to which one casts a spell first.

Thea arrives. She sits heavily.

"No cheque from your father. Oh dear, he is so unreliable. He promised."

I feel guilty for my father, uncomfortable towards my mother, resenting the tone in her words. I don't know what to say. I want to comfort her. I also want to say, "I miss my Daddy." Thea has explained that there is no arrangement between my father and herself. Money is a constant anxiety—it's in her eyes and voice. She says that, with my father, there is only a suspenseful hope that a bonus will come out of the blue.

"Your daddy doesn't pay for you," she says. Not for clothing, school, medicines, holidays. But he sends surprises, surprises which seldom arrive by post. A mutual friend, or some unknown person, will appear at the door, smiling, saying, "Louis asked me to bring you this." In his hand an envelope, or a small package.

I ask, "Where is Daddy, where does he live?" It has been a while since I've heard from or seen my father. I haven't counted the years. It feels long ago and far away.

"I don't know, Baby," my mother replies. "He still lives in New York, I think. He doesn't stay in touch."

On our next fortnightly visit to the big post office, Thea comes up to me on my bench with two envelopes, one white, one blue. One of my mother's black and white photographs has been bought by *Picture Post*. She works with Cartier Bresson and Capa at the Magnum Agency. A gallery in Paris has sold three of her paintings and she has a photo project.

"Gazpacho for lunch, Mrs. Mouse," she announces. This is a favourite treat—nowhere else can you find it. I skip ahead of her, away from the nickname which brings thoughts of Strasbourg, and words I cannot speak.

"Let's celebrate. We'll go to La Paloma."

The restaurant terrace overlooks the sea. We sit under an arch at a big square table. An iced dark red soup in a white tureen is put in the centre. Around it, a collection of tiny round dishes filled with chopped cucumber, onion, peppers. Señor Andres, the owner of the restaurant, greets us.

"Buenos dias, con mucho gusto. Las hermanas," adding, as he looks at my mother, "tan guapas."

Our lunch will be paid for with one of my mother's paintings. My mother has asked I continue to address her by her first name. We are to pretend we are sisters. The Spanish attribute shame to a woman unescorted by a man, and if there is a child with her, then where is the father? Without a husband, she can only be a woman 'sin verguenza'.

After lunch we walk over to the American Library. The librarian is a white-haired gentleman in khaki trousers, white shirtsleeves rolled halfway up his forearms. He wears white socks and loafers like a dancer in an American movie. Like my father. I stare at his feet with man-eating hunger. We return our books and choose another two each. There is the English Lady Eleanor Furneaux Smith who writes about aristocratic women who run away to Spain to live with the Romany gypsies.

"Real people. Of the earth," my mother says.

I take out two big books—*War and Peace* and *Anna*

Karenina, and an illustrated book about a secret garden. Back at the puerto, in the shady afternoons, I read about wildness and glamour and confusion and loss and happiness and unhappiness and despair and mad laughter. I love the constant change of mood that goes with the constant change of place; the description of clothes worn like stories told in long fluid lines; the way characters at table talk madly; the active use of conversation to get somewhere; the reach for god knows what, and what is God anyway?

I read and I want to leap up and dance on the page with the figures who open their mouths to sing and eat and talk of love and pain; who listen at the door to the cries of childbirth as if they were there because they know how to listen and see at the same time. Those who are jumping up on a chair, onto the table, out of windows; playing the balalaika; cry-laughing in one motion; running out in the snow; one day eating caviare, and the next day counting the potatoes. Those people dashing in and out of rooms— people together, people apart, hating and loving—all intertwine in and out of time and day. Their day is my day, in sentences that are paragraphs and page-long. This is where I linger, my mind floating on the loving details, and then it all takes off again at roller-coaster speed—and all are gone.

Every day I stare at the mountain facing the puerto from the roof. One afternoon, during siesta time of day, I take a book, an apple and tie a bandanna handkerchief around my belt. Observing my father's dictum of never to be out in the world without some token, I have St Christopher on a chain, a hand-rolled silk mouchoir dans la poche, or my

Hermès foulard Daddy gave me, like the one wrapped around Orlando, my marmalade pussycat.

A fly, big as a thumb, wings like gothic window panes, lands on my shoulder. I brush the big black thing off my white blouse. A thick spider's silk bars my path. I run my finger along the thread, fine as a knife's edge, silver in the sun. The way it hums under the touch of my finger, I feel a disgust and attraction. I lift the silvery thread and, as I pass under, say thank you. There is a presence at my side, not visible but there, which I hope is kind and gallant, but I'm not sure. It comes and goes wherever I am. Something happened between us, though I don't know what. I want to savour a moment of beauty I don't understand, or daren't speak of—something to do with forbidden knowledge, to do with a knowing of beauty in ugly things such as insects. Even the spider, the web, the tickle of tiny feet—the way a certain sensation can bring pleasure and after, or even at the same time, repulsion.

Strings of heat and sound-songs crisscross the musky scent of wild sage. I look back and down over the bay. A crow flaps slowly across, like sadness. The crickets are loud. The leaves of olive trees darken. I lift my thermos bottle of water to my lips, fill my mouth, chewing, swirling, swallowing bit by bit. The fine dust of the road slips between my toes inside my gym shoes. Sweat gathers on my upper lip tasting of salt and stone.

The road passes a field and a little way up, in the distance, there is a boy leaning on a fence. He has his back to me. His skin is the colour of chestnuts. I watch for a moment. He squares his shoulders, lifts his head and makes a rolling high-pitched trill like a policeman's whistle. From the top of the sloping field, a horse appears to be flying, mane streaming behind him in river waves. A black Pegasus. It gallops down and stops, just short of the boy, who quietly puts a hand on the animal's muzzle, then an arm over the panting head and his cheek against that of the horse. The boy is tall, his hair dark and thick and messy. He tells me his name—Rory. He jumps up on the horse bareback, turns to face the bay and myself for a moment, then waves as his heel gives the horse the command to go. This moment makes a mark in time. Miguel must have been with me that summer because we will refer to it all of our lives—a kind of proof of existence, witnessed and shared.

That day, halfway up the mountain, I leave the trail to take a rest under an olive tree. The puerto lies far below on the other side of the bay in a cluster of square and rectangular shapes. Their matte surfaces absorb a blinding-white sun. Two small shapes are black—Juan's car and the grocer's car. No bus today. One person walks along the jetty.

I open my book of fairy tales at random. There is a deer in a forest, and creatures and plants and trees and forgotten objects, all communicating in a language without words. I only speak of such things with my mother. She paints the secret space between things. I observe her drawings and learn to look at the space around and between, to draw the edges of the not-there space around a chair and, so long as I don't cheat and look for it, the magic happens and the chair appears without my having drawn one single line of it. That's how I see the in-betweenness that holds things together, how the atmosphere between people colours itself, expands, narrows, in all sorts of ways, how the feeling-thing we call love hovers inside houses and over towns and rivers and mountains… or not.

I read on, looking up now and then, coming back to the sound of crickets, the heat of midday. I put the book down, stand, look up through the canopy of the olive tree, make a covenant to never forget this moment, and set off back down to the house.

What's It Like To Live In One Place For Years?

Strasbourg, 1954

I am taught the management of a household. My aunt loves her garden. After flowering, the bulbs of tulips are carefully stored in the darkness of the garden cellar room, each with neat brown paper labels tied around their dying leaves. There is a cutting garden. I learn about things that grow, each in their way and in their own time. I learn where and when to cut. I am directed to vases of different shapes and sizes and asked to arrange flowers: for the dragon vase on the hall table behind the telephone (the rare cobalt blue one of my aunt's, 'Qing you must know'); and for the drawing room table between the French windows; for little arrangements in small pots for our bedside tables.

Aunt Agatha says there are many ways to a man's heart. I watch and learn that a woman serves her husband with flowers and food and is to give him her time. Uncle Edred does not like her to be working on anything that takes her away from home. I don't understand this, but I notice the arguments and how sad and dulled my aunt seems afterwards.

Aunt Agatha and I hold hands in the street on our way to the market behind the cathedral. Aunt A's hand is firm, not warm or tickly like Uncle E's. My uncle's hands are big and puffy, soft and careful as a bear's paw extracting honey. Aunt A lets go soon as we cross the street and touch the pavement on the other side. She is a tall lady, bony, taller than Uncle E in her heels. Her hair is long and blonde-white, like bone. Blue eyes, like me. It's the Celt in us.

"We are not English," she says.

She brushes it back from the crown of her head to the very ends, holding her arms out straight as sticks while selecting sections, braiding them like rope and tying them up in a coil at the back of her head. Hair arranging takes place after breakfast. Then there is attention to the face, finishing with a careful overall placing of loose powder with the aid of an ostrich feather puff. Last comes lipstick, colour of fuchsias, patting it with a Kleenex, pursing her lips. One more pat of the Kleenex, throw it away, open the handbag, light the first 'ciggy' of the day, snap the handbag shut, close the lid of the dressing table, ready for the day's business.

Aunt Agatha writes books. She writes about real life, not like my mother's fictions, she says. She has an interest in the criminal mind which takes her to visiting gentlemen in prisons across France and writing books about them.

"They are very interesting people, with an excellent, if rather dark, sense of humour," she says, with her cat smile.

She speaks of the importance of mental energy and the will to get on—which I possess, she says. I remind her of Elton Mayo, her father, in my love of conversation and the way that I observe and look upon people with a real interest. My aunt and I have conversations that make me feel able and part of the world. She listens well. There are pauses that give time for new thoughts. She advises, asks questions and avoids talking about herself.

Agatha also likes to sing. 'Tea for Two' is a favourite. And

Louis Armstrong's 'Without My Walking Stick, I'd go Insane', nodding at her gammy leg. She makes clever twists out of the lyrics of a song: "*You're the skin in my coffee / You're the turd in my shoe*," substituting 'skin' for 'cream' and 'turd' for 'lace', winking at Uncle Edred. There is the sad, sweet, Scottish song of a girl in the valley, singing to her loved one: "*Oh, do not lea-ve me*," my aunt stretching out the word 'leave' and something about 'sorrow' and "the remembrance of thee." Then there's the French folk songs from the Auvergne, and the 'Four Last Songs' of Strauss. All are strange to my ear, so different to Daddy's jazz and blues, or Tata's samba and merengue.

At the end of the day there is the return to the dressing table, the top flipping up to reveal the mirror glued to the inside of the lid. She retires to bed, hair loose down the back, tied halfway with a green velvet ribbon. It looks nice like that, like a curtain pull.

Aunt Agatha never hugs people and no one hugs her. Sometimes Edred pats the top of her head, or her hand on the dining room table, or her bottom on the way out of the front door. She limps on some days, and not at all on other days. Something bad like polio happened to her when she was very young. And there was that time in London during the war when she had to stand on the roof, ready to sweep off a V1—one of those bombs timed to explode a few seconds after contact. You heard its shrill whistling as it shot down, and then a terrifying silence. Aunt Agatha managed to sweep one off, seconds before the explosion, but was nevertheless thrown down and sprayed with bits of metal, one or two which stayed inside her.

There are many sighs chosen from an extensive

repertoire. My aunt will pull her chair out and sit down to lunch with a sigh. In the car, she puts the key in the ignition with a long, drawn out, thin, high sigh. She drops her arms into the sleeves of her coat and opens the front door with a high-pitched, breathy and abrupt huh-like sigh.

"Poor Pusskin," Edred says, in a sometimes grandiloquent, sometimes tired, sometimes irritated, sometimes teasing voice.

Conversation At The Dressing Table

Strasbourg, 1955

Aunt Agatha is at her dressing table. It's one of many Saturdays. I sit on the edge of the big double bed enjoying the ritual of face-making. There are little bottles and big bottles of cut crystal and tinted glass. One spherical-shaped bottle, almost heart-shaped, is kept in its box imprinted with a lace motif of delicate browny-grey flowers, like the veil drawn half-way down her face when she goes out to an important lunch with her diplomat husband. Across the middle of the perfume box, 'Femme' is written in white letters on a thick black band. Beneath, in red letters, 'Paris' and, underneath that, big gold letters for 'Marcel Rochas'—who I know is a friend of my father. My father uses a Rochas cologne called 'Moustache'. My mother has a dress designed by Rochas which lives in the trunk in the attic. I go up there to try on the dress—white satin, strapless, stitched with pearls and silver leaves. Year by year, it fits a little less well.

I am fascinated by the potions and objects on my aunt's dressing table. There are lipsticks in gold cases, a tiny lip brush, two sizes of hairbrush—one silver-backed and engraved with intertwining initials A.E.M. Several small combs lie beside the bottle of scent. I don't recall ever seeing my mother at a dressing table. I want to know these feminine mysteries—the how and what that goes into the making of a woman, starting with her face.

One day Aunt Agatha has her Siamese cat face on. I recognise the sly look, small and black like a spider, weaving and spinning thoughts in her eyes. She turns towards me.

"It is time you knew." Her voice is business-like. "You are turning your father into God. Daddy this, Daddy that." She returns to the dressing table, addressing her reflection while brushing her blonde-white hair. Carefully fixing into place the long thick coils at the back of her head, she continues.

"Your father isn't in the French Guyana jungle. His mining is over. The reason you haven't heard from him for so long is that he is in prison." She sighs. "Makes a change from jazz clubs and bistros anyway."

She pauses, puts the hairbrush down, reaches for the bottle of scent, moistens a second and third finger, dabs traces around ear lobes and on the inside of both wrists. There is a silence. Maybe I haven't understood.

She says more. "Your father is a businessman who deals in ways no one understands. Well… the many passports. Who am I to say?" she sighs, the exasperated, short, sigh I know so well since living the past two years with her. There's a pause. I'm thinking about how I'm at home here in Strasbourg. I have my own room now, and it's the first time I can remember being in one place for so long. My aunt is talking about my father again.

"What we do know is that he was caught smuggling gold bars across the Canadian border in his little aeroplane. A criminal offence in the United States, you know. Your stepmother, his new wife, and her famous acting connections will no doubt get him out on bail. There is an appeal, but it might take a few months. Could be a long time before you hear from him, but he's not one to keep in touch at the best of times, is he?"

Everything in this moment changes. The words my aunt speaks fall out of her mouth and spread like seeds around the room where they will take root and grow poison. Her voice takes on the tone she sometimes uses to speak of my mother, her sister—a tone made of pity, mixed with a clinical knowledge acquired, as she will so often relate, from having studied with her distinguished father, the academic industrial psychologist with a chair at Harvard University.

"She could be mad, you know. Really, my darling Mouse. When I think of you on my doorstep standing there like a storm-driven waif—a waif! I hope you know that I am your mother now. It's me bringing you up." There are tears in her eyes, not quite spilling out.

"As for your father. Never once coming to visit. All these years. How long has it been since you left America?" She puffs out another vigorous, exasperated sigh.

"Let go of both of them, Mouse, dear."

I don't know the word 'waif'. I will look it up in the dictionary.

Lolita Is A Spanish Name

Today the conversation going round the lunch table is about art and religion and existence and what is real and what is not real. I don't understand much but I love it. Just as we are getting up from the lunch table, Uncle Edred asks, "So, Mouse, how do you know that you exist, what would be your proof of existence–"

"Passport?" No one in my class has their own passport. I'm a little proud of this.

"Ha-ha!" Uncle E laughs his playful on-stage laugh. "Good," he says, "but not proof."

"The photograph of me inside it!"

"A photograph is not you."

I look into his eyes seeking myself. I see merriment. He goes on, "Think about it." A pause. "A story doesn't exist until it is told—"

"—a person doesn't exist until they are *seen*!" I say—near giddy with some kind of excitement.

My uncle looks at me. Now I do see, there I am, in the reflection, in his eyes.

There is a picture in the entrance hall of a large pipe, underneath it another drawing of a pipe, this one drawn with a frame around it and a caption *Ceci N'Est Pas Une Pipe*. It's a lithograph—an artist's *proof*, my uncle said as we were entering the dining room. My uncle smokes cigarettes in a tortoiseshell cigarette holder which has filters inside it, and now and then he fills up a pipe and puffs and sucks on that. Walking past the lithograph he'd held up his pipe towards the drawing of a pipe and asked: Which is the real thing? Is an image not real? He said the artist who knew how to illustrate these notions considered images traitors, that we are betrayed by them. What do I think?

Friends come for dinner. There are drinks in the drawing room beforehand. I am invited to join them for a little while before I go upstairs to my bedroom. There is a beautiful English lady called Joan, married to a Frenchman called François, who has brought a book he says Aggie and Edred must read—an extraordinary book, a masterpiece they say. I feel their excitement and listen because the name of the book is Spanish and right away I am happy.

The Taste Of Latin

At Notre-Dame-de-Sion, my convent school, there is Mass before lessons every morning. I am given dispensation from fasting because I have fainting spells. At communion, savouring the melting of the pastille on the tongue, its papery woody threads dissolving one by one, I am careful not to show pleasure. We have been lectured about pleasure, which leads to greed, and that greed is one of the very worst of the sins. We are taught the proper curtsy as we take a hand and are introduced to an older person. Right foot back, left knee very slightly bent, the two moving as one as you incline your head. It becomes automatic. I will do it until I leave Strasbourg when I am fifteen.

The Latin language is a sweetness on my tongue, another pleasure not to speak of. In class, Latin is different—the texts we are to translate are rigid, structured and always about war. In church, Latin is mysterious and fluid. Tongue and teeth come together in the inner realm of my cheeks, discovering lingual cavities I don't find in English.

"Patrem omnipotentem," the priest pronounces at the beginning of the service. "Judica me, Deus, et discerne causam meam de gente non sancta."

Sounds bring meaning. I crave them. My skin and bone long for them. Perhaps that is why my senses reach out, as the babe for mother's milk, while another part of me knows the sounds of my nursery—French, Persian, North African, Brazilian, Hispanic, Russian—are fading.

"Emitte lucem tuam et veritatem tuam." Endlessly shifting behind my closed eyes, are kaleidoscopic vibrations, geometric rhythmic patterns, arabesques, and words in all colours.

"Gloria in excelsis Deo." Pink and yellow fish quiver in a deep blue sea.

The priest opens the golden door of the sacristy, prepares his utensils, rings the sanctus bell three times. His voice is quiet, intimate, and personal to me.

"Hoc est enim corpus meum."

I open my eyes, both hands on the bench in front, stare intently which I know is forbidden. He raises his offering.

The nuns talk about being called because, they say, they are called by their name to be with God.

"How may we hear God?" I ask.

"God is everywhere. Eyes open, eyes closed, here, there," one nun says, pointing at me, the floor, the walls, herself. "He sees me, he sees you. He looks upon all. He is the very air that we take in, and the space that cradles and sustains and breathes us."

I love all of this.

I bring these words home to Edred and Agatha.

Uncle Edred smiles. "You might just sprinkle a bit of salt on its tail, Mouse dear."

Aunt Agatha says it is good nevertheless to think about these things. I should learn to think because thinking is good for the mind. The mind needs reminding, the mind minds about things. "How do we know what does and what does not exist?" Her voice rises, "How can we believe what we don't understand?"

She narrows her eyes, inhales on her cigarette.

Père Alphonsin, our religious instructor at Notre-Dame-de-Sion is a young man, handsome as a movie star. He strides the corridors, his long robe of heavy brown cloth swishing around his sandalled feet. The class takes in his every word. We duly fear the retribution he promises on God's behalf that will fall on all who dare to doubt, let alone challenge, The Word.

"Christ is returning," he reminds us, and instructs that God the Father, Jesus and the Holy Ghost business are one thing—this being as irrefutable as the most basic mathematical formula: two plus one makes three. I listen to every word, I absorb every inflection. I want to believe, and I am hypnotised, transfixed.

"Obey," he advises. Life is about what is. "Deum de Deo, Lumen de Lumine."

Some otherworldly presence takes its lodgings in me; I can feel it. It makes me think about the wolf Mummy said was under her bed when she was a little girl and maybe it's inside me now, making pain in my tummy. A doctor visits.

He pronounces, "Un problème digestif." He talks about "les intestins et le foie."

Unter Der Linden

There is a custom in Germanic countries to revere the lime tree. A village will have a lime tree in its square. It's Aunt Agatha who knows all about trees who tells me such things. It is a meeting place for souls to speak of their truth that day, and where medieval legal judgments were made *sub tilia*— under the lime tree. The tree could live to be five hundred years old and belonged to the goddess Freya. Proust dipped his madeleine cake in lime-blossom tea, *tilleul*.

I am on my knees in the church across the street from home. I drop in sometimes. I like the church, the wide path of crooked paving stones leading up to an arched doorway, the way hundreds of little roses overhang in summer and stroke the top of your head as you cross the threshold. It is quiet, and feels safe, like being with a grandparent, seated under a big old lime tree.

Today, a lady in black lace-up shoes like my grandmother Moko, is arranging lilies in a tall vase. She finishes and lights the beeswax candles on the altar. A smell of pine resin and honey wafts in the air, like in Spain where lilies grow on the beaches, where the pine trees are, where resin bubbles in a little fire on a terrace of the house where me and Mummy once lived together.

I wait my turn for the confessional. The dark burgundy red velvet curtain slides open and a person comes out. I have a need to talk about what is happening between me and Uncle Edred, though I don't know where to start.

The priest behind the screen asks for specifics.

"It's when he tucks me in. Reading. Saying goodnight," I say. "In the car, too. We sit in the back. Blankets on our laps. Aunt Agatha is driving and somebody is next to her. Mrs. Amber Mason, my uncle's mother, comes to stay. Aunt Agatha prefers to drive, she says my uncle is vague. How he was in command of the big ship in the war, she can't imagine."

I am on my knees in the confessional in the church across the street from home. I want to swallow my words back. The father shifts and leans closer. The legs of his chair scrape the floor, his face near-visible through the crisscrossing of the grille. I make out a shadowy figure with creased eyebrows and a big shiny nose.

"Every night?" he asks, voice long and flat.

"I don't know," I mumble. "Lots of times."

A silence. I feel myself shrinking, compressing my being into a speck, a black pinpoint sucking out the essence of my soul. I hold onto the sides of my chair as if about to fall.

"When did this start?" the priest asks, emphasis on 'when?'

Pause. "Day after my mother left. A Sunday."

"How old are you, child?"

"Twelve and a half," adding, "nine when we left Spain."

More silence. My knees are sore, the small of my back aches, my face is hot, prickles all over. I blush all the time. It's hateful. I stick out in class and at home. Uncle E teases me a lot, and I blush every time. When I pull my upper lip down over my front teeth he says I look like a wolf, snarling. I do it even more. He says this animal thing I do is a 'tic'.

The priest is speaking. "Recite one complete round of Our Lady's Prayer, two complete rounds of Our father's Prayer. Finish with the Credo, ten times. You are living in mortal sin. You must ask forgiveness if you wish Our Father to love you."

He sounds angry. I am very, very cold, shivering.

"Vous comprenez la gravité de vos actes, mademoiselle? Vous n'êtes plus enfant." He explains about ex-communication, about being in mortal danger. He says it is worse than death, that I am damned. Do I understand what it means to be in a state of sin? I am to recite the prayers every day and I am to tell my uncle everything he has said.

Urgency takes hold of me.

The priest draws the sign of the cross over the grille, reciting, "In nomine Patris et Filius et Spiritus Sancti."

Aunt Agatha is in the kitchen preparing the afternoon tea. A tray is laid with the Sarreguemines china teapot and tea cups, her favourite. It is a privilege, when I am asked, to lay the teatime tray myself. It means that I am part of the house, that I belong. I have a room of my own, and I feel I am home. Today the arrangement of tea for two is set on a lacy white cloth, with a pot of sugar and the little milk jug round as a belly, my favourite piece. I love teatime almost as much as breakfast time, and even more than the midday or evening meal times.

"Where's Uncle E?" I look away from the tea tray. I sound wild and strange to myself. I want to speak French, Spanish, anything but this tongue of my mother's—a tongue without edges, soft, where you don't say what you mean to say.

"Upstairs, Mouse darling. Reading, probably. Tired." She adds, "He might be dozing. Knock, won't you, Loïs. Tell him tea will be on the terrace."

Uncle Edred is on the bed fully dressed, a book open on his lap. I stand in the doorway.

"Hullo, Mouse," he says, the usual cheeriness of his greeting questioning the unusual timing of my appearance. A pair of brown suede lace-up shoes is neatly positioned under the bedside table. I address myself to them from my place in the doorway. I haven't prepared my speech and I don't know how to line up, in some reasonable way, the thoughts in my head made up of French and Latin.

I speak fast, blurting, "The father—in church. I have been to confession—just now. He said I was living in mortal sin. You and me. It has to stop. I will lose my soul. I am damned." My words come out full of throat, scratchy. "The father said I'll never be allowed in church. No communion."

The strip of bare floorboards spins round the room while the Persian carpet design seems to run like spilled ink around the stool legs at the foot of the bed, up to the bedspread fringe. I glance up at my uncle, meet his eye and, in that same moment, see myself running down a tunnel, going deeper and deeper down, smaller and smaller. The bond between us, whatever it is made of, stretches, unwinds like string, pulls apart, and snaps like a gunshot.

My uncle has not spoken a word. Something terrible has happened, though I can't give it a name. Still standing on the threshold, I wait—longing, absorbing whatever it is. A sensation of stain spreads up my legs, groin, belly, chest, throat. I take a step back, close the door, cross the hallway, enter my bedroom, close the door. I have trespassed. I know that I am to hold my uncle's silence and never to speak again of this moment. It's my fault. I have broken my mother's rule never to confront, never to hurt another person's feelings.

Uncle E doesn't come up to my room to say goodnight anymore, nor does he read to me, or help with any of my Latin, mathematics or history homework. Our 'goodnights' are said downstairs. My aunt, not a tactile woman at the best of times, never used to come up to my room in the evenings to tuck me in. She would be in the kitchen putting dinner away while Uncle Edred and I held our goodnight rituals. I didn't miss her, but now I do.

A need to know squirms inside me. I sit on it. But I want her to explain and make sense of things. How can something mean so much when it is not said? How can empty space feel so heavy? Aunt Agatha is so good about understanding the world, can't I ask her? Will I lose her if I do? She talks a lot about hurt feelings.

For a long while I don't notice that it is only in public that my uncle speaks to me. I don't know that this is sulking.

"Edred is preoccupied, preparing his speech," Aunt Agatha says. "Ask him later today."

That afternoon I take my homework to his workshop.

"Hello, Uncle Edred." I feel guilty and shy speaking his name. Uncle Edred looks up from his desk to somewhere past my left shoulder.

"Latin. I'm stuck. Caesar again. Wars, and something about building a bridge over the Rhine. Just two paragraphs…"

My aunt says the teachers responsible for switching me

over from left to right are nincompoops and have confused me even more. Uncle E doesn't look up, continues writing his speech.

"I'm busy," he says.

Under The Lamplight

One evening in winter, after we had moved to the house with a garden, when the days were short and the city smelled of bonfires and pine and cumin, I walked home instead of bicycling. I crossed the last bridge. The church of St. Paul, built in the dark pink stone of the Vosges mountains, stood central on the island. As I emerged around the darkened building, a man in a beige raincoat stood under a lamplight. His stillness caught my eye standing under the golden triangle of light. The man mumbled strange words, flapped open the two panels of his coat.

"See?" he said.

I hurried past him to the big avenue and two more streets. The man's footsteps were steady and close behind. At the corner of my own street I ran through the iron gate. Uncle Edred was in his study overlooking the street.

I burst in. "Uncle E—a man. He's followed me," I said, out of breath.

"Show me," Edred said, in his voice of the once distinguished commander of a ship in enemy seas. We stood behind the catalpa tree at the front of the house. The man was there under the lamplight across the street, diagonally opposite my bedroom window. Something waved from between his trousered legs.

"Go to your room," my uncle said.

Aunt Agatha was out. It was Josephine's day off. I waited on the edge of my bed. My cat, Albert, lay in his usual fossil position next to the pillow, asleep. I stroked him behind the ears, he stirred and began to purr. The shutters were closed, curtains drawn. My uncle came in, turned straight to the window, drew open the curtains, opened the window, pushed out the shutters—all with one hand as in the other he held a rifle which now he lifted up to his right eye, and took aim. Two shots rang out in quick succession. Albert jumped off the bed and ran out of the room. A high-pitched whine resonated in my ears. I didn't move. My uncle turned, eyes small as pins, walked out. Not a word was spoken, the man under the light was gone. I was safe now.

Closing my eyes and going to sleep means going into the dark where the black dot-thing swirls in eddies, wrapping itself around me, sucking the marrow from my bones. Once it starts, even with my eyes open, it's there—solid blackness, deep, magnifying, behind me, around me, below, above. A speck, a dot, miniscule and elongating, a snake and a tunnel. I don't talk about it. Images emerge from behind my eyes with a will of their own: my mother and father in an open car, top down; Daddy driving; car catches fire; car crashes; Mummy and Daddy dead. I cry myself to sleep.

Someone is shaking me.

"Mouse, wake up. Mouse." The voice is far away, serious. I open my eyes. My aunt. I stare at her. What are we doing downstairs?

"You've been making such a racket. We thought someone was breaking in."

As we slowly ascend the stairs, my aunt holds me by the

hand, pulling me up. She asks, "What were you dreaming about? You kept opening and slamming doors, opening and shutting drawers."

I don't tell her of my dream about the sea. The way the horizon lifts into a tidal wave rushing towards the shore, a black wall on the move. I stand, staring, paralysed. Sometimes the black speck finds me in the daytime at school. I see it coming from far away, slowly swelling, fattening, hungry for me. Classroom, teacher, students, sharply outlined like paper cut-outs, recede.

A doctor comes to visit about the sleepwalking and the asthma attacks.

"C'est votre âge. Douze ans. C'est normal, ça passera," he says.

I use a squishy thing that blows air into my mouth. I'm scared of things. I love things. I hate things. Sometimes I am so happy I could scream.

One Thursday, half day at school, home early, no one in the house except for me and Madame Walter in the kitchen, tidying up after lunch. She has her back to me, standing at the sink washing dishes. The way she says, 'Yo-yohh' in her Alsatian lilt makes me laugh, and then something comes upon me which I can't stop, a near-winding energy, a feeling of mad wildness—I don't know what. On the radio, a gospel song 'He's got the Whole World in His Hands'.

I pull off my navy blue school sweater and throw it high over the top edge of the open window.

"Mein Gott in Himmel!" Madame Walter cries out.

I unbutton my white shirt, crumple it up into a ball, and

out the window. My dark grey flannel skirt and tie follow. Clothing flies as if winged—Pegasus, I think, remembering the horse in Mallorca—past the Catalpa tree, over the hedge and wrought iron railings, into the street. Next a shoe, the other shoe. Socks, underpants, Navy blue bérêt. At first, Madame Walter laughs. Then she stops. I laugh louder. Without a word, she goes out in the street. I stop laughing, watch her through the kitchen window as she picks up my things, one by one, and brings them back into the house.

"Heavens, Mouse. How cross you look," my aunt remarks one afternoon.

Cross? I feel accused, alerted to something inside me that is threatening, like an animal charging. The need to speak is urgent, but I don't know what about or to whom. I teach myself to block bad thoughts about people who are in range of hearing. No space is safe anymore, not even behind the skin. A darkness inside me grows thicker, denser, made up of feelings I do not yet have words or names for. I sense how it moves from one part of my body to another—liver, kidney, lungs—snaking a way, curling up, waiting to strike, longing for its expression out there—a dance.

Dancing In Circles

Strasbourg, 1956

Before dinner, or more often after dinner, we listen to a record right through to the end, as if in a concert hall. My aunt sits in the armchair and I sit in the corner of the sofa on the other side of the room where the books and the gramophone are. Uncle E is in the armchair next to the sofa. Sometimes I sit on the floor between his leather slippers, tremors of music running through his legs and along my back.

The gramophone lives inside a tall, white, tower-like box. I can stand just high enough to reach over, remove the heavy square lid, and put on a record. I especially like Spanish music. Sometimes, when there's no one in the house, I put on Ravel's 'Bolero'. The music draws circles in the air and, spontaneously, I dance round and round until I'm dizzy and sort of let go and float downwards like a twirling leaf upon the ground.

'Sponte' is the Latin root of the word spontaneous and translates as 'of its own accord'. Doves fly home first in circles before entering their dovecot. Dogs go round and round before settling down on their beds. Cats lie nose to tail in a perfect rounded shape. It is said that when we are lost, or in anger, we pace ourselves in a circle. Instinct gathers itself into safety. As storytellers, we sit in a circle by the fireside. And so spontaneously, I instinctively dance myself into a mandala, a healing space with the dove, the cat, the dog.

"Careful," Aunt Agatha says, her voice lodged in my head. My mother's whispery almost-song voice is hardly there anymore. My aunt's voice is strict and I take heed of her words. "Once a record is scratched it's scarred forever, Mouse dear, like skin." And, as my hand lifts the gramophone arm, the diamond tip ever so slowly comes to rest on the edge of the record. "Hold your breath, Mouse. That's it. Stops you from shaking."

I soon get the hang of this holding in of breath, of every twitchy nerve, so that by the time I am ten and eleven and twelve, I can control my body from head to toe, my face near-perfectly stilled. One day people will say how serene I am.

"Listen, Mouse dear," Aunt A says one evening, her voice high and girlish. She has a new record. An American jazzy version of an opera.

"*Carmen Jones!*"

Instantly, Spain is in the room: the pinging tram bell of the streets of Barcelona; the bullring on Sunday afternoons; the man in his black ballet slippers in the blue and gold suit pouncing on the ground, calling out, "Hé-hé… toro!" I stand in the middle of the sitting room waving at my mother, her friends, Alvaro my mummy's fiancé, my cousin Monsieur Moustique-Miguel, Tata Leïla, Daddy—their faces, everything, all of it, bursting through a secret window inside of me, pumping my heart to bits. The music tells me to stand up and fight until I hear the bells. The voices sing about there being a café round the 'cor-orner'. And something about you talking just like my ma and walking just like my pa which is how I see my parents on the faces of movie stars.

I march across the drawing room green moquette, my dressing gown with the embroidered rosebuds twirling round my legs. Aunt Agatha and Uncle Edred clap in rhythm, my aunt's voice high and sweet. She stands and performs a crooked dance.

"Charleston!" she laughs, breathless.

Uncle E protests, "Charleston, to this! Really, darling. Surely not."

Aunt Agatha giggles, and in her English-accented French, "Poohquoi pas, poohquoi pas?"

I continue in pasodoble fashion. The matador enters the arena. I wave the panels of my dressing gown at the bull who is about to charge. We go out into the entrance hall. My aunt's feet rub diagonals and exes on the parquet floor, and she hops in little skips. I remember the time I asked her to adopt me and how she answered, "No, Loïs. We will not," in her no-nonsense voice which I will, one day, love a little. Loving makes me happy, but my aunt is difficult to love. Either some part of her, or some part of me, always gets in the way.

At school I've been asked: "Where are your parents?"; "Are they alive?"; "Why don't you live with them?" When I tell them that they don't live in the same city, that they live in different countries even, the questions persist: "So why don't you live with one of them?"

A shame runs through me to not have an answer.

Aunt Agatha explains to me, one day, about adoption.

"You see, Mouse. It wouldn't work. We would want you to have our name—Loïs Mason. Your father wouldn't allow that. You are Loïs Vincent de Damas and that's that. Though where on earth he got the 'de Damas' from nobody knows." The omission of my mother's feelings, vis à vis me being adopted, punches a big hole in the air. I can't see it, but I sense it because it hurts so much inside my tummy.

Aunt Agatha leads me into the sitting room. We sit together on the little tapestry sofa under the window.

"Do you drink tea?" Aunt Agatha enquires.

"I don't know." Tata comes to mind. "I like hot water with lemon and honey." This new aunt returns a moment later with a tray laid for two.

Agatha and Edred are childless. At some length she relates how, having been through all the required tests, they'd come to accept not being able to make a child together. They had been thinking of adopting and had entertained this possibility for some time. Just as they were considering the next step, I happened to them, as she put it.

"Out of the blue," Agatha continues, her voice different, pitched somewhere high between the white notes of long-suffering and the low black half-notes of exasperation.

"We received a telegram from your mother." She reaches deep down in her black leather handbag with the horn and silver clasp and pulls out a telegram.

"LOIS ARRIVING MONDAY AFTERNOON TRAIN STOP LETTER FOLLOWS STOP. DESPERATE STOP. LOVE THEA STOP. "

Agatha pulls a white lacy initialled handkerchief out of her sleeve and blows her nose. I note the hand-rolled edges and dislike it intensely. Only Daddy has hand-rolled handkerchiefs. She hands me the telegram.

"I couldn't believe it," she continues, "though knowing your mother, I had to. So I cabled back: BRING HER HERE YOURSELF STOP LOVE AGGY STOP."

She laughs girlishly. "And here you are! The almighty certainly has his ways of answering prayers."

Aunt Agatha finishes with a sigh. The telegram returns to her handbag which is snapped shut, and she tucks the handkerchief back up her sleeve. I note the handkerchief again, the pretty lace not at all like Daddy's, so very different. I decide that I like my aunt's neatness and precision, her snapping turtle handbag, the way she turns sad things into funny things. I like what she calls 'irony' and 'wit' that make me, by some trick, laugh even when I don't want to. I enter her mood-place. I like how her eyes are shiny and how they go up and down. It makes me feel less far away.

Routine Is A French Word For When Things Keep Happening And Become Normal

In the evenings, Uncle E accompanies me upstairs to my bedroom. Tucking me in, he takes up his position at my side, and reads. Diction, voice, and pitch are soothing. I love being read to. It feels safe. The book might be *A Tale of Two Cities*, or perhaps a poem-story, 'The Rime of the Ancient Mariner'—about a wedding, a ship and a great bird that flies in the ship's wake. The bird is white and very big. The bird will be slain, but still its spirit follows.

One hand holds the book, while my uncle's other hand creeps under the sheets. It finds me and begins its knitting and tickling.

"… And I am next of kin," Uncle E reads. "The guests are met, the feast is set."

Uncle Edred talks about his school, Eton, about the kisses and cuddles between the boys and matron, their longings expressed between the sheets, the headmaster's flogging stick, or the belt—the whip-snapping sound it makes as it pulls through the loops of trousers.

I search the faces of men actors. James Mason and Danny Kaye are my uncle. Gene Kelly and Robert Mitchum and Clark Gable—Daddy shows in all of them. I peer into their faces for signs of love in their eyes, at the position of their bodies when they approach a woman. I stare, as if by staring I will catch the feeling of love hiding inside their gestures, as if love were a thing invisible—but a thing nevertheless which would be mine, if only I could touch and feel it.

I don't read the Russians anymore. Uncle Edred gives me a book called *The White Rabbit* about an Englishman who knew to keep silent even when he was caught and tortured by the Germans, fingernails ripped off. I reread the sentence about how he kept silence. Uncle Edred talks about the war. He says he knew *The White Rabbit* man and he tells the story of a French lady named '*La Chatte*'. She was a famous spy.

"I was enlisted to take a woman across the Channel in the middle of the night. We anchored a mile offshore. I rowed her over to a creek. Brittany. A bad coast. The vast tides. Shipwrecks. We were lucky, the sea was only a swell that night, but it was black-dark. Her face was a half-moon in the mist. And her scent—unforgettable. Lemons and jasmine, that's how I recall her scent," he says, head lifting like the fox's catching a scent on an air wave.

I like these stories. My uncle was commander of a motor gun boat which led the attack on St Nazaire in German occupied France. He talks about the sea, an estuary, nighttime, touching bottom twice, then search lights, shellings. I lose names and dates, while imbued with a near-overwhelming and exciting sense of danger. He says he wore a beard then and that it was red, and he was known as Red. He says the war was a mess. No one knew what was going on. The English were always in a muddle, terrible at organising, yet their eccentricity was useful and became their skill. Their boats flew the German flag to delay the enemy from understanding what was going on.

"We were good at fooling the Germans," he says. "Still

are." Uncle E chuckles his usual three laughs: Ha ha haah. I see the sounds and the letters they draw as they emerge from between his lips thick and fast as thieves.

The stories my uncle reads and tells become a world, sometimes secret, sometimes more real than the day we live in. There is 'Owd Bob', the old man to whom no one speaks, who lives with his dog in the Highland hills. Uncle Edred turns himself into the old man—the transformation happens as he speaks. I see the mountain air swirling round tree bark and scree, and the spitting of waves and rain, and the muting effect of mist on nature—all this comes alive in Uncle Edred, his voice carving out of the invisible air between us the very thingness of things he reads to me. Sometimes he'll stop and tell what is not on the page. He describes something or someone he has experienced himself. Then, when a chapter comes to an end and the book is closed, after a nice long pause, and the story's images are given time to settle, he says, "Next chapter… tomorrow."

I read about a little girl who is secretly a princess and lives in an attic. And about a secret garden. And French fairy tales by the Comtesse d'Aulnoy, one about a blue cat and a bird. And Kipling's stories about the boy Mowgli who is adopted by a black panther, Bagheera. I read out loud to myself so I can hear Bagheera—she's there, inside me.

And there are the ghost stories my uncle reads to me also at bedtime. The one by his school provost, M. R. James, 'Oh, Whistle and I'll Come to You, My Lad', leaves me terrified of sleeping in a room with two single beds for years later. Uncle Edred says that Monty, M.R. James, is haunted by God. He says that can happen even if you don't believe. He says M.R. James was a scholar who had translated ancient manuscripts of Christian texts.

When Uncle E reads those stories, his eyes stretch into long glassy telescopes with scary things at the very far end of them, laughter falling out of his mouth in little glassy, clinking, spooky, tee-heees—a bit like when he looks at my mother, patting her bottom.

Uncle E has helped with homework since the beginning of my schooling in Strasbourg. He knows things neither my father nor my mother ever spoke of. I love the way he remembers poetry, and the words and names of people and places, the way he quotes from a story, from a poem, sometimes even whole phrases in Latin or Ancient Greek, I love knowing about the roots of a word, as he says, growing in the darkness of forgotten meanings. My languages are good—French, English, Spanish, Italian, and just a little German. Spelling, music, art, religion. But Latin, the grammar so strict, the stiff uncompromising upside-down inside-out placing of nouns and adjectives and verbs—the dreaded conjugations. I hear the words, but they won't stay together and make themselves into what the teacher says is 'structure', they just don't go in, however hard I try to make them. There is an oddness in my brain that blocks me, like a hog in the doorway, a vast and hot body of something refusing to give way.

The tickling, the fiddling—that's what I call it one day when I am married and my husband asks—started on a Sunday, the morning after my mother drove away and my aunt said they were not going to adopt me. Uncle Edred and Aunt Agatha always took their breakfast in bed punctually at nine o'clock on Sunday mornings.

"You may join us," Aunt Agatha instructed. "Collect the newspapers from the bench downstairs and take them up to your uncle. I will make up the breakfast tray."

I accomplish my task of the newspapers with a sense of importance, warming to the hint of privileged responsibility in my aunt's tone of voice, that this was part of being at home and accepted. Uncle Edred isn't wearing pyjama bottoms. Lifting the sheet to get in, I see and, looking, I ask, "What's that?"

Patting himself, my uncle says, "Why that's me." Lifting the edge of my nightie, he says, "And this is you."

All my senses confuse me, so many of them. Everything comes alive at once. Little strokes feel nice. Then he stops, "Ssssh." A clatter in the kitchen downstairs is followed by the slam of a door. A nest of sensations in my body goes still.

Uncle Edred sits up straight, rustling the sheets of tissue-thin newspaper over his lap, "Mmm, good smells. Here comes brekker."

I too sit up straight.

Aunt Agatha enters the bedroom, puts down a large tray on the folding table erected for the occasion by her side of the bed. I move over to make room for my aunt. I have two soft-boiled eggs with toasted soldiers, a small glass of freshly squeezed pink grapefruit juice. There is a pot of tea with aunt Agatha's own mix—two teaspoons of Assam with one teaspoon of smoky Lapsang Soochong. Now the conversation of the day takes place either side of me, newspaper pages carefully folded back and forth, sounds of chewing toast and the sipping of tea. I am thinking about the night moth I learned of in class. How it begins as a caterpillar and protects itself from predators by making a cocoon of stuff from its own insides. First it builds a framework and then it spins a silk miles long, winding it round and round the framework. Inside, it is safe to do what it must do to grow up into its new form. The teacher showed us pictures.

Later, when Aunt Agatha is downstairs washing the breakfast things, and I want to get rid of that strange itch which is somehow nice and somehow not nice. I ask my uncle to do what he does to make the itchy tickle go away.

He whispers, finger on lips, "Not now, later."

I go downstairs to help Aunt Agatha in the kitchen and then we get dressed to drive out to the countryside because it's Sunday, and Sunday is the day for walks.

There are good times, bad times, happy times, and times I have no words for. The long, empty, dark spaces where something happens and the day isn't day anymore and a podgy hand sneaks its way to my lap under the lunch table. Or on Sunday afternoons driving back home when Uncle Edred and I are in the back seat of the car, his right hand tucked inside my outdoors coat while Aunt Agatha drives, and sometimes Uncle Edred's Mama is up front on a visit, sitting beside her, and they're both talking, talking, talking.

"It is so very nasty and cold in England after Christmas." Uncle E's mother pauses, pats her well-coiffed head of red hair. "My poor old bones do suffer so."

I say, "It's cold in Strasbourg too."

"Oh, but don't you see, the sun doesn't come to England the way it does here. You lucky people. The damp…" she begins to explain, then forgets the rest of her sentence.

Something is said about a village name ending in 'heim'

like just about every other village in Alsace. I know 'heim'
means home.

Oh, do look at that lovely line of poplars by the river.
Almost there.

The car-chat changes, becomes distant.

She sounds like a bird, but has a tiny nose like a cat's and
wears hats that look as if they are about to fall off, with
ankle-length puffy skirts and shoes with buttons. She walks
down the street in small steps, in tune with an emanation of
motorbike-like little farts. There is a touch of the regal in her
gestures and the feeling of a good piece of furniture which
has somehow been left in a junk shop. She purrs and fusses
over Uncle E as if grooming him from ears to tail. I hate her,
and I hate my aunt Agatha.

Edred calls his mother 'Mah' and 'OhMa', and 'Mahz-zi-
pan'. At home, at the sound of his mother's step on the
stairs, he lowers his voice and says, "Okay men: here comes
Omahaaha." Most of the time he is either cross with his
Mama or pandering to her. They argue, picking at each
other.

The hand slows its knitting and weaving. It comes to a
halt. Suspended, I am dangling like a wee spider at the end
of her silken thread. I squirm. I feel a longing. Mummy. The
hand starts up again. The longing goes. Now it's like music.
I'm in another element, swelling, lifting, floating. The out-
there outside the window comes into focus, friendly; I
belong. Trees are whizzing past, blurry bushes. My feet are
inside my feet, I feel the woolly scratchiness of the inside of
my socks, the moist leather of my shoes from today's walk in
the mountains, the solid support of the seat against my
back, the ticklyness of the blanket's fringe on my tummy
skin. I'm about to fall. I let go. I love caresses. I am

remembering Ninin caressing my forehead and being able to close my eyes, just be there, warm, falling asleep as my grandmother leaves the room, quietly closing the door, and I have—I have fallen, I am asleep.

Uncle E is strange and moody when his mother comes to stay—a whole fortnight. I see him back in wartime space, sniffing out the enemy. He gets mean with aunt Agatha and accuses *her* of being strange and moody.

"Having a bad day, isn't she?" he'd say when my aunt defends herself.

He complains that his shirts are being ruined by Josephine's ironing, or about the food saying things like, "Couldn't the kitchen be more imaginative?" He asks Agatha if she couldn't wear any colour other than beige: "My dear, you do look dull in dun."

But my aunt has her ways too. Less obvious and less moody, but more subtle and more clever, deadly rational, which makes my uncle go red in the face. I see how my aunt herds him, picking up the trail of books and papers that he leaves lying around the house. I see how she says nothing in a studious and saintly manner, and I can feel it turning into poison, though I don't know how her secret recipe works.

"What a child you are," she says, sighing long and slow, "oh, do grow up," just as uncle Edred is by the front door in his dinner clothes, ready to go out, and one eager step, caught in mid-air, hesitates, to land as if on quicksand.

She nags him about his map reading, about how vague he is. He snaps back, or sits inside a silence as impenetrable as fog, or walks away, dull and closed-faced like one of those apples stored for too long on the drying shelf. I feel sorry for him and, at the same time, impatient. I wish, with all my might, he would talk back.

"Talk back, Uncle E," I say in my head. "Stand up and fight until you hear the bells."

But he never does. Whatever fumes inside him never comes out. Instead, he looks accusingly at others—my aunt, myself, any woman—and closes down, wordless and sulking.

Or he asks, "What's the matter with you?" and I shrink, intuitively preparing myself to be entered unlawfully. All the while, good or bad, my aunt and uncle address each other in their elegant cultured voices made beautiful with reason, logic and erudition. I do like how, somehow, a sense of courteousness and grace remains. Over the years it lies on my memory like a patina—hard, and shiny, but also protective. I love them. They are my home now.

It's Rude To Stare At Ruins

I don't know what to do about my aunt's unhappiness which swells the space she inhabits and, by some dark magic, enters you, sometimes: *You must make me feel better*, it says. I watch when it falls on Uncle Edred's shoulders, how they hunch up. He makes little noises of the tut-tutting kind saying, "Poor Pusskins," while looking the other way and carefully placing one of his Player's cigarettes in his tortoiseshell holder, sucking on it with clenched teeth, and the tip of his 'ciggy' glowing, walks out of the room. I don't know how to shake off my aunt's mood the way he does. I don't even know it's got inside me until it's too late.

Aunt Agatha is always in pain. She informs the household of this several times a day. Plaintive, she speaks a line from one of Pushkin's poems: "Your time to bloom is mine to die."

She says only Dostoyevski and the cat, Albert—whom she occasionally addresses as Prince Myshkin, the perfect innocent wisest of creatures—understand her. Whatever comforting you may have achieved is forgotten the next day, as if it had not been given, as if it was never received. You are permanently the guilty one.

*

I think about how silence can be wild, penetrating, and ghostly. How the invisible thing has a way of haunting the visible thing, like a draft creeping up from under a door, its coldness wrapping itself around your legs. I am vigilant, on edge. Frightened, all the time frightened but I don't know of what. Only that it is big, and bad.

It is just before dawn in that uneasy light between night and day. I am woken by an ache in my lower back. I curl up inside my shell. A stickiness. Lifting the sheet I look and see dark stains. Blood everywhere, streaks and blobs of it on the sheets, on my nightdress, on the inside of my thighs.

My aunt takes me straight to the bathroom, sits me on the stool by the linen cupboard door.

"Ah, so the curse has arrived. Life is vile in this way. You are menstruating," she explains. She turns down the lavatory seat, sits down opposite me, "You know about that, don't you?"

"No," I say, "I don't."

My bare feet on the white tiled floor are cold. I am crying. I'd spent a night at my friend Marie-Louise's house not so long before. She had shown me her mother's underwear, giggling. The gaps in rising arches between the suspenders had throbbed with meaning, but I hadn't dared ask because it would have meant admitting to my ignorance.

"Really, Mouse. You are twelve years old. Surely even the nuns can't avoid teaching you something about anatomy. Well…" Aunt Agatha sighs one of her prolonged dramatic sighs, and begins. Words like 'oestrus' and 'menses' and 'vagina' and 'penis' and 'semen' and 'ovum' and god knows what else pour forth out of her mouth as she explains a woman's bodily functions. Some of it sounds Greek, some of it sounds Latin. I take in the words while understanding none of them. I nod and shiver as Aunt Agatha's words swirl about in my brain, refusing to anchor. My aunt, apparently oblivious, sails on.

"A man positions himself," she says. "Well, it's all a bit of a bore and undignified."

The lecture abruptly ends. Later, in my own mid-life years, I will learn that, as a couple, my aunt and uncle were celibate.

"Take off your nightdress, Mouse. Cold water releases the molecules," she says, turning the hot and cold taps on. "Blood gets cooked solid in hot water. Soak for half an hour. Scrub with soap." She shakes a box of Lux Flakes over the water and, vigorously, both hands swirling like egg beaters, produces a froth. The nightdress is dropped in and pockets of it float upwards as she pushes down on the air bubbles trapped in the cloth.

"There. Now leave it. Wash yourself in the bidet and get dressed. I'll tell Josephine. She will put your nightdress in the machine later this morning for a proper wash. Bring me the sheets, they can go in with the nightdress. Don't fret so, Mouse." Aunt Agatha sighs again, this time in her girlish high-pitched way and hands me two Kleenex tissues, some long cotton strips of stuff wrapped in muslin to hold between my legs, a lacy white suspender belt with the big archway for the front and the back, and my first pair of stockings.

"Sorry," I say, my arms hanging, feeling a familiar mix of blankness and awkwardness and guilt, and above all, confusion. Always the horrible sense of mess and confusion and of looking up from the bottom of a well, a circle of light above receding and contracting until it is but a pinpoint.

"It can't be helped, I suppose," my aunt replies, and then she smiles and I long to put my arms around her, but she gets up and limps away before I can.

The moat around me widens.

Sundays are for walks in the mountains, exploring the Vosges. Aunt Agatha and I will have prepared the picnic—everything carefully wrapped in freshly ironed kitchen damask cloths. Aunt Agatha drives and Uncle E map reads, though, once we're out and walking, Aunt Agatha pockets the map. We each have a bag made of khaki cloth and basket weave which fits on our backs. Paths are soft underfoot, made of dark pink sand and pine needles, leading us through foresty rooms and foresty corridors. Uncle Edred whispers that the woods don't like to be disturbed and in springtime the wild boar will be tricky. We walk in single file. The path steepens, narrows. There are little boulders and big boulders covered in moss and lichen. Some are big as a car and open up into caves. Uncle E shows me how to read which moss indicates north. We come to a fork and my aunt stops. Leaning back on her cane, she shakes the map open and sighs.

"Oh, Edred, honestly! I knew we should have taken that first right turn. How did you ever get through the war, I ask you?"

My aunt often asks this question and, just as often, Uncle E does not reply, not directly.

"There's more to navigation than maps," he remarks. "You forget the sun, Pusskin, and the moon, and the stars. And one other thing," he turns to me and in a stage whisper, says, 'the hunch'. He looks at my aunt. "In the forest, intuition is science, my dear." Not so vague as he pretends, my uncle, but he zigzags with his words and I'm never sure of where I am. Sometimes I want to look behind me when he's talking. I don't know why.

While Aunt Agatha and Uncle E are bickering, I cast my attention downwards onto a trail of ants making its way across the path. We walk for another hour or two. It rains a little and my wet trouser legs flap around my ankles. I'm getting tired and grumpy. Some of the bickering from earlier on sticks to me. Or perhaps a mood has come over me, as my aunt will occasionally say.

We come to a clearing. Aunt Agatha announces, "This will be our picnic spot."

There's a wooden structure made of long poles and crooked branches rising to a platform at treetop level, with sides and a cover of matted twigs and leaves.

"The hunter's hide," Uncle E says. "For the boar. He'll sit there for hours, perhaps until night falls." Uncle E wrinkles his face and makes his nose look snout-y. "He'll hear them rooting and rustling." He grunts and shuffles his feet in the pine needle soil. "Pigs are very fond of nuts and truffles."

We climb up and gaze over tree canopies. Misty plumes of fog trail in the valleys.

Aunt Agatha points to a spot beyond and says, "That's Bischeim," and then to a second spot, "and that's Hohtenheim, where we'll go for tea." She shows me the trail for our return walk on the map, and where we will come to one of the Vosges' many great castles, this one a ruin from the thirteenth century.

"Eguisheim," Aunt Agatha announces.

"Castle Eggies," Uncle Edred says.

After the picnic, we set off again. Our footfalls are silent.

There is an exquisite feeling of drowsiness, a tinge of warmth, and the evergreen resin-scented forest is subdued. Our shoes make a soft, thuddy sound on the thick carpeting of pine needles and foresty humus. Sometimes an echoing underfoot. The air is milky.

My uncle points downwards and then, an index finger on his lips, he says, "Chambers," and after just a little pause he adds, "things going on down below." Light beams of sun tilt and shiver through the trees. The sun comes and goes from behind clouds. The woods open and ahead are the ruins of a castle on a bluff. It is so big. Some of it looks like a cliff, steep, broken up. Three straight up, squared towers. Uncle E talks of Neolithic people and Celts and Romans, all remembered by these forests. We come to the foot of a monumental stairway of granitic rock.

Castles, according to pictures in my books, are formidable, impenetrable, everlasting structures. I have never seen a ruin before. It is intimidating, and fascinating. It feels rude to stare. Narrow planks of grey-eyed wood are laid across a steep drop. One at a time, Edred first, me second, Aunt Agatha behind, we walk across holding a thin iron rail.

"Don't look down," my aunt instructs.

But I am drawn to the abyss. I do look down. The pull to leap into nothingness is a sensation palpable between my legs.

"Steady. Vertige has arms with which to pull you over," my aunt says, a hand on my shoulder. This wisdom will stay with me all my life, the times of depression wanting me to jump out of a high window. We walk through open-air spaces that were once rooms and long passages. A staircase that ends in mid-air. Grasses and weeds growing over a stone floor. A well.

Uncle Edred looks around, finds a stone the size of a small potato, and gives it to me to drop in the well. As it falls, he counts out loud, slowly, in an unusually authoritative tone of voice.

"One, and two, and—"

Sound of an echoey splash. "Ah. Nineteen point five metres," he says.

I am standing in my bedroom staring at nothing for minutes on end. I walk up to my homemade altar—the shelf above the radiator in my bedroom. I undo the arrangement: shells, collected in Spain; twigs tied together as a cross; pine cones from the hills of the puerto; and the two seal-shaped stones from one of the walks in the Vosges that Uncle Edred had suggested were the halves of each other, and for a moment I had put back together. Also the big grey and white stone that Père Alphonsin had given me, which he said represented the foundation of all things. Lastly, Soeur Elise's card of Mother and Child from Nôtre Dame de Paris, tucked inside the silky pages of my missal, which now went behind my shoes in the armoire.

Everyone is gone, the house is quiet. Gathering all the bits and pieces, I go to the far end of the garden by the boundary fence, dig a hole and bury the lot, big rock on top. I break the crucifix twigs into small pieces and scatter them behind my aunt's flower beds. I feel bad and know I will be punished for such heretical behaviour. I don't care. I feel free, though of what, I have no idea. It's a feeling I have not felt before and I like it. God is nothing and nowhere and he is not coming. I am thirteen now and I wear stockings.

*

One day a phone call from my mother, from Paris.

"We have a home, Loïs," is what she said, pronouncing my name the American way. She is remarried now, not living in a tiny apartment in St. Germain anymore. There is room for me, and I am signed up for another school nearby.

It is evening when she calls, after supper, and my uncle and aunt and I are in the drawing room listening to an opera, *Dido and Aeneas*. As ever, my aunt cries at the end.

"You're coming to live with us," my mother continues. I note that my nicknames are gone. No Monkey or Petit Loup or even Mrs Mouse. I am fifteen years old now.

My aunt has answered the telephone on the hall table, her tone remote and serious. One or two words float back to the drawing room—'moody', 'difficult', 'are you sure?'— before I am summoned to the telephone in the front hall.

Standing in the doorway, my Aunt Aggie relays the message.

"It's your mother, she wants you back."

She retrieves a lacy handkerchief from a sleeve. "We will miss you, Mouse. It's not fair."

I look at my aunt. My heart contracts. I cannot speak, or say I don't want to go, or say that I do want to go, because I don't know what I want. I don't know how to put so much, or so little, into words. I am afraid of saying the wrong thing, which Mummy has told me would hurt a person and then I'd lose them.

So my voice stayed behind, in Strasbourg. And I left for Paris.

Part Two

1960-1972

Paris Maidenhead New York

Quito Geneva London

Kicking The Conkers

Paris, 1959

Thea and Philippe live outside the gates of Paris in St. Cloud, on a hill, on the eighth floor of a modern apartment building. My new school, the Lycée de Sèvres, is at the bottom of the hill. I walk down a wide avenue of horse chestnut trees, shuffling through the rustley clusters of five-fingered leaf formations scattered across my path. I kick at the conkers in their spiny covers, lying half-hidden like bits of my own misery. Inside, I am a small person crying for her mummy. We don't play anymore. She's not on my side. She's strict and my stepfather doesn't like me. I will reach for his hand in the street, and he shakes it off. He looks like a messed up portrait of my father, mixed with the twisted faces of other men in my mother's life, such as Alvaro in Spain. I'm longing to go to New York where my father lives now. I'm even missing Strasbourg.

The Lycée is huge, at least three times the size of my school in Strasbourg. It is one of the first international lycées—co-educational, with classes of up to thirty pupils. You don't need to pass an entrance exam—all that is required is to be foreign and, since I'm born in New York City, I'm classified as American.

One afternoon, the history lesson in full flow, the class door bursts open, its mottled glass panel rattling loudly. My mother marches up to the teacher's desk.

"Voleuse! My daughter is a thief," she says in her fluent, but slightly accented, French. It is soft and modulated as always, though in a lower register than usual, its pitch deadly.

She turns towards the class, facing my row at the back of the room.

"She is wearing an item of clothing that belongs to my husband."

The history teacher, putting down the book he had been reading from, summons me up to his desk where he stands with my mother beside him. There's a shuffle of feet. The classroom, until this moment dull, comes alive with whispers and snickering. Thea takes hold of my hand, pulls me out of the classroom, down grey corridors and hallways with their metal cupboards, lined up along the walls like sentinels. Out we go to the recreation yard, straight through the massive wrought-iron gates, up the steep hill and the avenue of horse chestnut trees, to the apartment on the eighth floor, with the balcony with the view of the Tour Eiffel—so far away. Not a word is exchanged between us. I am in anguish and I can't speak. My mother is not the person I remember from Spain.

Once inside the apartment, Thea turns to face me. I take off my stepfather's sweater and hand it to her. She shakes it, spreads it out on the kitchen table, folding it carefully. It remains there for me to give back to my stepfather when he returns in the evening. My mother explains how she had been looking for my passport—(how I hate her breathless endless explanations without pause). She said there had been a possibility of me going to America that summer and my heart skips a beat for my father—not seen since his flash-visit five years ago. Unable to find the passport, however, my mother had called the school and, unfortunately for me, it was lunchtime.

The Lycée receptionist had replied, "Mademoiselle Vincent is always absent during the lunch period—in fact it has been months since she has been seen at the school canteen."

The news exposes my delinquency. I have been using my lunch money to buy things like underwear and handkerchiefs with hand-rolled edges, and other things my mother disapproves of (like bras which she says I'm too young to wear).

So I do not get to America that summer. Lucky for me, I am invited instead by Tata Leïla to stay for the whole month of August. Leïla keeps track of me and knows everything. She lives in Geneva with her four children, including Miguel—her firstborn from her Brazilian marriage—whom I haven't seen since Madrid. It feels like it's just in time, and I can't wait. I have my fifteenth birthday surrounded by cousins, and we are soon back to communicating in our own macaronic language. This is where I feel wanted, where I belong. It is home, and I am one of them.

Tata takes me shopping. She says I am 'une jolie jeune femme' and that I am to enjoy it. At the end of the month, when I return to Paris, I will have a suitcase full of Tata Leïla-style luxuries: cashmere sweaters; a Chanel suit—the silk lining hemmed with a fine gold chain, a signature of true couture which adds weight to the fall of the jacket; and a little pile of silky underwear. Except for the bras and panties, my mother takes them all away. She says such garments are inappropriate for my age. A few days later she's wearing one of Tata's cashmere sweaters.

I bury myself in books. I write down the phrases that make me feel alive because, in French, I am more alive. The words are beautiful. They give me energy and I dance with them. I read Flaubert out loud to hear him there beside me: "Ce ne sont pas les grands malheurs qui font le malheur, ni les grands bonheurs qui font le bonheur, mais c'est le tissu fin et imperceptible de mille circonstances banales, de mille détails ternes qui composent toute une vie de calme radieux ou d'agitation infernale."

Learning To Steal

In the first term of the Lycée, I make friends with Tomi, Béri, and Barbara, sister to Tomi. The three are of mixed nationality, French and Russian. They are well-travelled, tri-lingual like myself (in different languages), tough and impatient with those who are 'weak' and 'ignorant'. I am in awe of them and pray never to be on their bad side.

Barbara arrives every morning in class declaiming something poetic and politically chic like, "Rappelle-toi Barbara, il pleuvait sans cesse sur Brest ce jour-là." It is a line from a poem written by Jacques Prévert, poet and writer of song lyrics like 'Les Feuilles Mortes', and 'Je Suis Comme Je Suis', sung by Piaf and Juliette Gréco. She mimics her namesake and the man in the poem who was remembering a girl standing in the rain, that day, in Brest.

"Épanouie ravie ruisselante," shaking out long locks of thick blonde hair, her words soft, falling like drops of rain.

Barbara takes me in hand to the department stores of the Grands Boulevards in the centre of Paris and initiates me into becoming, as she puts it, "Enfant du Paradis—grande artiste de l'air et du vol!" The word 'vol' meaning both thief and flight gives more weight to the idea of being 'artiste'. It was a political necessity, in her view, to stir up les bourgeois. Off with their vacant heads! I have no idea of politics, nor what it means to be political, but, so what, I'm swept up by the energy of my new friend, by the ease and skill of her speech, and the use of such terms as 'existential'— (pronounced existe-en-ciel, exist-in-sky)—and by her reciting entire paragraphs of Sartre and de Beauvoir.

Barbara practises her rhetoric loud and clear on the métro ride back to Sèvres for all to hear and join in—and some people do. She makes me laugh as I haven't since being with my father and Tata Leïla. We laugh with such free-falling abandon that one day, as the métro train motion throws us back and forth, bladders bursting, we open our legs and let the golden liquid run freely, running out just as the sliding doors open to our stop, Michel-Ange Molitor.

That was the year of the films *Zazie Dans Le Métro* and *Les Quatre Cent Coups*. Barbara and Tomi were the children of an avant-garde film director, their mother a journalist who covered left-wing culture and politics. Béri's parents were the owners of a restaurant that specialised in the regional cuisine of Burgundy. Our daily lunch boxes were supplied with patés and salamis and portions of salads made up of waxy potatoes, lentils, plummy tomatoes, bits of foie gras left over from the previous day's menu, and we took all this beyond the school grounds to eat.

I revel in the new friendship, the daring fun of it, the escape from the increasingly unhappy atmosphere of my new life with my mother and stepfather. I am not wanted there—but in Strasbourg I am, in Geneva chez Tata I am, in New York with Daddy I am, (aren't I?). My stepfather, visibly under the spell of mad love for my mother, is in awe of her artist's sensibility. He gazes at her and speaks incessantly of her beauty, her finesse—this last word poisoning the air we breathe. The atmosphere in the apartment in St. Cloud is thick, loaded and hostile. You feel it, or at least I feel it as soon as I cross the threshold. My stepfather drinks a lot of red wine—and brandy. In the mornings he can be found mixing the dregs of bottles consumed the previous evening, tasting and commenting in his gravelly voice on the difference between this or that vintage. He is not a happy man, but I have no understanding for someone so hostile to me.

My bedroom is a small, almost square room, painted white. The bed, pretty to look at in its frame of wrought-iron flowers and leaves, also painted white by my mother, is cold and hard to the touch. There is a basin in the corner shielded by a folding screen of bull's blood red silk panels. This is where I stand in the mornings and evenings to brush my teeth and wash my face, bare feet freezing on an uncarpeted floor. The kitchen, in the shape of a long corridor, has a narrow refectory table where my 'beautiful' mother, stepfather and I just fit in. There is a drawing room, with sofa and armchairs positioned too far apart for intimacy, and no side table for a cup of tea.

One evening when my mother and Philippe are out, I enter their bedroom and explore Thea's wardrobe. Blouses are tight, skirts too long, high-heeled shoes too small. Even the ballet flats I look at longingly belong to the feet of a person I no longer know. I open the chest of drawers and find a man's dark, anthracite-coloured v-neck sweater. In the mirror I see how it falls loosely over my hips, the way Barbara wears her Dad's or her brother Tomi's sweaters. Turning this way and that, I welcome my reflection. Maybe I can be as pretty as my mother. Maybe I can be stylish like *Zazie Dans Le Métro*. Maybe I'll wear it to school tomorrow.

In Between Times

Paris was a disaster. My mother and my stepfather and I cannot live together. I am sent off to a so-called finishing school near London. Away from home (only by name), with some relief, I work much better. I like working and I like studying, nevertheless somewhere unspeakable in me there is a turbulence.

Marion Milner, a British psychoanalyst and artist, was a family friend whose name and profession as an independent British psychoanalyst I'd registered during family dining table conversations. It was said she worked with young people and was particularly interested in the minds of artists and writers. It must have been through Aunt Agatha that I made my way from the finishing school in Maidenhead to Mrs. Milner's practice room in London. It was 1959, I was just fifteen, very shy, navigating by the antennae and instruments of intuition which told me I needed help.

Mrs. Milner sat at a large mahogany desk, enquiring politely about my aunt, and my beautiful talented mother. There were piles of papers, notebooks, two pairs of reading glasses, paintbrushes, pens and pencils and, to one side, a thick pile of postcards. I looked avidly upon all these things. I liked her voice. But when she spoke, though I heard her words, I could not relate to any of them, nor take in their meaning. It came back to me that she had worked with my grandfather, Elton Mayo, a respected Industrial Psychoanalyst—my mother's and Aunt Agatha's father. How could I tell her bad things to do with my family, whom she spoke so highly of? Perhaps her person was simply to serve as a go-between. This I now surmise as, decades later at a memorial to my mother in the Long & Ryle gallery in London, there was Marion Milner, now ninety-two, wandering from painting to painting on the gallery walls. I stood afar in the little crowd of admirers of my mother's work, remembering what I didn't say, and wondering what to say so many years later. The moment passed. Once again, I was in that space beyond words, where the silence of womankind has filled thousands of years.

After my long silence, Mrs. Milner leaned forward across the desk and handed me the stack of postcards. "Choose three," she said, and suggested that I look at each postcard, describing what I saw without looking at the details on the back. All were of artists' work. It was exciting, now I had so much to say. Words and images. Art. A world I loved—my mother's world. And that was it, but in that hour I was given much more than I realised at the time. It was like a fairy tale, where a crumb can lead to treasure, or disaster.

I knew she wrote books and, upon leaving, I found a bookshop nearby and asked for books by Marion Milner. I was told there were none and discovered, after some months of sleuthing, that she wrote under the pseudonym of Joanna Field. Her books were a thread, a lifeline, and one day in fairy tale time made of decades leading me all the way to Jung's Depth Psychology, as it was referred to then, and to living what Jung called one's personal myth. For over thirty years, I kept *On Not Being Able To Paint*, and *A Life Of One's Own* by my side, reading and rereading. And when it was my turn to listen, as a psychoanalyst, to the words (and silence) of others, I had a stack of postcards to offer.

But first, at the end of the finishing school, there was the promise of a summer in New York and, at last, a meeting with my father whom I hadn't seen for years.

The World I See

Manhattan, 1961

"Ninin?"

"Oui, ma chérie?" This is my grandmother's voice, always a little vague.

"Comment tu sais que j'existe?"

"Ah, la la, ma fille," she began, in her accented English that she liked to show off. It became more accented with every passing year, and she stressed the letter 'R' with that French back-of-the-throat roughness. "You are my first grandchild qui cherche midi à quatorze heures, et tu as toujours été comme ça."

She was lying on her bed in the pink lace dressing gown I'd given her for her sixtieth birthday last May, her toes twitching like chubby little antennae. My grandmother was logical about the what's-what and the what-is of it all. Never ask why, she would say. "Ça ne sert à rien, le pourquoi change à chaque heure."

"You will come and live with me," Ninin had said on the day I was told to leave my father's house. At the end of the summer holidays, my father had asked what I wanted to do about returning to Europe.

"No thank you," I said. Europe meant my mother and I

was not going back there. I'd also had quite enough of schools. I wanted to stay in New York, but my father told me I couldn't live with him.

"Your grandmother will take you in," he said, living up to a favourite motto: never complain, never explain. I said nothing.

Ninin, speaking in English when talking business, laid down the house rules.

"I take in students who pay rent. I will count on you to do the same, ma chérie. Seventy-five dollars a month. Your father and his wife have a life—not for you. Anyway, it is too late. Forget your parents. All of them."

Two waves of a hand expressed her dismissal.

"Your father does not make the connection—accidents, loss, never (pronounced ne-vairr) his fault. Change de maison comme de chemise. The warehouse with all his belongings burns down, so he curses the landlord who he hasn't paid for months. He curses God. One day he will see the face of bad luck is his own! Then my poor son will pay."

I would ask my father some thirty years later and he would reply, straight out, that my stepmother had refused to have me live with them. She had pronounced the legendary phrase of all bewitched stepmothers, "It's her or me." Decades later, across the ocean in England, married and preparing for my elder daughter's wedding, I had sent an invitation to my stepmother out of politeness, never thinking she would accept. But she did... and she came. Showing her around the grounds when she arrived, we reached the little stream at the bottom of the garden, and she stopped.

"Oh, Loïs," she exclaimed in her theatre-trained clear-cut voice, "I think I have lived long enough to admit what a bitch I was when you came to live with us. How you survived your childhood, I really don't know. I think I've lived this long to give me the chance of saying so."

At that moment, before she reached the end of her cri de coeur, something inside me melted, something heavy became weightless. My shoulders dropped and my body seemed to rearrange itself, bitterness turning into sweetness. I had no idea I cared, that I still hurt from all that time ago. We continued our stroll through the garden, now laughing now tearful and talking fast, discovering how much we had in common—the love of literature, poetry, art and Chekhov, dear old Chekhov. This little moment, short in human time, lives on in me, bestowing its mix of truth, beauty, regret, a sometimes generosity of spirit, and grief whenever needed, a role model for acceptance of one's own dark self.

Ninin lived at the end of East 52nd Street in a duplex apartment by the East River. The East River is not, in fact, a river at all, but a tricky salt water tidal strait that frequently changes its mind and, like all larger than life things, such as whales and elephants, appears to move across one's eye at a slow and meditative pace.

Across on the other side of the ruffled tidal waters were long, low factory buildings of a dark maroon brick. Day and night, the huge red neon eyes of a Pepsi-Cola sign blinked above their roof lines. My grandmother's building was part of a group built in the thirties, façades decorated with Art

Deco touches of wrought iron, stained glass and shiny steel. Four wide steps took you down to a lobby of stone and marble, with the look of a grand, old European hotel. The doorman touched his cap as you passed by, opened the doors and helped you with your shopping bags and suitcases. The lift had heavy folding back gates made of zigzaggy iron bars, and it rumbled, agonisingly slowly, up and down its shaft, tremulous under its passengers' (and its own) weight.

The entrance to Ninin's apartment consisted of a wide landing space giving onto a high-ceilinged drawing room. Beside the galleried balcony, in a corner by the coat cupboard, was a small round table with ivory-white 'Princess model' telephone, notepad, agenda book for appointments, and two small, gilded reproduction Louis XVI chairs with their flirty turn of legs. At the other end of the entrance hallway, a dining table, four chairs of similar Louis XVI style, a doorway to the galley kitchen and on the other side a doorway to a corridor leading to two bedrooms and their bathrooms.

The drawing room had a fireplace and three tall windows, each with cushioned seats. A square card table was set up permanently beside the middle window for Ninin to hold her consultations and readings, using a special set of playing cards. They were the kind with the crowned heads of kings and queens, and beside them sat two sets of Tarot cards. When she had finished working with the cards, a stack was neatly returned to the left-hand side, where it would cogitate as chat expanded into a conversation about the hidden meanings, associations, and memories of a life.

My grandmother had created for herself a career out of nothing—or so it seemed at the time quite soon after a severe illness had come upon her. A friend brought her a book while she was in hospital. Diagnosed with arsenic poisoning, near-paralysed for months, she was unable even to turn the pages. Her friend returned daily to read to her. The book was about the stars and the planets and their relationship to mind and body. Doctors had pronounced that she might get out in a wheelchair in six months if she was lucky. But she defied them all. Instead, she walked out on two canes and soon these were discarded.

And so, in her late fifties, my grandmother embarked on earning herself a living as an astrologer, horoscope reader, palmist and life diviner. This was not the image I had of a grandmother's persona. She might as well have put on a turban and sat in a circus tent reading the fortunes of others, I thought with typical teenage prejudice. But Ninin worked hard and would quietly become another role model for me in my own later life when, divorced and single, I would work as a Jungian psychoanalyst with clients of my own.

Ninin blamed her ex-husband for her illness, of course—my grandfather whom we all called 'Papa'. She referred to him as 'Ce monsieur', who belonged to 'La dernière race après les crapauds'. I barely knew my father's father as the two were not on speaking terms. One had lied and stolen from the other in some unmentionable business deal in Monaco soon after the war, each accusing the other of being 'le voleur'.

"C'est comme ça," she'd say, "mon mari, fils d'enfant trouvé!"

When I asked about my great grandfather, the enfant trouvé, she'd only say that he was 'un bon monsieur, quoique triste et sévère', while informing me, and the world, that his son—her ex-husband—sent her funds that were not even enough to feed the dog (a small white fluffy thing named Zina). Indeed, not many years later, she would have to move out of her beautiful apartment on the river into two rooms under the 59th Street Bridge.

"Ah, quel Bandit des Grands Chemins," she would say, her words spiky with derision.

We talked about my mother and my father only when the cards showed their presence, which was seldom. I had a Russian boyfriend and Ninin liked his surname, its grand connotations, a name that appeared in the great Russian novels, but the cards did not give him a good prognosis, so he was not to be trusted: "Attention, ma fille! He is not for you. Do not tie suspenders on a lobster!," another of her favourite expressions.

Ninin's last paying student, whose room I moved into, was a French woman. 'Une jeune fille de bonne famille', as Ninin would say. She had a lovely name—Isabelle Colin Dufresne. After she left, she invited us to tea in her dazzlingly white apartment—chairs, sofa, fluffy rug, curtains, walls, everything white. Isabelle transformed herself during the next few years into Ultra Violet, as part of the Warhol entourage and one of his official girlfriends. When she invited me to a party at a big warehouse—a huge open space full of people dressed in electric colours, talking about nothing—I had no idea where I was or what to say. There was the presence of a studied ennui. I found myself uneasy and bored.

A few days after moving in with my grandmother, I woke from lying in an open grave, looking up at three men in black and at the same time looking down on myself in the ground.

One of the three dark figures said, "It's too soon."

Waking from my dream, I tried sitting up but couldn't move. I called out. An ambulance took me to hospital.

"Meningitis," a doctor said. "Consider yourself lucky. It's not the worst kind."

It was a few days after I'd been thrown out of my father's apartment. Ninin said I was in shock—apparently, I wept every day calling for Daddy. What was left of my dreams structuring a world, had collapsed.

"Eh, bien. Nous sommes jolies toutes les deux. Moi, comme une vieille chaise. On s'assied dessus quand on est fatigué et puis bye bye. Et toi, un paquet oublié à la poste restante. Viens, ma chérie. Ne pleures plus. Ce soir, nous allons bien dîner. En commençant par un verre de champagne."

I was sixteen and I earned a living as a gofer, typing up scripts for the producer of the Metropolitan Opera's Saturday afternoon broadcasts on the radio. Thanks to my six years in Strasbourg I was at home with opera. It was familiar to me and, however different to the blues and to jazz I'd known before, it spoke of emotion in another way, even though you didn't want to dance with it. My boss, Geraldine Souvaine, said I could barely tell the difference between a typewriter and a washing machine, but she liked my "conversazione," as she put it, and that I had a feeling for the arts and this was what mattered. The job was seasonal, so there was no pay cheque during the long hot summer months. I stood in the dole line, sweating through June, July, August.

*

I took jazz-dancing classes and evening life-drawing classes at the Arts Students League. My Russian American half-brother, Stefan, introduced me to his America. He was a little wild, in that Russian way, or perhaps in our mother's way. He took me to a celebration at his university where young men like himself ran down the corridors half-naked, roaring with song and chanting, "Let's be balling it." On my knees, I lost my virginity to his best friend, a man called Brud who made movies. He talked about the soundtracks to his films, whistling a tune while taking me from behind. It hurt—I didn't know it would hurt. No one talked about, or explained, sex to me, nor did I dare ask. But it was there all the time and you learned in silence.

I danced up in Harlem in Smalls Paradise, the nightclub where the only white people welcome were French. I was promiscuous—not a word I knew—and didn't know how not to be. Older men were attracted to me and then the inevitable happened—I got pregnant. It was with the Russian with the grand family name who Ninin had warned me about.

Abortion was against the law. It was a crime, but being pregnant was terrifying, and being a mother unimaginable. Stefan, the only person it felt safe to tell, found me the unlisted, illegal telephone number and contributed half the fee to pay for the business—two hundred dollars. His support was matter of fact, without judgement, brotherly in the best of ways. When I called, a voice on the telephone instructed me to take a train to New Jersey and stand on the platform holding a pink newspaper. A man wearing a hat and a long dark grey coat approached me. No names were exchanged, he gestured to follow him down a dilapidated street behind the station.

We walked to a tenement building, up three flights of stairs, into an unfurnished apartment. Unpainted floorboards, loose and broken. Like a movie. I felt not-real. Two large white porcelain sinks, buckets under a dirty window. I was to lie on a table beside the doorway to the kitchen. No undressing. Remove panties. Lift up my skirt. Something was inserted inside me and a woman wearing a dirty green apron said, "It will happen later, within the next twelve hours."

I had lied to my grandmother about being away on the weekend with friends in Long Island. I returned to the apartment of my Russian lover, a man in his late thirties. In the middle of the night, a pain spread through my lower back and I tiptoed to the bathroom, determined not to wake him. I stared, for a long moment, into the toilet bowl, waiting for feeling, meaning, image, voice… anything. Nothing came. Only the reddish-brown messy bloody stuff against the white porcelain.

A week later, during the summer holidays, I flew down to Ecuador. My father had moved to Quito, from where he commuted to work on a river mine near the borders of Columbia. I was continuing to bleed, and it became heavy and infected. I lay in bed, pretending the altitude was making me ill. I didn't trust my father, fearing him as much as adoring him, and I certainly would not have risked consulting my witch of a stepmother. Somehow, I found my way to a doctor, up a steep hilled street, who gave me something for the infection and, after a few days, the bleeding stopped.

*

My father gave me driving lessons, teaching me how to double de-clutch in the middle of a corner then, against all instincts, accelerate, feel the tyres grit the road, and go. After this, he arranged for official lessons so I could have a driving licence when I went back to New York. The driving test took place on a mountain road in a taxi driver's smelly old car, which I had to manoeuvre backwards around a hairpin bend, as well as start on a hill and, without backsliding, move forward. My Ecuadorian driving licence came in handy for escaping parking tickets back in New York.

One morning, my father took me up in his small Cessna aeroplane. To gain sufficient altitude, he piloted us upwards, round and round in spirals, to pass over the canopied jungle of very high, very green Colombian mountains. We then came bumpily down, following the snaking course of a copper river to the runway—a short stretch of dirt track which had to be attended to daily in order to fight back the speed of jungle growth. The camp was a mess of tents, equipment and scattered machinery. Larry, my father's manager, explained that there'd been another attack by the Jivaros, the nearby native head-shrinking Indians. My father wolf-whistled: "Well, hello!"

The jungle, during the day, was spooky-quiet, but, as evening fell, the noises began—the monkeys, wild pig, mountain lion and the leopard they called 'tigrillo'. Snakes were everywhere, and the whispering presence of insects, big and hairy and sticky and shiny.

We walked over to the main tent, which was being put back in order. There was a large black box on a table—a two-way transmitting radio which crackled and hissed as we communicated with Lionel and Lara—my very young and beautiful white-blonde haired half brother and sister, and their mother (the witch also beautiful), in Quito, confirming that we had arrived and were safe. I had to remember, before speaking, to wait for the other person to pause, then flip the switch from 'receive' to 'send', and only then could you speak.

"Listen to this," my father said one afternoon, back at the house. Brushing particles of dust from the gramophone turntable, he held a record by its edges with sensual care, dropped it and then, holding the diamond stylus, gently let it rest on the outer grooves of the disc. A melody began. A young woman's voice emerged, pure, clear, confident. No tremolos. With each note, the lyrics rose up high and then higher. A circling of sounds filled the room like doves coming to roost. It was so familiar and, incomprehensibly to me at the time, so sad.

"Listen," he said again, "it's never been sung like this before, so slowed down."

True, I'd never heard it sung that way either—a long and easy stretch, cat-like.

"La chanteuse est une jolie-laide," he said, making a gesture on his face, "with a big nose. Elle s'appelle Barbra Streisand."

The song played once more and now I recognised the melody, and the lyrics of 'Happy Days Are Here Again'—sung almost the way my mother sang it, humming something about blue skies, in Spain, barefoot.

On some weekends my father and his wife gave parties and we danced, short of breath, in slow motion. Quito is high, surrounded by a tight circle of rusty-coloured mountains. Clouds gathered predictably, punctually, every afternoon, so all flights were scheduled to land before two in the afternoon. In bed, a blanket on the chest felt too heavy. Polo games were slowed down as the horses struggled - there were cases of equine heart attacks. On other weekends, we drove down to the lakes where native women stood on the rocks, slapping cacti against a platform of stone, collecting the foam to turn into soap. Indian men with long hair tied back, and women with the faces of smiling crocodiles, and their children—barefoot, too poor to own shoes—all wore a black flat-topped sombrero.

The Saraguros tribe, high on spirits of their own as well as on alcohol, expressed their feelings for the sacred on Sundays by squatting on the side of the road, the wife, head lolling, lying in the husband's lap, out of her mind with drink. They took it in turns. Next Sunday it would be the husband's head in the wife's lap.

My father's house, once the Mexican Embassy, stood in a big garden with palm trees and monkeys. Driving out to the countryside, the landscape changed within two miles, turning into desert with nobody and nothing other than strange-looking cacti evoking inhuman creatures in various states of rest that might, if you looked away, run up behind you in a game of Grandmother's Footsteps. Everywhere there are the sounds of the music of high mountains, the panpipe, the mandolin, a small guitar-like instrument that emits a metallic sound of splashing raindrops, evoking an energy of giddy, laughing, poignant ecstasy.

Meanwhile, although the bleeding had stopped, something inside me was not right. Too afraid to look, I ignored signs of continued infection until I got to Europe. I was to spend the month of August with my cousins in Switzerland. My aunt Leïla would meet me in Paris and we would travel back to Geneva together. But first I visited my mother, whom I had not seen in two years. I was longing to see her lovely, anxious Ingrid Bergman face again and to talk to her, as we used to talk, about anything and everything. There had been perhaps two telephone conversations in our years apart, but long distance calls were awkward and the lines crackly. Sometimes I couldn't hear her at all and once I had to shout my name three times, my mother asking, "Who? Who is calling?"

Now, as she opened the door, I burst into tears. "Mummy!"

I blurted my story—abortion, bleeding, Quito, infection. And the smell in me down there, what did it mean? No one spoke of such things. I usually didn't dare ask, but now I did. I needed my mother's reassurance, and her love, so much.

As I stepped closer, I registered a stiffening of her body, her arms held down at her side as mine were opening for an embrace. She stood block-still in the doorway.

"How sordid," she said. I was not invited to cross the threshold. I turned my face away as if I had been slapped. The years between us, any love for me I might once have seen in her eyes, was gone.

I pulled back the creaking gates of the elevator, closed the glass door, stared at the floors going down. She didn't call after me. I walked out into the street, along the Quai de New York, to the Place de l'Alma, up the Avenue Montaigne and down two side streets to the Hotel de la Tremoille where Tata Leïla was staying.

I was shivering. "D'où tu viens, ma chérie? Le North Pole?" Tata Leïla said. "Tu vois, c'est pour ça que ça s'appelle une nervous breakdown," she continued, gesturing 'break' and 'down', and lay me out on the bed wedged in with the baby pillows she always travelled with, and a clutch of the hotel's cushions.

After a moment she called out from the bathroom door, "Your bath is ready!"

I had never had a bubble bath before, let alone had one prepared for me. I lay in the warm water, spreading the white foaminess about my breasts and shoulders, listening to the crackly bubbles, watching them pop and melt. We talked about frivolous things like lacy underwear and couture clothes, about my watch which she had given to me on my fifteenth birthday (hidden from my mother when I'd returned to Paris). For the past few days, it had been skipping ahead of time, even though I kept resetting it.

"Your watch is having une nervous breakdown too," she said. It needed to go back to Cartier, and I needed to go to her family doctor, "Un gentil vieil ours," who would take care of me. Then the watch and I would be as good as new.

Tata was not one to hug and embrace and stroke and yet it felt like that when she twiddled strands of my hair and cooed her Brazilian terms of endearment.

"Mi coraçãozinho. You have saudade, ma Louloutte chérie." I knew this word had many meanings to do with yearning, sadness, regret, nostalgia. I said it to myself sometimes, saoh-dadje. It was comforting. Quietly now she asked questions. She wanted details and listened to my story from start to finish. I asked her to say 'coraçãozinho'—little heart—again. I loved the sound... cora-saow-dji-nyo.

And then, "Ma Louloutte," she said, tone critical-funny.

"Your hair. Catastrophe. Coiffeur tout de suite!"

Sometime at the end of that summer I also met with Aunt Agatha. We'd kept up correspondence over the years. As ever, she was practical, clinical—perhaps I mean pragmatic, or all three. There was humour and efficiency, but not warmth. And yet it was care. I was taken to meet with her doctor too, and then to the hospital where I was looked after. It was explained to me that gonorrhoea was a serious disease. It could leave me unable to bear children.

So it was like that. Life on the threshold, in doorways, on station platforms, on the tarmac. Stories and more stories. Father, two aunts, grandmother, cousins—and brothers, sisters, even if only half. I was one of six. My mother aged forty-one would have one more child, a girl, named Sofya, and my father was keeping another ménage on the side. I was nineteen when he invited me out for a day in the month of August. A surprise, he said, one hand on the wheel, one arm leaning on the open window of the car.

We arrived an hour later, somewhere outside New York, a clapboard house with a porch overlooking Long Island Sound. A young woman, French, smart, very pretty, with a small child, sitting up.

"Say hello to your little sister," my father said. "She looks just like you when you were a baby. Her name is Laïsha. Born the same month as you." The unsaid grew tall in the colluding silence. It happened so smoothly, apparently so easily, on a sunny day. It would take decades for me, my brothers, and my sisters to cut our way through the net of rope and its thousand knots.

*

My father is telling a story. We are in Paris, Chez Castel. Red leather banquette. Hand-rolled silk handkerchief in suit pocket, shirt open, tie undone, hand-made cowboy boots, slanted heel, stitched in Quito. The story of where we come from begins. My father talks about family, about my great grandfather, Alfredus Josephus Vincentus. Glass in hand, twirling an inch or two of Delamain, his favourite cognac, admiring the shapely trails of the amber liquid running down the sides of his goblet, he says, "Mm, nice legs." I remember more—how he leaned forwards, elbows on the table, looking down into the grain of the wood, evoking the whole of France, crossing the Mediterranean, two fingers tapping their way to the Middle East, arriving in Damascus.

Now it's Syria, 1860, the year of the massacre of some ten thousand Christians. Europe is in shock. France sends down her best officers and one picks up a little boy, perhaps five, perhaps six, and takes him to Alexandria, to the monastery of the White Fathers, St. Vincent de Paul. The boy with blue eyes has no memory of himself, of family, of language, nor even of his own name. The trauma has wiped his mind clean. There is nothing to remember. There is a medal of St. Christopher around his neck and so we know, my father says with some pride, that he is Christian. Later, as a young man of sixteen, Alfredus goes to France in the hope of finding records, even locating relatives, but there is nobody. My father says he has Barakah.

"What's Barakah," I ask.

He whispers, "Don't tell anyone. We all have it. Negative luck: a kind of blessing in bad times. Just when you're about to give up—it comes." The positive as a presence—life! It never occurred to my father to give thanks to a higher being.

"If God exists," he would say, as a man who relied on the evidence of his own senses, "why doesn't he show himself?"

It's late, near dawn. Streets are empty but for clochards and the carefree. My father zigzags at speed, double declutching around corners, down the narrow streets of St Germain. He knows by heart how the one-way system is laid out—the short-cuts, the slip road down to the river, up and across the Pont Royal, through one of the arches of the Louvres Museum, zoom round and round the Concorde, tilting the car on two wheels, one or two more zigzags, arrive at destination, and park on the pavement. Perhaps this time it is by the front door of La Calavados, the after-hours piano bar. He saunters through, cowboy boots making their own soft clip-clop sound, gesturing a salute to Joe Turner at the piano who is immaculate in white shirt, suit and tie, a half-smoked cigar between the lips, striding the ivories with the 'St. Louis Blues' or, when he sees my father, 'It's Just One Of Those Things'.

Another day, another month, another city. Tata Leïla tells the story. It is afternoon time. Cup of tea, slice of lemon floating in a pale amber liquid. We are seated on divans or sofas or on her bed amongst her pillows. She has eyes the colour of palm tree dates—sometimes a little scary in the way they gaze straight at you, unflinching. Tata lies back in her lazy-lion position, one leg propped up against the other, a bare foot delineating little circles in the air. She twiddles a strand of hair, hers or mine. There are pastries, a dish of loukoum.

Tata begins, and it is like this: "There was a baby in a basket, his eyes were blue." A stream passes through the pages of my imagination, reeds bending as the little craft passes by with baby Moses. "Mais non," Daddy's voice comes to mind, and interrupts the Sheheradzean embroidery from his place across the world. "Mais non, when he was found he was a little boy, six years old, white skin, blue eyes, and the medal, don't forget the gold medal and chain around his neck. He was Christian."

Slowly, developing into itself like a black and white photograph in its alchemical liquid, my psyche weaves another thread of the family story. A country where the alphabet is born. A city with narrow secret streets, and people running in and out of doorways. A child keeps hold of his mother's hand, crying, "Monkeys! Mummy!" An ocean-wave made of hands and arms and legs tears him away. Hours, perhaps days, perhaps years later, when the city is quiet and smells of smoke, the boy is lost. Wandering this way and that, he makes his own way. A boy without memory, origins, or name. He is in me. I feel him stirring my guts whenever the story is told.

Whoever told the story always ended in the same place— the orphanage in Alexandria run by the White Fathers and Sisters of St. Vincent de Paul who gave the boy, and us, a name: Vincent de Damas. Alfredus-Vincentus was his first name, de Damas his given surname, and later, as a family man with a business of his own, the 'de Damas' is left behind and the Latinate 'Vincentus' becomes the surname 'Vincent'.

The Full Catastrophe

New York, 1965

Years pass like clouds, shapeshifting.

It was on my way up the stairs to a friend's party I met a man sitting by the top step outside the apartment door. He was taking the bar exam, he explained, the following day. I sat down beside him and fell in love. Leaning against the wall, me on the step below, he on the one above, we never made it to the party. His looks took their hold on me—his olive-skin, his thick near-black hair, inch-wide eyebrows, stocky build, combined with the fact he was well-informed on just about everything—politics, history, religion, economics, and poetry. He also talked a lot about the law, about being true to self, and about the must of a moral code as a practising Catholic.

He told me his name in full: "Theodore Alexis Bergmann. But call me Teddy." He played the piano, composed a bluesy melody, and wrote lyrics about our meeting and his feelings for me—the lost child who needed salvation. This was a pattern in his life, a match with my own. One of three sons, Teddy was the one chosen to rescue his murderously alcoholic father from police stations, from pavements, from bars—over and over again. One day he also had to rescue himself when his father, in one of his many moments of madness, threw his son off his yacht, trying to drown him in the waters of the Long Island Sound.

We went for long walks downtown, uptown, across town, and one evening Teddy took me down to a small jazz club in the Village. There, a black lady sang out of her mind. Angry and ecstatic, the energy of the divine inside her as she stood at the piano, slamming the black and white keys, singing 'Mississippi Goddamn'.

Soon, we were engaged. Teddy's family was of German and Italian descent and were religious about things. Being Catholic, sex was not allowed before marriage. We lay together sometimes, fully clothed, one body awkwardly rubbing against the other. The aftermath was Shame with a capital 'S'. To Teddy, we were in sin, and we had to talk it over and take it to the confessional.

On the surface, life went on together well, while below, the waters were not so still. During the three or four years of being engaged, whenever it came to set the date for the wedding, Teddy called it off—once, twice, and then a third time. It got as close as choosing the silver, the lettering on the invitations, the spelling and position of our respective and very different family names. One year, we even got as far as booking the church for the month of May. That time the problem came from my side, for not having the proof of being baptised Catholic. I had to be indoctrinated, given instruction, and finally baptised—for the third time. The first time was in New York as Episcopalian, the second time as Catholic in Madrid, and now, with Teddy and his family attending, a third time Catholic.

Each time Teddy's feet went cold, there would be more talk and more opinion, with louder hints of his increasing concern about my 'louche' father as he put it, my traumatic background, the careless, incoherent and peculiar upbringing. It happened, more than once, that a person—upon hearing to whom I was related—would turn away or get up and leave the table. There were others, though, whose faces would light up and say "Ah, so you are Louis' daughter. You know you must write about him. How is Louis? What a life!"

Teddy was an avid golfer. I would follow along the greens dutifully—bored and, down-down-underground, angry. One Sunday, a month or two after the last cancellation of our engagement, Teddy ran into an acquaintance, another avid golfer. This other man, who didn't talk as much as Teddy, communicated a free spirit—or so I thought. He had an easy sensuality, and joined us for the rest of the day. He called the following Monday, inviting me out to dinner.

"Hi, it's Bobby Pratt," he said, "I want to see you." He asked a lot of questions and talked much more about me. I was beautiful, he said, and he wanted me. Making love was nothing to be ashamed of and, at the end of the evening, he proposed… and I said yes.

Home at two in the morning, the light showing under the door to my grandmother's bedroom, I tiptoed in. She always waited up for me, and she was delighted with my news. Robert Gibb Pratt. She knew the name.

"Enfin, voilà un jeune homme de bonne famille," she said. "Acceptes-le. Tant pis pour ce monsieur Teddy qui change d'avis comme de chemise."

And so on Friday, four days later, Bobby and I eloped. I was twenty-two and Bobby was thirty-two. He made me feel taken care of, and the following week he took me to meet his family in Long Island on the unforgettably named Skunk's Misery Lane. The drive was a mile long up a hill, circling round to a large house overlooking Long Island Sound. It was two-storied with a front porch, portico and columns. It felt grand and overwhelming, with pale green walls, reproduction furniture, no jazz.

His mother looked at me with a tired and kindly déjà-vu look in her eyes. Later, she told me I was Robert's fifth wife. He'd been adopted aged four during WWII. I came across an article about the big time crime boss known as 'Lucky' (Charles) Luciano. It was the photograph that grabbed my attention—tall and gangly, with the long face, the thick straight-across eyebrows, the wide lips, that hungry smile. The resemblance was uncanny. Bobby—Luciano or not— was a black sheep. He spent his days playing high-stakes backgammon at the Racquet Club or underground gambling in New Jersey. Invitations would come from the best hotels in Las Vegas, offering free first class travel and a suite at the hotel—a privilege reserved only for the big-time loser.

On the first evening, after a brief explanation of the protocol at the craps table, Bobby handed me the dice.

"Blow," he said, "shoot me snake eyes." This meant throwing two 'ones', known as 'aces'. The odds against this throw are 1 in 36. All eyes were on me. I had to throw hard enough for the dice to hit the other side of the table. A childhood parked in nightclubs and on bar stools with my father playing the dice game Quatre Cent Vingt Et Un, '421', rose up to serve me. Cupping the two dice in my right hand, rolling them back and forth (ivory warms to the touch immediately, like skin), I blew softly, fingering the gently rounded corners of the dice with my thumb. Opening eyes wide, lifting my chin, leaning forwards, showing off my décolleté—which Tata said was even better than Thea's—I threw. The dice rolled across the green baize, hit the far end, and rolled back. There was a collective sigh.

When we returned to New York, Robert told me what he'd put on the table as he was turning the key in his apartment door—two thousand dollars. A few weeks later there were phone calls and hang-ups when I answered. Then came the threats—the message that my husband should return the call or else. Bobby showed me where he kept a rifle hidden on a shelf behind his suits, and how to use it. He'd come home around nine or ten in the evening, and, without a word, shave, change shirt and suit, and go out again. There was an underground craps game in New Jersey. There were women. I couldn't take any of it in, though its atmosphere of suspense, danger (denied), excitement, was strangely familiar.

One evening when Bobby came in, expecting some delicious amuse-bouche from his French wife before going out again to try his luck at a game, I dished out what I called 'Hamburger à la Sauce Marchand de Vin'. I had prepared meat from a can of Alpo dog food, binding it with egg white, adding handfuls of finely chopped parsley, and freshly ground peppercorns from my travel-sized treasured Peugeot pepper mill (which I kept in my handbag). I sat there, watching Robert Gibb Pratt eat dog food, chasing it up with his standard drink, Bourbon on the rocks.

The months passed, and I eventually told Tata of these things. She suggested a trial separation.

"Ne pleures pas trop, Pussinetta. Viens passer l'été avec nous." She sent me an open ticket so I could fly back when ready to face my husband. We'd only been married four months. The word husband was only a word.

While abroad, I wrote countless letters to Bobby, hoping, explaining, analysing, describing. Then, upon my return two months later, there they all were, stacked on the hall table, unopened. I dropped my suitcase by the apartment door and there it remained for the next two days. I folded in on myself like an accordion in the big arm chair facing the window, staring out at Second Avenue. Traffic going uptown, skyscrapers, daytime turning into nighttime, while thoughts crowded my mind—thoughts of my father, husband, the church blessing we'd arranged after the elopement, our families attending, my father asking if he could walk me up the aisle.

"Too late, I'm married, my husband wants to walk me up the aisle," I'd said.

A photograph of my father standing at the back of the church, leaning against the wall, his face so sad, would haunt me for years. I didn't know I could be so cruel. More images passed before my gaze. Leïla's telegram a week before the ceremony: J'ARRIVE STOP AVEC TROUSSEAU STOP. A suitcase for the silver, a bigger suitcase for the sets of linen sheets with pillowcases embroidered with my initials, fine cotton lace baby pillow covers, just like those on her bed. And then the clothes and accessories: two Yves St Laurent couture dresses with short Jackie O style jackets; a Chanel coat; a gold brooch from Van Cleef with matching earrings in the form of open flowers and little diamonds in the centres.

Bobby's charm. My father's charm. My mother—who didn't even come—her charm too. I thought about all of this. And Ninin, in her mink pillbox hat for special occasions, a little askew on her head. The défilé of these pictures finally stopped around midnight and I left the apartment. I decided I must apply for a divorce, so I was hardly surprised when a few days later Bobby burst into my office. I was working full time as a designer and buyer in a department store. Bobby stood in the doorway weeping and declaiming I was his saviour, he couldn't live without me. He took me home, to bed, and I woke the next morning sick with the realisation of my self-betrayal. The lawyer in charge of my divorce explained that, by returning to the conjugal bed, I had given up any chance of support. We'd been married less than a year, but it would take six years for the whole mess to undo.

It was time to live alone.

My apartment—the first three months rent funded by Teddy—was an L-shaped room on the 13th floor. It was listed, however, as the 14th floor as this was a superstition of many of Manhattan's high rise residential buildings. The apartment overlooked a long and wide flat roof and, beyond turrets—thirties-style castle tops on surrounding buildings, water towers on their stilts and, sliced between two skyscrapers, a piece-of-pie view of the tree tops in Central Park. On a summer's night, I could hear the coughing throatiness of lions in the zoo on the other side of Fifth Avenue. And, as ever and always, music. As soon as I crossed my own threshold, just as my father did wherever he lived, I put it on—blues, jazz, opera, Beethoven, Brahms, or Ravel's eleven-minute *Bolero* that I used to dance to in secret in Strasbourg—a need fulfilled.

There was a deep yellow velvet two-seater sofa which pulled out as a bed—this was the guest area. Guests would be my father, or Miguel, arriving from Brazil.

"Get on the floor," he'd say, deadpan, putting on a record and lying down, "Put your ear to the floor." An eerie echoey howl hummed through the room, sounds I'd never heard before—an electric guitar twanging itself into a violin, reverberating through the floor into the bones of my skull.

My father would drop in from Ecuador, stay for a night or two. Walking into the bathroom he'd say, "Ferme tes yeux, j'arrive." Caught off guard, I'd obey, muted by surprise.

A wall-to-wall dark green moquette carpet, exactly the same colour as the carpet in Strasbourg, stretched across the one room apartment. Opposite the guest area, a table just big enough for two, and a pair of open armchairs. A free-standing bookshelf divided the living space, a single divan bed on the other side, with a big comfy armchair piled up with clothes I seldom put away. And I had a Siamese cat called Tallulah. She talked a lot about being confined indoors while staring at the pigeons on the flat roof outside the window.

I listened to music in my L-shaped apartment on the thirteenth floor that didn't exist. There was a song from a new film about raindrops falling on your head, and not giving a goddamn. When the song played I was happy, carefree—life was easy riding. It said, jump on...jump off...never mind the cliff...hey ho Monkey, away we go. Sometimes I'd walk to the Baptist church two streets away where I'd stand at the back, the only white face, swaying to the Gospel choir, clapping and stomping in rhythm with the congregation.

At this time, I remember watching a documentary about the massacre of big game in Africa. *Mondo Cane—A Dog's*

World had an exquisite musical score that floated over unbearable images of piles of bloodied elephants, their ivories torn off, mutilated and maimed. I had to walk out halfway through, but I still bought the record of the soundtrack. Drawn to the melody which put a spell on me, it gave me a violent longing for something I had no name for. I danced with that invisible pain—the pain that runs through a family—to The Charleston, rock and roll, batucada, merengue and samba. The *Mondo Cane* melody haunted me for years, right up to my forties when I embarked on psychotherapy and Jungian analysis. My dreams drew a portrait of an inner unrecognised self: dreams of maimed animals, abandoned creatures left starving, wild animals charging—rhinoceros (blind aggression), a tiger (man-eating). I learned Jung's dictum about living the symbolic life and I experienced aspects of this opposing 'other' in me. With time the *Mondo Cane* musical spell would lose its power over me.

I wrote what I called story poems: of Alma, mirror to the man doing up his tie; the mermaid who sat for centuries on the big rock calling out in vain for a sailor to take her to land; the old lady, a Russian refugee and her cat Olga; and the nightingale that sang all night long. An editor from Knopf read a draft of my poems. He said I had a feel for language and to come back when I found my feelings. I took this literally, not really understanding what he meant. Back at the apartment I tried cutting myself, on the top side of my wrist. But nothing came to me other than a sting as the knife cut through my skin. I had not yet read Yeats' statement that it takes a lifetime to find our feelings, and then longer to believe them.

And meanwhile I struggled daily with fatigue, as if I were dragging heavy iron chains around my ankles. A doctor prescribed a pill to be taken once, or even twice a day if I felt the need. It made me light and chatty and zigzaggy with energy lasting a day. The name was Dexedrine. Only years later, living in England, no longer available over the counter and had to stop, did I understand what I was being prescribed was speed, and why I felt so awful for one whole year after.

I had debts, regularly visiting the big pawn shop on West 57th Street, past Henri Bendel and Bergdorf Goodman. I hocked the Van Cleef gold and diamond earrings and brooch in the shape of flowers that Tata Leïla gave me. The gold bracelets and necklaces from my father also went, and a brooch made of Brazilian semi-precious stones which belonged to my mother but was left behind in the care of Leila when she left New York.

Sometimes, on a Sunday, I wandered downtown armed with my precious Konica camera through Wall Street's deserted echoing canyons, back uptown through the Bowery, drawn to the down and out figures and places. There was a middle-aged man, unshaven, overcoat lapels turned up, arms folded on a shelf, staring out of a bar window from under the brim of his hat. I took the photograph. That's more than fifty years ago, but the black and white photograph still stands in my cloakroom. Every time I see this black man's dulled face, vacant eyes, I catch something of myself in the window's reflection.

*

On an evening when an urge to roam came upon me, I would dress for the occasion. This could take an hour, maybe longer. I tried things on. The dark maroon velvet trousers, the black tie Yves St Laurent pantsuit, the long red silk jersey shirt dress, the striped red and black Sonia Rykiel sweater worn with a wide shiny black belt and flared black skirt.

I'm standing on the corner of 60th and Third. Humidity, heat, and yellow taxi cabs on their way uptown. A red light says 'Don't Walk'. Behind me a wall of light from Bloomingdales' windows spills across the sidewalk. I note the summer dress on one of the mannequins. It calls me to go buy it tomorrow, but I don't have the money. So what.

The light turns green. 'Walk', it says. Crossing Third Avenue, the tarred surface of the road is cushiony-soft from the heat of day. My high heels sink in the black spongy tar, cars panting on my right, the heat of their engines breathing on the calves of my legs. I jump to safety on the sidewalk. The wave of traffic roars down the avenue past me. The restaurant on the corner has a glassed-in terrace. Tables for two with candles, cave darkness beyond the glow.

Walk on. Past the dive, faces in candlelight. Round the block, and back. Music, talk. I want to go in, but I don't. There was the smart little Gristede Foods Store two blocks away. I bought a pack of the bright red twice-ground hamburger meat, a box of frozen French fries, a hamburger bun, two brownies, and a box of Fig Newtons. Home, back at the apartment, I prepare my supper, take out the tray painted in a green and white and black-like dappled shade, covered in glass. I look down into it as through the canopy of a tree, my face reflected there. The wood frame and handles are painted glossy black. There are black and green and white napkins to match. I lay out my supper the way my aunt Agatha taught me: glass, knife, fork. Salt and pepper mills at the top. Napkin on the left.

Almost midnight, my time to watch movies. I turn on the all-night channel and search for the 'Late Late Night Movie Show'. Movies about love, about adventure, with Gene Kelly, Rita Hayworth, Ava Gardner, Gregory Peck. I gaze into every face *and feel something*. Happy-go-lucky. Lucky Strike cigarette packet on the pavement. Step on it—brings you luck, the ad says. Station platforms, taxis and aeroplanes. Running across the tarmac, plane with a single propeller rotating clockwise—always clockwise, that's what Daddy said. Ingrid Bergman and Humphrey Bogart. Suits and open-necked shirts, hand-rolled handkerchief in jacket pocket, wide belt, cinched waist, flaring skirt, click clack high heels crossing the avenues of Paris, Madrid, New York. Isn't life exciting, magic? My father said that when I was a little girl I said 'hello buff' to the bus.

Hello tree.

Hello bird.

Scared. Sit down on floor—hug knees—humming Daddy's music.

I write something, anything, to keep myself together.

Twenty-five and pregnant, again. This second abortion took place in a private brownstone in the East Sixties—a clean and elegant part of Manhattan, across the street from my friend, Debby. Although the procedure was legal by then, anaesthesia was refused, the clinic receptionist oozed disapproval. The pain was severe enough to keep me fully conscious of pain and guilt. A nurse squeezed my hand as I moaned. The doctor said I had one healthy ovary left but would most likely not bear a child after this termination.

When Life Walks In
Looking Like An Englishman

My right hand on the telephone, poised as on a Bible. I was alone in my apartment on the non-existent thirteenth floor. I made a promise to myself—an oath.

"C'est fini. No more men—no French, no Russian, no American, no Italian, no Spanish. Nada."

A few weeks passed when Debby called to say an Englishman was coming to dinner. It was his first time in New York and I should come and talk to him, so I promised her I would. And that was when I first met Julius T. Gallagher. From the moment I laid eyes on him, I was running. Tall, strong, copper-coloured hair, no eyebrows—well, none that you could see. His skin was pink and white and covered in freckles, and—unlike the others—he was honest, reliable, solid, informed… and right about everything. We argued, how we argued!

Julius felt foreign to me, but I could never put my finger on it, the attraction so insistent, a secret geomorphology underlying us like two magnets unable to keep themselves apart. I argued with this attraction. He wasn't my type—such pink and white skin; no eyebrows; his socks were too short (I sent him home the first time he came to take me out to dinner). I sensed he would be difficult and swampy-moody, but perhaps no more than my own man-eating tiger moods. For all his brilliant education (which I envied), he wasn't interested in Tolstoy or Balzac, and he was bored—bored, how dare he!—by Chekhov.

Like Robert, Julius proposed within a day of our meeting, only this time I said no, and meant it. I wasn't divorced, but it made no difference. Julius was a terrier with a bone and I nicknamed him Milou.

Walking along the beach one summer evening Julius spoke some words made of soul and I was taken. Words spoken a certain way run up and down a woman's spine and spirit rises from its slumber, as the snake to the fluid notes of the flute. I fell under a spell, and this one was to be lifelong.

"Come gentle night… give me my Romeo… and when I shall die… take him and cut him out in little stars…"

"Again," I said.

Conversation between us became—erotic, electric. He would say that he was agnostic—or was it atheist? We argued about this too. But I felt safe. Neither gods nor demons disturbed his sleep. And then, once again, I fell pregnant. The fighting between us was now filled with pain. It felt like we were up against a dead end. Even Julius had to admit defeat. The erotic, the electric, all gone.

But, this time, I had a gentleman at my side. Julius made the necessary arrangements and I was looked after in the safety of the Leroy Hospital on Park Avenue. An immense sadness filled me—one that I had not felt the other two times. The next morning, lying in my bed looking out on Park Avenue, I realised that this was the hospital where I had been born.

Julius and I agreed that this was the end of our story. He

returned to London. Well that's over, I told myself.

Ten months later, the telephone.

'Alló, oui?'

"Bonjour." A man's voice I didn't recognise, speaking impeccable French, pronounced my name à la francaise—an irresistible touch. Julius had taken an eight-day intensive Berlitz course.

"Viens à Londres," he said. He even pronounced the liaison correctly—*vienzalondres*.

London. A hotel room. Marvelling at the magnificence of this man's shoulders, I asked, "Qu'est-ce que c'est, 'Rowing Blue'?"

Julius explained about Oxford University, the Boat Race, team spirit, the brutality on the muscles of arms, legs, shoulders, everything.

"Feel my thighs," he said, "go on, punch them."

I sighed theatrically, "Oh la laaah… dûr comme oak tree trunks."

He spoke about many things and pronounced the unpronounceable name of the town where he was born.

"Vaizagapotam."

"Vaiza-quoi?"

"Vai-zaga-po-tam. I was born in India."

I told him I was (maybe) Syrian on my father's side, and of the legend of my great grandfather.

"You must write a book about that," he said. Oh why, oh why, was I told this again and again over the years by so many? And why was I so reluctant? The poets write that the creative act begins in chaos—from therein no control, no order, they declare. Lie down beside your fears, befriend your terrors.

We spoke about the thirst for knowledge. Did I know of Scott Fitzgerald's '*College for One*'—the reading list of one hundred books he drew up for his lover, Sheila Graham? Later she would write about her affair with Fitzgerald, using his title. The books changed her life.

I asked Julius what the list was made up of.

"I'll tell you," he said, "in the next twenty-five years." A pause. A knowing smile, "Grow old with me. The best is yet to be."

Underlying life, I believe, is a secret geomorphology, an irresistible natural force that draws one person to another. Like a pair of magnets, they are (almost) impossible to pry apart. And so indeed, I stopped running. Julius was my fate—or was it destiny? Mektoub. I resigned from work, pulled up my American roots, packed, and prepared for my emigration. I have often wondered at what point in the crossing of lands and oceans does the emigrant become immigrant. I had watched and learned throughout childhood how this works—with tears and then, face blank, turn away, walk on, no looking back. I sorted my apartment and its small amount of furniture. I said goodbye to my cat, Tallulah, and gave her to one of the lady singers in the Baptist church around the corner. The rest, nicknacks and books and clothes, fitted into one trunk.

While my belongings were taken to be shipped abroad, I stayed at Debby's house, returning to my building every other day to pick up any post and final bills.

One day, at the doorman's desk, two men in overcoats and hats addressed me.

"M'am we're looking to get into Apt. 14E. Is that you? There's been a murder reported. We're looking for the body of a girl."

The three of us went up to my apartment. They inspected the fridge, the oven, the dishwasher, cupboards above and below. I stood nervously beside the trunk in the middle of the room feeling surreal and wondering why on earth I should be feeling guilty. Open the trunk, they said. Then the two men left, without a word. And I left America, the country of my birth—home, empty of thought, empty of feeling.

"When you left America you left Loïse behind. She is still there, waiting for you," Tata Leïla would say years later.

Part Three

Two Marriages Eleven Changes Of Address

1971-1973:
Chelsea, Holland Park, Clapham

1973-1983:
Manhattan, Bedford (Westchester County, USA),
Katonah (Westchester County, USA)

1983-2009:
Richmond, Fulham, South Kensington,
Blakeney (Norfolk),
Houseboat (Chelsea),
Letcombe Regis (Oxfordshire),
Cousin's cottage (Oxfordshire),
Uffington (Oxfordshire),
St. Cezaire (South of France),
Chelsea, South Kensington

Heads In Buckets

London, 1980s

One summer day, walking into my local delicatessen, there on a chair by the door was a neat-looking khaki cloth bag—square, with a netted window on the side. Inside there was a bird, the size of a pigeon, with a parrot's beak and wings of many colours.

I walked up to it. The bird cocked its head, and I cocked mine.

"My bird," said a woman standing a few feet away. "I rescued it, and it's recovering. We're so pleased—though it has no song, yet." She carried on about its health. I interrupted. "The colours! Where is it from—do you know?"

"Brazil," the lady said.

"Brazil! " I cried out. "Babushkina. Que tal? Hermosa pajarrrrito." Rolling the rr's, I went on—whatever came to mind. "Quieres bailar? Papa-zinha, Mama-zinha. Coraçáozinho." The bird twirled on its tiny perch, little baby feathers fluffing up from under its wings.

"Goodness—are you Brazilian?"

"No, no," I said. I wanted to sing and dance. "Karina poopoochka," I cooed. "Dostoyevska Chekov-nanachkaya!" The bird made little clicks with its parroty beak.

"It's sending you kisses—I don't believe it! " the owner said, not sounding too pleased. "It never sends *me* kisses."

"Do you have knowledge of birds?" the woman wanted to know. "Can I have your address?"

Oh dear, time to go. I was shaking with tremors inside and out. An incoherence of images whizzed through me: café terraces, cobbled streets and wide pavements; the dry clicking of palm tree leaves waving in a warm breeze; le salon dans sa maison; the Russian who came to tea; the Portuguese who stayed for lunch; conversations in Brazilian, German, Spanish, bits of English, Russian, Italian.

"Is it the 'me' in all of this that I miss?" I asked myself, standing on the street corner, looking up at the English sky—the implacable flat grey ceiling of it—my life passing by underneath—unlived. I remembered the sun in my eyes, bare feet in the sand, the tinkling of ice in my glass, lemon on the lips and my father calling out, his arms raised and clapping his hands, "Garçon! Deux citrons pressés s'il vous plaît."

For a moment, I stood back in time, when mountains were just mountains and days were just days—as many as I wanted, as long as sea-waves. I walked back to my car, sat at the wheel and wept; homesick.

Some books take a lifetime to write. We experience our lives afterwards. You don't know at the time that you are watching, that you are listening. It all takes so long. It is Yeats who says in his autobiographies that It is so many years before one can believe enough in what one feels even to know what the feeling is. And I know now, nearing the end of my eighth decade, that the act of looking back, really looking and feeling, is to consciously re-enter an event, vulnerable and alive and present to the moment in a way that one could not be at the time.

In the very early years of being married and always keen to travel, Julius said, "Let's drive to Alsace, stay at that famous hotel your father knows about and we can visit Strasbourg and you can show me where you used to live." Quicker than lightning, like lemon on the oyster, my whole being drew back into itself. No, it said. No. But why, and how to say? I couldn't think, so I said nothing. A few days later I could feel something unpleasant going on in a part of my body that I didn't want to know about. Arrangements were made. Our two daughters, at that time six and nine, Rose and Kate, would stay with their grandmother, my mother-in-law. My father, who knew everybody in the business of fast cars, American movies, the best restaurants and hotels just about anywhere in France, booked us the best table and the best room in the ancient and famous Auberge de l'Ill.

We set off, crossing the Channel on a ferryboat, a turbulent ride which in itself increased my malaise. The drive across Northern France was scheduled as part of the adventure. We took two days stopping on the way for one delicious meal after another. By the second day I could barely sit. The pain between my legs unbearable. We were in the middle of lunch when, blushing, sweating, in tears, I pleaded, "Julius. Get me to a hospital."

The French doctor, examining me, expressed surprise. Why had I waited so long, he wondered. And how interesting, he'd never seen such a big specimen—a vaginal cyst, an abscess named after its discoverer, Casper Bartholin, a Danish anatomist of the 17th century. The thing would have to be cut out, there was the need for anaesthesia, but I would be immediately relieved of pain, he reassured me.

I had spoken little of my time in Alsace, perhaps once mentioning en passant that my uncle used to 'fiddle'. It was the only word I could think of. Such things were not spoken of, didn't have a name, and sat well-behaved inside their well-kept silence. We are lived by forces we pretend to understand, W. H. Auden said.

We never made it to the Auberge de l'Ill, let alone to Strasbourg. It was perhaps ten years later, in analysis, talking about the psychosomatic that I put two and two together. But I digress—marriage, children, husband, however beloved, are not in themselves my story. It is in the writing act that I seek to get behind them, and find the individual self. I have in mind a moment in Karen Blixen's story, Out of Africa, when she has lost almost everything. She leaves her headman to wait several hours outside the bank where she hopes to be granted a loan to save her home. He responds "Time is of no matter. Now I will live."

Jung says marriage is the king and queen of relationships, that it demands compromise, adapting to the differences, transformation, none of which is possible without the mystery of love. My marriage to Julius would indeed become a life-changing adventure. London for our first two years together, when and where Kate was born, then New York almost ten years, where Rose was born, then back to London. We moved house eleven times. I was overcome by the restlessness and too muchness of it all. It was after thirteen years together that we separated, divorced and, after nearly four years, would remarry, the second marriage lasting fifteen years. Counting the years of separation (destiny never did let go however hard we fought it) our marriage was of thirty-one years. Though we live apart, the bond still holds some twenty years after that. We have a conversation, and we share our pains. The mystery of love indeed. As long as we stand apart, we are a couple.

So it was when first time separated that for the first time in my life, I owned a house. And I was writing, fulfilling my dream of life in a bohemian world. And yet though thrilling, inside I was unhappy and full of questions. I began seeing Dr. Cobb, a consultant psychiatrist and psychotherapist at The Priory Clinic in Roehampton. I started sessions at a distance of once a month, fearful of a closeness to something I intuited as dangerous… then twice monthly, then once a week.

Dr. Cobb would explain to me that everything in the dreams I brought him—people, animals, landscapes, weather, even objects—were all images representing emotion, the shape and movement of e-motion, all an aspect of what was in motion inside me. It reminded me of how my uncle Edred had talked about there being herds of animals inside one's tummy. Many sessions passed telling stories about my family, my children, my husband.

"You talk about your father. You talk about your mother. Aunts and uncles and grandmother. But where are you? What is your story?" he asked. "Julius says this, Julius says that. Your husband is not here yet the room is full of him. Depending on his moods, and yours, Julius has turned into some kind of giant. Your rock, you say. Hero of giant proportions, and poet and provider with capital P. How can he live up to any of those projections? And by the way, the poet is you, and yes you are wedded to a force of nature—in my thirty years as a consultant psychiatrist and psychotherapist I have never met anyone with his kind of power of persuasion. He should be listed in the Guinness Book of World Records, and you may tell him I said so. While you need to ask yourself how that relates to your history."

Meanwhile Dr. C and I continue to examine my life's inner events. It means digging up things forgotten—or buried, as he puts it. Dismembered and remembered. Such as coming upon both my parents' heads in buckets of water, stored in a garage. Dead bodies, frozen limbs, threatening animals—a bear, a lion, a rhinoceros, and an alligator—all after me. For nights on end wounded, raging creatures appear, some threatening, some caged, some in desperate need of care. How about the man-like gorillas in a compound, bodies skinned, raw? Dr. C wondered aloud what might I be making of this rawness. The gorillas look like a Francis Bacon painting, I suggested evasively. "Never mind art," Dr. C said. "You need to think about your own neglect, how feelings are compounded in your unconscious. It is your responsibility to do something about those big miserable monkeys."

Visits to Dr. C continued. I brought him more dreams, drawings of my dreams, music, and books. He accepted recordings of Verdi's *Requiem*, and the opera *Macbeth*. Those bushy eyebrows of his unusually stilled.

"It's the 'Dies Irae'," I explained, "and the 'Witches' Chorus'. You must listen."

"Thank you," he said, nodding. "I'll refrain from taking the murderous themes personally."

I brought him a book called *The Pregnant Virgin,* by Marion Woodman, a Canadian Jungian analyst whom I had recently met and whose once a year week-long retreats I would join. This time he looked pleased, in fact he seemed to have trouble remaining seated.

"You are intuitive, sometimes frighteningly so," he suggested, holding the book up. Then, leaning forwards, he said, "I have impregnated you."

His words were too close too much too soon. I took his metaphor literally, and recoiled.

I was wearing my silk and linen Prince of Wales jacket. I dressed carefully before going out for these sessions—handkerchief with hand-rolled edges puffing up from the breast pocket, Fedora hat, pleated trousers. And one of my leather chokers—I wore chokers with everything.

Now Dr C mused that the chokers that I wore made him wonder about enslavement. What were my thoughts about this? Again, I said nothing. Anger and fear inside me. Don't let out the beast, I remembered my mother's saying, and yet here I was learning the opposite. Dr Cobb went on talking—about emasculation, and that in dreams people, animals, landscape and weather, even objects, all being a universal aspect of ourselves, however horrible, are in need of acceptance.

Marrying Julius for a second time marked a new beginning, and to me, in terms of effort and transformation, it would be the real marriage. As I saw it, the first marriage was for fun, even for joy, for being unconscious, free to build our lives as we wished. Then, the second time, as I was learning with Dr. Cobb, there was responsibility—to become conscious of how one's own pain and woundedness could cause harm to others. I wanted to know what was behind the harm already done.

It was two years into our second marriage that Julius, aware of the restlessness regarding his working life, left the City. As he put it, we had a year of freedom (from the need to earn a living). What to do during such free time?

"How about going around the world?" he suggested.

"Oh, dear God, no." Hotels, taxis and aeroplanes passed by me. I heard myself say, "Let's go for a walk."

"Walk? What do you mean?"

A bit surprised myself, I fished for words, "Well .... You'll like it because we'll be moving all the time.... and I'll like it because it's terra firma."

To my surprise, Julius liked the idea. But where?

Whilst going back and forth about where to walk—not up mountains I prayed—we happened to be invited for a weekend away at my mother's house in France, near Toulouse. There, in conversation on the subject, my mother came up with the idea of going from the Mediterranean to the Atlantic… Yes, that was it!. Our Walk now was awarded importance with a capital letter, and took on the quality of myth-in-the-making.

And so we would walk across France. From sunrise to sunset, from East to West, along the foothills of the Pyrenees. I was forty-four years old and had never engaged in sports of any kind. Without such experience, it didn't cross my mind that the simple act of walking would challenge me from top to toe. It would be yet another first step in the process of something inside transforming and it would serve for the rest of my life whenever the thought 'I can't go on' rose in my mind - which it would all too often.

When we returned home, I wrote a book about the experience. My good friend and editor, Buz Wyeth, at Harper & Row in New York, loved it. In a letter to me, he wrote that he read the manuscript sitting up in bed, passing page after page to his wife beside him. A month later he wrote back saying that his publishing house—oh such a good one and he a legend in the literary world—was being taken over. Books were now being chosen by a committee and my book had been voted out. I threw the manuscript down the stairs, all two hundred and eighty-two agitated pages.

So, in the end, it was Julius who would write a book about walking across France with his French wife. He had the maps he'd scrutinised all the way to go by, plus his knowledge of history, time, and place, as well as my scribbled on-the-road notes, which he asked for and which I, as good muse, gave him for the feeling of things. The book was published, and it was a success. I was pleased, really pleased for my husband, while for myself I felt confusion, numbness, and loss. At least the story was out there, I told myself—thanks to Julius' ability to imagine, create, execute—make real. Which it seemed, I could not; yet.

But Julius' book was not my book—or my story. This realisation resonated with Dr. Cobb who asked me to differentiate between my life, and the life of others. My story of The Walk is a collection of moments that would shape the course of my life. Like the woman in Narbonne, who sat on the bench opposite me on our bistro terrace. How at ease she sat, thighs widely spread, string bags full of groceries on either side of her sandalled feet like obedient canines; the way she stared into the shade of the plane trees; her swollen ankles; face in repose. It made me see that I never did this—I never sat to pause for thought on my way home from daily errands. Sitting on a cafe terrace was so much part of my childhood, and that day I promised myself that when I got back to London I would take time to sit and watch the world go by, to be present to fatigue, give time to my muse who wants me to write. Today, writing this, I think of the times I have read my mother's autobiography. The first time I was saddened to see how little I featured in her life story. The second time, five or ten years later, I was surprised how much I did feature in her book. Another five or ten years pass by then struggling to write my own life as memoir, I can admire how my mother keeps to her own world view, inadvertently revealing herself. I come to know my mother and accept her as I couldn't before.

After we returned from the walk, we sold the much-too-big house (so it seemed after a month living with backpacks) we had bought two years before upon remarrying. We moved to Norfolk, to a smaller house in a village by the sea that Julius had bought during our separation. But it was too far away, and so we moved (again) to Oxfordshire, closer to London and to the boarding schools of our two daughters. It was an old manor house with a stream at the bottom of the garden where the kingfishers came; where I watched *Out of Africa* thirty-one times when Julius was away (so much). We lived there as a family of four for almost ten years—a record for us. "At last, we are settling and putting down roots," I remember thinking with passion. It was here that I wrote, and drew, and sculpted. It was here that I walked every day on the Downs, along the most ancient of roads, the Ridgeway. And it was here that the girls' problems with addiction manifested and where my youngest daughter, Rose, made her first suicide attempt, aged eighteen. It was in this house where I woke up to my role as a mother, where I had failed my daughters and might be granted the time to mend.

Although my second marriage to the same man was different—even very different to the first—the same patterns tracked me down. I could not escape them, but at least now I was present to the struggle to differentiate between mine and my husband's. Julius was away more and more on his new venture of emerging markets in Africa. I was also reading more and more analytical literature, and the vast works of Carl Jung, which led me to question my husband's way of life not being my way of life - an eternal dilemma of the loss of soul. I was visiting Dr. Cobb on a regular basis now. We explored the walk, what was being asked of me to invite such an outgoing venture, what was to be sacrificed for its realisation. To go on the walk, I had had to abort my first attempt of a novel—I had almost finished a first draft. I had had an upsetting dream about my sister having to have an abortion. She was unexpectedly understanding and accepting of the loss, leading to a gift from her husband—a pearl necklace. Dr. C remarked on the exchange of values that the dream was pointing at, and how the qualities of wisdom in my sister were representing a part of myself that I was unconscious of. I didn't know how much I loved (and needed) my husband.

Grit In The Oyster

France, 1989

As we walked across France, I got to know a part of Julius and a part of myself unknown. A map, to me, bore no relation to the look and feel of a place, but I was beginning to recognise and admire, even envy, Jules' spatial sense and ability: the apparent ease of handling myriad signs, lines, numbers, dots and dashes; the ability to see mountains and rivers, latitudes and altitudes on the page; the ability to execute and achieve; the ability to get what he wanted, no matter what.

The idea for the walk came from me, my imagination, but it was my husband who made it real. How often in my life in New York, as a young woman, had I been able to fulfil the desire to go for a walk in the rain, or to wander down Wall Street on a Sunday afternoon and take photographs? I did, but once or twice only. How hard I found it to make a social call, a friend, instead remaining in my one-room apartment, weekend after weekend, as if paralysed. The loneliness of it, the near madness. In the first years of my first marriage to Julius, I would not travel without him. We walked hip-to-hip like Siamese twins. Our friends would say that we were the most together couple they had ever known.

*

It was maybe a week into our journey, while I was struggling up a hill, that I heard a car coming up from behind and I jumped to the side.

Julius called out from behind, "Don't!"

"Why not?" I asked.

"Do the opposite," he explained. "Step to the middle of the road, make *them* move."

Goosebumps rippled along my skin. How his words and sentences—erudite, witty, sharp—flashed by, like motorway traffic—so much of it, so fast. This is what would happen between us.

Dr. C said that this was typical of a masculine dynamic. I needed to learn how to let go of my tendency to question, explain, interpret, which is what drained me far more than my husband's style of debate. In other words, as Julius would say sometimes with a smile, "You don't have to rise to the bait."

On our third or fourth night on the trail, we had dinner at The Muscadelle, a little gite near Carcassonne. We'd gone down to dinner promptly at seven thirty, ravenous. The restaurant was crowded and it was easy to tell it was a favourite with the locals. The lady of the house had her own distinctive manner of flirting with the room, moving as in a dance, her feet swiftly sliding and scuffing along the polished floorboards, hips in an easy swing as she weaved between tables. She answered calls, depositing a little dish of something extra in one continuous movement, passing here and there, plates balanced on both forearms. A miniature dish of ratatouille was tangoed up to Julius.

"Here you are, just to taste. We made too much. Allez-y cher monsieur, dégustez."

Julius occupied himself with a cassoulet. For me, a dark andouillette, the grilled sausage that smells of leaves and wet earth, with caramelised onions. I learned the love of food from my father. He was a very good cook, and I became one too. His specialty was sauces. We would call each other, continents apart, and exchange ideas on the latest secret ingredient, such as handfuls of fresh mint leaves crushed in the blender with a little veal stock, red wine and a dash of mustard, to go with roast lamb. "Not that English thing, confiture avec la viande."

Food is a moody business, like weather and sex. Going to the market, the handling and choosing of produce, the tasting of a Muscat grape, pressing two thumbs at the top of a melon, or tugging at its curly stem. The foreplay acts of preparation and presentation—peeling, chopping, slicing— in accord with the shape of things, following the uneven curve of a potato, extracting half-moon shapes from the pear. I thought of all this as I watched the lady at The Muscatelle. The pride of service shown in the movements of her body, the expression on her face, the artful smile for her clientèle—the theatre of it all well familiar to me. Cookery and poetry books piled up on my bedside table. I devised my own school of cooking and became a very good cook, perhaps filling in the gaps where I failed as wife and mother. The table was laid, the food was delicious, jazz in the background, the fireplace alive with flame, day and night whatever the sturm und drang in our lives.

Julius devised that, on the walk, we would stop and rest every hour and a half, and for no more than five to seven minutes. A bit military, I privately thought at first, but I learned how right he was. After each short break, I was ready to get going again. Any longer and my limbs became so stiff that it would take an uncomfortable hour—if not the day— to get back into my stride. How magical those five minutes were. Off with the rucksack, drop, lie, look up through the leaves. My body at one with the ground, aligned with earth and sky, drawing itself into the six lines of an I-Ching hexagram. So deeply sensual. The pleasure and pain of grit in the oyster making its pearl.

Two nights later, at the Hotel de la Gare in a tiny village, a wedding supper was being prepared. Our room was above the dining room, and the so-called double bed a little small. It was decided (by Julius) that, since he was the larger of the two of us, he would take the bed. Uncertain about this, but unable to articulate my hesitancy, I agreed in silence. After a while, I drifted off to sleep. Trains rumbled through the night, once or twice every hour, inches from my head, their colossal engines vibrating inside my pillow. Lying in my narrow bedding on the floor, wrapped in the one sheet and blanket stolen from the armoire down the hall, I rocked as if in a canoe in the wake of passing battleships. The live wedding orchestra pulled and dragged me out of sleep-mists with songs I hadn't heard in years. 'Les Flons Flons Du Bal'—that was New York, my grandmother Ninin. 'La Vie en Rose'—wasn't that Paris? My twenty-first birthday party chez Moustache—'Mousse' as my father called one of his oldest war buddies. Oh, and just before falling asleep, strangely comforted by the familiarity of the melodies and their lyrics, 'Il Y Avait Un Rat Dans Ma Chambre', Strasbourg, an image of Uncle Edred floated by.

*

On the next day, our sixth, our walk took us past the grounds of a small chateau with a farm. As we passed by a big open courtyard, a chorus of wild barking erupted, followed by a rush of dogs stampeding in our direction. I kept my eyes to the ground. Julius turned round and round on himself, keeping a sight on each dog. Two were huge—one black with a square face, the other an Alsatian which jumped up at me.

"Use the alarm. *Quick*," I said to Julius, "for Heaven's sake." I was in a whirlpool of dog, furious and terrified. Julius didn't reply. The smaller dogs of the pack fell back.

"I think they're okay," Julius said at last. "They only want to play, look," he pointed, adding, "the alarm might have frightened them."

"Frightened *them*! How about *me*?"

"Their tails are wagging. Look," he said again.

Just ahead, the Alsatian and a different black dog, perhaps a Labrador, led the way, as if our escorts. Julius continued in silence and my words echoed back at me. I was ashamed of my fear. Moments passed and the two dogs trotted on, nuzzling each other, friends at play. Then one, the Lab, turned his head and ran up to me. Struggling to master the rough sea of sensations inside me, I asked Julius—who'd been brought up with dogs—why the dog kept doing this.

"They smell your fear," he explained. "That's why they go up to you, not me. They want to know what's wrong with you. They don't want to harm you. Really, they want to lick you better." As he spoke, the Labrador jumped up on me once more. I stiffened, but made myself look at him and saw that his expression was gentle, not hostile. He returned to his friend.

I had been unaware until that moment of just how afraid I was of dogs, of how much fear I carried—as Dr. C had put it one day—and that not all of it was mine.

When we were about halfway, Julius suggested we have a rest day, and that I call my mother. "See if she can drive down and join us for lunch tomorrow," he suggested. "If she says yes, it's heads, and we stay. If it's no, it's tails, and we walk on."

Thea, separated from her third and last husband, now lived in Quercy, barely two hours away. When we last talked about our adventure, she had been madly keen, wanting to hear of our progress, and had even wondered about meeting up with us, joining in on the walk, just for a day. I had misgivings about my mother's wounded persona, drawing and demanding constant attention. But it was generous of Julius to want to invite her now. He was usually wary of my family, in this case my mother's siren-like persona which could be at once enticing and ambiguous to a man who would be elevated one minute and dropped the next.

As Julius wandered off, I spotted a cabine téléphonique just off the square, a modern glass cubicle with steel ribs and joints. I stepped inside, closed the door, and dialled the number. As my mother and I were talking, I became aware of the intensifying heat. I pushed at the door with my free hand while holding the handset to my ear with my other hand. It was rather like a shower door that slides and folds back on itself, however this one resisted. I tried pushing it with my bottom, all the while continuing to talk. The problem eventually overtook the conversation.

"Is something the matter?" my mother asked.

"I'm trying to open the door. It's rather hot in here," I

said, shaking and pushing and pulling, and now sweating profusely.

"Are you alright? What's happening… hullo?"

"I'm suffocating." Hysterical giggles taking my breath away. Sudden recall of my mother and me in Spain. For all the sadness, how we laughed together, got the giggles. She was such a young mother—too young to ask for help.

"It's boiling in here."

"I'll call the police—where are you? Samatan? Oh help, what's the number? Don't worry, I'll call them now—call you back."

I dropped the receiver and banged on the glass door with both hands. An old lady a few steps away looked in my direction, hesitated and came over. I shouted through the glass, laughing despite myself.

She peered and pointed. "You can't open the door," she remarked, stating the obvious, her voice muffled through the thick glass. She gave the door an ineffectual push.

"You don't like it in there?" She now thought it was funny.

My mother's voice squeaked metallic-like out of the dangling receiver.

A man came over, drawn by the commotion. A small group had gathered for this quiet afternoon's unexpected entertainment.

"You want to get out?" asked the man, deadpan.

I just looked at him. One energetic kick, a shove, and at last I was free. I breathed long breaths of air. There was a round of clapping. I blushed, feeling naked—anger and grief and humour exposed, even ridicule. But I thanked my new friend, who looked like the singer, Yves Montand, and conversation with my mother resumed. She had not hung up to call the police after all. "Yes," she said, "I'll come for lunch tomorrow."

Heads. We had a day off.

My mother arrived and I observed them both, mother and husband. Both sandy-red-haired, they attracted attention. Julius's Apollonian proportions, the Rowing Blue oarsman's shoulders and height at six foot one. There was my mother's movie star figure, the red silk shirt left unbuttoned quite low, tied at the waist, shirt ends fluffed out. The narrow trousers, cropped, showing the perfect ankle. I knew her age—sixty-two not even looking fifty-two—because my father knew, and he'd told me. Whatever the number, that air of youth and beauty never left her. I looked away, feeling big-boned, clumsy. There was envy between us. Hers for the apparent security of my life. Mine for the artist milieu of her life… and those ankles.

Julius and my mother chatted amiably. I noted myself holding back, how my mother didn't ask questions, neither of Julius, nor of me. She talked only of what mattered to her, of what she knew, and would dismiss anyone who didn't 'get the point'. This evoked an empty landscape to me. I was thinking of her paintings, the naïf style, the stick figures, engaging and playful. But over the years, the palette had changed—mostly greys of different intensity, and whites, trees without leaves, closed shutters, no figures not even as sticks—all pointed to the presence of the artist, and no one else.

After lunch, three or four hours later, Thea asked if she could try on one of our rucksacks. "Just to see what it's like," she added. I took her upstairs. Her interest felt invasive.

Maybe I was being paranoid. I was relieved when, at last, it was time for her to leave. But, when I watched her roll down the car window, wave, and drive off, I was tearful.

"I might join you," she called out. "Maybe on your last three days. Don't forget to call!"

"God, no," I thought, pulling myself together—"not our last three days. How could she even think of it?" There was so much I didn't know about my mother. That mercurial side—there one minute, not there the next—skittish, volatile, erratic (some of me there?). And where was any memory of love? I asked myself as the red Peugeot turned the corner, and a familiar pang of emotion jammed up inside me, brought on by memories of suitcases, taxis, aeroplanes, and station platforms, my mother in tears, clinging to me. "I mustn't cry," she would say, walking off or driving away.

"In the desert
I saw a creature, naked, bestial,
Who, squatting on the ground,
Held his heart in his hands,
And ate of it.
I said, "Is it good, friend?"
"It is bitter—bitter," he answered;
"But I like it
Because it is bitter
And because it is my heart."*

Stephen Crane, from *The Black Riders*

A Rose Is A Daisy Is A Rose

London, 1990

Back at home, I was returning to my childhood more and more often, wandering around like a dog looking for its best bone. Where was it buried? Fragments of memories came to me—the trilling of tree frogs, podgy hands, tickling fingers, a dark corridor, leaning over the toilet bowl being violently sick, the taste of capers. Real or not, I couldn't tell, nor some chronology with space and time. The images were so vivid, present, unrelenting, terrifying, unexplained. Voices woke me up at night. I couldn't tell if they were in my head or from a radio next door. I didn't tell anyone I was hearing voices—not even Dr. C. Sometimes they called my name, waking me with a poem. Once, in our first marriage, I'd suggested to Julius I needed to speak to someone. He'd said, "What on earth for, do you think you're mad?" I'd replied of course not—and that was that. But I was worried, overwhelmed, afraid I was going mad. I remembered Aunt Agatha had thought my mother mad, and I was afraid of that.

Dr. Cobb suggested I start to write things down. "Use your left hand," he said. I liked the idea of that. My mother was left-handed, so too my Russo-American half-brother Stefan, my half sister Sofia, my daughter Kate. It made me feel part of the family.

I wrote slowly, carefully, enjoying it and concentrating with crossed eyebrows, as if back at school, learning in the company of classmates. However hard I tried my capital letters, E and D and P and K, all insistently looked left. "Arrested development," Dr. C explained. I had probably been made to change from left to right as I was being taught to read and write. I was picking up parts of self left behind. Jung remarks on the process of becoming conscious—in this case, a child's self joining the adult self. As he puts it, islands of consciousness growing together, closer, becoming a continent.

I was writing and painting and sculpting—at last in relationship with my own artistry. It was a difficult relationship—as with an elusive, unreliable, though exciting lover. In fact it was even a reflection of my childhood, exciting and terrifying. Sessions with Dr. C informed me about the child who, sexually abused before the age of reason, stops playing because playing has become dangerous. The creative young soul gives itself away under the illusion that, in exchange, it will be loved.

One day I brought Dr. Cobb one of my clay sculptures. He thanked me, his thanks made me blush. I was pleased for its recognition, giving it value. He said he liked the way the snake uncoiled its way up to the rim of the plate. He asked if its tail was stuck or if it was pulling free from what looked like stones at the bottom of the sea.

After months my hands wanted something rock hard to work with. I found a quarry and a sculpture teacher and worked on a piece of speckled black soapstone the size of a giant's foot. After hours of unrelenting work, something emerged from the dark matter—the finest thread of a line—could it be a whisker? I carved and carved in some agitation and excitement, gauging—according to the wavering line—which of my sculpting tools to use. Carefully, I extracted ear, eye, jawline. I looked deeper, chisel carving into the stone until, bit by bit, with stealth and passion, a panther's head appeared. Matisse said he didn't paint the table, he painted the feeling that came to him when he looked at the table. I loved the stone. I loved it. I wanted to bite it, kiss it.

Days later, using the finest grade sandpaper, I rubbed down the rough edges of stone under cold running water, until my hands were swollen and red. The polishing went on, the observing, the looking, a loving meditation. The matte of stone beginning to reflect light, to become sheen. Does pain require light, I wondered, can there be healing in isolation, in darkness? The idea of finding one's feelings—as the editor who commented on my poetry put it so long ago—took on meaning for me. It was about experience - living the self vs thinking the self. When sculpting, I felt and saw the inside of stone, of clay. I felt ravenous—a need to work, a need for space. I thought about a moment I had had on the bus, overhearing two women in front of me talking about a mutual friend being in a lonely marriage. The phrase struck me. I took it home and there it stayed and would not go away.

For a while Daddy called me on Sunday mornings—8am my time.

"Loulouchkax? You talkable? Listen to this."

I groan. Strains of tinny piano tunes float down the long

distance wires. A crackly voice sings, "It had to be yooo,"

I mumble.

"Haven't had your café croissant yet?" Now he sounds puzzled or maybe pretend-concerned. "I'll call you back."

I fall out of bed and tumble down the stairs like Winnie the Pooh. I make my coffee and I'm reading the Sunday papers when the phone rings again.

'Louixette!'

'Yes, Daddy. Morning Daddy! I am talkable now."

It's 10 a.m. my time, 2 a.m. Daddy Time in Los Angeles. We talk about life, war, Kosovo, history, jazz, and family. He's a born storyteller, so he invariably tells me a story or two, and then I tell him a story or two. Most are stories we've told before, but each time there's a glint I haven't noticed before, a turn of phrase that I wonder at, and that I write down.

Today he says, "Eighty! I'm going to be eighty! Can you believe that?" and he continues, "What the hell. I'm ready. Ready to go." And then it comes, the phrase that I write down. "So if it's not tomorrow, the day after tomorrow."

That's one of the many things about my father that amazes and delights me—and confuses me. How does he do it? Let go like that. The letting go of life. Live it, let it go. The letting go of people too. One day he's there, one day he's not. "See ya next time I meetcha," is another of his phrases. I envy what appears to be carefree—or carelessness?

One day I asked Daddy about flying. "What's it like to fly?" I'm not sure I understood his answer, but there was something in his instructions that conveyed pattern, poetry, even bravery. I wrote it all down. I wanted whatever it was that could give me wings, free me from fear.

So, I asked again, "Daddy, what's it like to fly?"

"Aaah, flying," he said.
"You glide—gliii-de on the wing,"
"Then you turn—and fall."
"Recover and dive."
"Then… up!"
"Hang on the prop,"
"And just before stalling, turn on your back—"
(a pause)
"—and now the la-azy eight—"

My father always liked things, wanted things, a lot of things. The 'thingness' of a big house, the thingness of children, friends, jazz, a Bugatti in the garage. I know he regretted not having achieved any of it. Instead, stupefying debt.

My meetings with Dr. Cobb became difficult. I was worried about Kate and Rose, especially Rose. Was I projecting my childhood wounds onto her? Dr. C spoke of the self-destructive aspect of the creative person. "Think of your mother," he said. Was my concern and worry for Rose, or an anxiety of my own? But I was worried, truly frightened for her. Something was wrong. I knew it in my heart, in my guts. Small things like stealing sweets, and lying, and cheating—all these things, however superficial, indicated to me a deeply troubled young soul. To see into the depths, one starts with close observation of the surface, Dr Cobb remarked. The watercolour she'd painted for her father's birthday of a sea wave so high that there was only an inch of sky-air left on the paper was reflecting something ominous. Each time I viewed the visceral beauty of her painting, the feeling was of being submerged, suffocated, drowned. And yet, she also had her own mix of gaiety and humour.

There was no pretending about my younger daughter. You knew how Rose was at any moment. She didn't pretend to be what she wasn't. Her feeling preceded her into the room, and just in case you were a bit slow, she'd inform you. Sashaying, wide shoulders, twirling her keys. The child, the girl, the woman, all in one. "Hello! It's me. I want lots of attention."

An early memory: one morning Rose, four feet tall and five years old, enters the kitchen.

"Good morning, Rose," I say.

No reply.

"Good morning, Rose," I say again.

"I am not Rose," my five-year-old daughter says, pronouncing her words as if she'd just taken an elocution lesson.

"Oh?" I say, "so who are you?"

"Daisy," she replies. "I am Daisy."

"Well, hello Daisy. Do sit down and have your breakfast."

And so she was Daisy until some weeks later, another announcement: Rose was back. Daisy was gone.

Later, aged nine or ten, back from day school, little backpack full of books hanging off one shoulder, Rose hummed in tune to a jazzy song on the radio. The perfection of her beat, the natural phrasing kindred to the blues singers I had loved so much as a girl, whose songs played in the background of my girls' lives. Rose sang the blues, Rose sang gospel, and one evening when Julius, Kate, Rose and I were in a little café in Norfolk, Rose sang 'Ave Maria'. It took us all by surprise, the whole café went quiet. She loved Verdi's

Requiem, a piece of music played over and over when in a certain mood. Rose was a little person with a big personality, like the wren, that small dun-coloured bird with the lion-sized heart belting out its song. And there was 'The Singer', the song which Rose said scared her because as I remember it (paraphrasing), she couldn't answer the question: *She comes and goes / but nobody knows / is she the singer or is she the song?*

Another memory takes me by surprise. Julius and I are inching along from desk to desk, behind all the other parents at an end of term meeting, receiving from the relevant teacher news of their son or daughter, about their grace, their beauty, their talent, their work. We come to the last table, the most important one and this is what I remember. A delight out of nowhere flooding through me. About being a family. About beloved daughter Kate, my first born whom I call Pooch and Poochienetteski, is taking the Baccalaureate. We are well. We are complete. We have driven to Oxford from Norfolk where we are temporarily anchored and the happiest Julius and I have ever been. We will be driving back the same day—three or four hours each way. It is a perfectly ordinary day and yet I will never forget how that day filled me to the brim, love and happiness all mixed up.

Perhaps it was time to talk to a different psychotherapist. A woman… about art, spiritual things, nature, the unknown and unspeakable. Dr. C told me about the time he'd been to see a Jungian analyst. It was after his mother had died.

Though it was a help to him, he didn't go back. Jung's ideas about the religious instinct in mankind was not a language he spoke, but he thought it might well suit me. However, he suggested that I should first go on a retreat. There was an Anglican place in Wales. When home, though uncertain, I wrote a letter of enquiry and posted the envelope in the big red letterbox on the corner of our street. It made a nice, soft, cottony sound as it dropped inside.

What Do You Do In A Convent?

I stood at the sink peeling a potato. Ten to go. On the small curved-back chair under the big mirror lay the sleeping cat, head tucked away under hip and paw. I longed for the same. Peeling another potato, staring into the whiteness of porcelain tiles behind the sink, then interrupting myself, I spun round. Half-peeled potato in one hand, peeler in the other, I walked out of the kitchen, across the hall into the study, looked through the stacks of cassettes on the shelves while wiping my hands, dropped the peeler into my apron pocket, and pulled out *La Bohème*.

On my way back to the kitchen, passing under the hallway skylight, I reached for the potato in my kangaroo pocket, threw it upwards: blue sky, blue sky. The orchestra struck up just as the half-peeled potato dropped back down into my cupped hands. I returned to the sink, shifting my weight from one foot to the other as my legs ached all the time these days. *Bohème* in the background moved to the foreground, waves of sound washing over my thoughts.

I took a taxi to Paddington Station as directed by the letter in my handbag. If Paris was grey, London was brown. Streets meandered like rivers, unpredictable. From the air, London looked like a jumble of old toys. This might be home, I thought with gratitude, but I don't belong.

The train to Wales took two and a half hours. I read a

little and looked out of the window. It was cold. I put my coat back on, and smoked, and smoked. Suburbs. Countryside. Thoughts that had been closing in on me like sharks changed direction and swam off. Open skies. A cow under a tree, legs folded into a rectangle, drawing herself into sacred geometry. The taxi ride to the convent took a half hour up and down the Welsh hills. The landscape was gentle, though the blue-black country road ahead curled around the slopes of hillsides, ominously tentacle-like.

"What do you do in a convent?" I asked myself, trying to remember my school days in the Strasbourg convent.

The front door was ajar when I arrived. No bell, no knocker. No one in the wide silent entrance. I stood on the stone floor listening for any sounds of life. A fly scurried like a minuscule grey mouse across the open guestbook on the hall table, the tappety-tap of its insect feet on the page just audible. A printed card tacked on the wall above an old-fashioned square black telephone specified: 'Incoming calls between 4 and 6 p.m. only'. I inhaled the promise of no interruptions. Peace and quiet.

A nun materialised, as though through the wall, hands tucked inside wide black sleeves. She stood there, still as furniture. Sister? Reverend Mother? I wanted to say 'Bonjour Ma Mère'. I recalled the card depicting the 13th century statue of Virgin and Child from the convent in Paris that Sr. Elise had given me when I was six years old, and I wondered if I still had it somewhere.

"It's alright," the nun said, and reading my mind, she introduced herself: "I'm Sister Veronica, just one of the ancients. No titles. Welcome, my dear. Follow me. Most of us are in silence today, but there is Sister Paula, our official greeter. She will visit you in a little while."

The elderly nun indicated various rooms with a respectful nod of the head as we passed: the library, the back entrance, swinging doors to the kitchen, dining room, glass doors to the stone porch. "See how the columns frame our dear old Welsh hills."

At an ornate door at the foot of the stairs Sister Veronica opened the door with a curving gesture, almost a bow. "This is our chapel, you may join us, or not, as you wish. You'll hear the bell."

I looked through. Cow parsley in a tall glass vase, a smell of wet grass and incense, fine dust particles in slanting sunlight.

The sister led the way upstairs. Opening doors along a corridor. "East or West?" she asked. "You will be on your own this weekend. Choose any room you like."

We came to the last room, around a corner, filled with sun.

"This one," I said.

I unpacked my bag and stood barefoot facing the window. Stretching, I pulled my arms high, see-sawing on stockinged feet. Loving the silence and solitude, a rush of energy like an incoming tide flushed my cheeks. I did a little jig.

There was a wash basin—bath and lavatory down the hall—an armchair and a window seat. The bed was a skinny thing with a metal frame and a mattress with a dip in the middle. A hanging space for clothes revealed itself behind a floral linen curtain by the door. On a mantelpiece, a jam jar of wildflowers and above, a plain chunky crucifix carved out of pale wood, fine-grained, hung on a brass picture hook. I lifted the cross off the wall, stroked the inlay, the pleasing texture of the thing fitting neatly in the palm of my hand.

"I'm Sister Paula, my dear. Welcome." I jumped. A young nun stood in the doorway. I'd forgotten how these ladies, in their long black and white robes, came and went like whispers. "Welcome to the Priory of Our Lady. If you wish to talk, I will be available late mornings."

"I would like that," I said, sincere, but at the same time in a near-panic about what to talk about. Replacing the crucifix on its hook on the wall, I stood there feeling large and awkward.

"I am Catholic—no, Episcopalian. I mean, I was baptised three times, but my papers are lost—different schools," my hand zigzagged in the air, "cities, houses, rooms, countries." I paused. I sounded like a telegram. "I'm multilingual. In English, I'm not even half of me." I looked out of the window. "I'm tired. I've lost faith, if I ever had it."

I sensed that what I was not saying, or could not find the words for, was being heard.

When did this *ennui* steal into my heart? I thought of Rosie's recent remark that I sounded bitter. Sister Paula and I sat by the window. She replied, voice quiet, easy, "You are in the right place." I felt blessed, taken seriously. "This is meant for you. God is in your centre."

I didn't know what this meant, but my heart knew because it soared. Sister Paula's dry, cool hands soothed the heat in mine.

'Do you have a prayer?' she asked. Again, I didn't know what she meant, but I replied something about loving to read. The conversation turned to books. She said writing began as an act of prayer. "Homer begins his odyssey invoking the Muses. We're all praying for something."

After this talk, the first of four, I went downstairs to the library. I opened one of the books Sister Paula had spoken of. Then another, leafing through that, and on to the next. I continued along the shelves, taking out a number of those recommended, plus two more. That was Thursday. I woke before dawn on Friday, went back to sleep, and woke again at six-thirty to sit in the armchair by the window for most of the day, face washed, without makeup, reading, writing, and thinking as I had not done in years—perhaps ever.

Sister Paula came by for our second conversation not long after. She spoke of heart-centred thought, being different from mind and intellect. I then read ten, eleven hours throughout the day and deep into the night: ancient writers; modern writers; mystical writers; poetry; a novel about silence and apostasy by a Japanese Catholic writer, Shusako Endo (I pronounced the name whispering to myself, luxuriating in the texture of esses, the breathy 'o' beside the finality of the 'd-oh' sound); then the letters of the nineteenth century French priest, the Abbé de Tourville, defining the state of sadness as *error*, or 'off the mark' as sin. He wrote about the danger of compromise when it leads to the betrayal of self. I took to bed with me a line about the Holy Spirit, 'black on black humming in the night'.

"Do not put down permanent roots," Sister Paula said the next morning, and spoke of 'The Hymn of the Pearl', a Syriac poem from the third century. She talked about how the search for origins was not the same as the need for identity. I thought of my father, endlessly telling and retelling the story of his grandfather, our ancestor, whose identity we would never know. "No need," she said. "It's inside you. The books you read will lead you in."

Texts broke down into a particularity, each with their

own timbre, rhythm and tone. I read Blake aloud in my room by the window, the plainsong rhythm, writing lines of poetry and prose. My notebook filled and ideas moved through centuries and across the pages as I read from Plato to C.S. Lewis, *The Cloud of Unknowing* to Julian of Norwich and Flaubert's letters in French. Oh the joy, the energy when reading French out loud. Flaubert, who'd found his felicity, as he put it in a letter to his dearest friend, George Sand. "You have no compassion for your women characters," she'd written. In his novel, *Emma Bovary*, there is a servant whose name is Félicité who is fired from service by Emma. Twenty-five years later, Flaubert wrote a short story about this character Félicité, an ordinary soul who suffered loss after loss, yet without bitterness, without that ennui that had plagued him and his 'Emma—c'est moi' all of his life.

Writers crossed over the lines of time, writers that knew of each other, quoting, interpreting, reinterpreting, redefining the big questions until, it seemed to me, that one spirit was breathing through each and every writer—a candle's flame eternally seeking itself. I felt privy to a discourse held between *it* and *them*—a discourse I could be part of. I was coming home. As the sun crossed the sky into late morning, names that had been unknown to me at dawn became familiar. Morning rolled into afternoon. I read a sentence, reread it, stared into the space between the lines, an idea rooting there, then followed it out of the window where it linked itself to place, to event, to a person past or present. I was back in Spain reading *War and Peace* in the shade, my mother talking about life and death and war and God and the things we want to know and don't talk about. I was back at the table with the grownups, eavesdropping on their conversation, their questions. How I loved their questions—that they could ask *so many* without getting answers.

My gaze returned to the convent garden—the flower beds by the house, the lawn and the apple orchard, the intelligence of nature, of background. Fruit trees stood in tall grasses, thistles and buttercups in the lee of a high wall of beech, and a white horse chestnut, a maple, and one very tall cypress. A cockerel crowed throughout the day and a magpie hopped about on the lawn and up on the back of the mossy grey bench and down again—winged pirate with a black patch on one eye.

I ate alone in the evenings in a luxury of silence, slowly chewing the plain goodness of home-made brown bread, while my mind absorbed and digested impressions of the day. Memories opened like windows. Time ahead, time to myself, empty time, time vast as sky. I savoured sounds of my own gestures, single as islands: the rattle of the cup on its saucer; the teaspoon's little whirlpool dissolving milk and grains of sugar; the tap of knife edge against eggshell, salt crystals; and drops of yolk on buttered toast.

At the top of the stairs, off the landing to my bedroom, was a small anteroom: a table thumbtacked with a blue and white checked oilcloth, a kettle, a jar of instant coffee, a plate of biscuits, and a jug of milk covered with a small square of muslin hemmed with turquoise beads. After lunch, I would make myself a cup of coffee, another later in the afternoon. The little beads tinkled against the neck of the jug of milk, punctuating portions of hours, marking the day like miniature church bells.

After lunch on the weekend, two ladies appeared and introduced themselves.

"I'm Olwyn," the older of the two said. "We're the

volunteers from the village, we come twice a week to help tidy up."

"Sue," the tubby one said, putting out a hand.

Olwyn said she had wanted to be a nun but was turned down on medical grounds. "I took it badly. I felt personally rejected by God. I was bitter for a long time." She described the hardship of the nuns' lives. "They are tough women." Their life was not only spiritual—it was a very physical business as well. You came to God—and the worst of yourself (and possibly the best)—in silence, while scrubbing floors, mending roofs, and peeling potatoes until your back broke.

I had no idea of this, imagining, at most, something white and fluttery in the sky. Or a nun, young like Sister Elise, whose hair you were allowed to brush, transcending the body, its heaviness, its ugliness.

"Oh no. They go on and on," Olwyn said. "They become very strong. Their bodies build their spirits, you see. Not the other way round, and not with sweetness."

How different it was to be amongst women. I registered the difference, surprised to find my French self emerging through an Anglican (English!) spiritual context.

A thunderstorm. White forks of lightning pitched into the metal grey centres of clouds. It rained all afternoon. On Sunday the skies cleared. Traces of mineral and stone and humus rose from the ground, tickling my nostrils like pepper. I sat in the orchard in damp tall grasses, observing the world of insects, the little rustlings of them going about their business.

After lunch, Sister Paula came for a fourth and last

conversation. She recommended Kipling's masterly tale of 'Purun Bhagat'. I wrote down the strange name. Over the next few months, I transferred the story's title from notebook to notebook. No one I asked had heard of it, not even Julius. The story was not listed in any of Kipling's short story collections. It didn't occur to me to look in the children's section, and after a while I forgot about it.

And so it appeared in its own time and manner—in a *The Second Jungle Book*, lodged between 'How Fear Came' and 'Letting In The Jungle: The Miracle of Purun Bhagat', a story about alchemy and transformation. I wasn't on that path yet, or was I? I intuited my way would have to do with the study of the work of C.G. Jung. What also came to mind was T.S. Eliot's phrase about finding the soul 'at the cost of everything'. Would my marriage withstand such a change in priority—being myself?

When I left the convent, the hall was as empty and silent as on the day I had arrived. Nothing had changed, but I felt different, and vulnerable. I reached for the wooden cross in my pocket. Just as I was leaving the little bedroom, suitcase in hand, eyes forward, mind blank, my left hand had reached up—the same hand which had chosen the books from the library shelves, the same hand I had not been allowed to write with—and lifted the little crucifix off the wall, dropping it into my coat pocket.

Two o'clock. Taxi driver waiting.

We drove through the valley, green, leafy, mysterious. The road no longer seemed tentacled and ominous. The driver told me that he had been here during the war and, recognising it from childhood, swore to return. It was all he could think about, getting back, back to 'his' countryside and at the end of the war he did so. He had set up his taxi business and had not tired of it since. "Every day is different. Every season, every year, I see how beautiful it is."

I was early for the train. It was sunny. I stood on the platform, back against the warmed brick wall, eyes closed, face lifted towards the sun. Anticipating my return to London, I remembered Julius driving me to the station, saying, "Existentialism—what's that?" He had sounded irritated. "Means nothing to me."

"Let it be," Sister Paula had said. "A thing defined is no longer infinite. Celebrate your husband. Celebrate what is difficult for you to accept in him, for as you accept him, you will accept yourself."

I looked forward to the next two hours on the train, looking out of the window, saying and thinking nothing, safely gathering and storing my senses' impressions. Still leaning against the wall, I opened my eyes and looked straight into Julius's face. "The thought of him is making me see things," I said out loud to myself. I closed my eyes, took a deep breath. There was a giggle, and something as solid as stone and as hard as head tackled my stomach.

"Mom!"

I opened my eyes again, put out a hand to touch the skin, caress the hair. Rosie, my daughter. My husband. I couldn't speak. I was both entranced and appalled.

"You look as if you've seen a ghost!"

"Yes."

"A surprise. Rather a long drive, Rosie thought."

"We hid behind a column!" Rose shrieked. "You walked right past us, and we tiptoed all the way over to you when you closed your eyes."

My hand went from daughter to husband, to his

shoulders, to his face. Rose took my hand. The texture, the sum of four days, the view from my room, the retreat—all of it passed beyond my grasp, a pearl in the water falling, in horizontal stages, in vertical stages, landing somewhere down there, beyond reach.

Letting go of my husband's hand, I reached in my pocket for the cross, stroking its edges.

It was not until two and a half years later I posted the little wooden cross back. I kept seeing the empty hook on the wall whenever I thought of the retreat, until finally I couldn't stand it. Two weeks later, a reply from Sister Paula saying: "It is my birthday on Sunday, what a lovely present you sent me—the best I can remember! I cannot recall what you look like, nor the sound of your voice, but the depths of your distress, that is very vivid to me still, and it is good to know that you are together. May you continue building a lifelong friendship. How we walk our relationships is the making of our paths. I send you back the little cross with our love and blessing—vague as I am I did not even realise it was missing. Keep it. Perhaps it is made of an olive wood from the Holy Land—you ask, but I don't know. I have framed your poem. It hangs in the little bedroom where you slept, and your book stands with our books in the library for our guests to come upon. I tell them a writer slept here, but I don't tell them your name. It is best to let it be, for each to have the joy of their own discovery should they come upon it and read your inscription."

The Agony Of Healing

Sometime in the late 1980s I embarked on an analysis with a Jungian analyst, a woman in her late fifties or early sixties. Her name was Cara, which I assumed was Italian. This assumption would be my first introduction to the phenomenon of projection. "When God wants to see something, he creates an image," Cara would say, leaving me to wrestle with what that meant, though there would be an occasional reference to the fact that the psyche can never see itself and so she throws out an image and steps into it.

Cara was discreet. She seldom disclosed the personal, though when she did, it served in the form of a story. It was different being in therapy with a woman. The surprise was that while I had been able to talk, discuss and even argue with Dr. Cobb, I was near tongue-tied with a woman. In the beginning, I found myself staring at Cara's freckled legs—always bare, feet in ballet flats. I had an embarrassing impulse to crawl over and hug them. I never admitted to this. That is how I understood, after a long while, years of reflection in fact, how difficult it is to speak of love to anyone, even your therapist. One day out of the blue it came to me unasked that I had been seeing---projecting---my mother's freckled legs, my mother's bare feet in those ballet flats.

*

I would meet Cara in her small study on the top floor of a little house in Chelsea. A life-size sculpture of a horse's head lay a little sideways on the mantelpiece and there were books—novels and poetry and plays—alongside the twenty tan-coloured hardback volumes of Jung's writings and the books by his colleagues and disciples. All of which would eventually sit on my bookshelves, with paintings and objects, a flower in a small pot, a stone, a shell. I loved her practice room. Alive and full of story. It was there I entered the process of transformation—the idea of transformation exciting and enticing, the process of transformation—trans/for/ma/shun I repeated to myself out in the street—exceedingly uncomfortable, at times it was painful and disorientating to the point that I walked home zigzagging the streets. Thing is not you that is transforming—you are the pot containing something boiling and burning your insides as it transforms, the fuel is what we call 'e-motion'. And so while I was being undone and rebuilt, at home family life unravelled. Though Dr C had said he saw me as sister to my daughters, now Cara said Rose in trouble was the making of me as mother.

Sometimes Cara kept me waiting downstairs while she finished a session—a half hour, even occasionally an entire hour. I would politely be asked to wait in her neat, formal dining room as she climbed back up the three floors to her study. Should I sit? Should I stand? I would wonder this each time, while staring at the long branch of ivy that had broken through the outside wall above the window, making its way halfway down behind the curtain rail. In a few more months, or years, it would reach the floor and then what? I puzzled over this evidence of laissez-faire, or perhaps neglect, but then after a while I observed the judgemental questioning going on inside me, the restlessness and irritation at being kept waiting. This too, like the 'legs' attraction, I never spoke of. Maybe it didn't matter, I told myself—as I did in childhood.

Dreams during my Jungian analysis were different from dreams when in session with Dr. Cobb. Shooting stars zipped through a night sky: a straight line made of light which, as it moved towards me, drew itself into a wheel, spokes and all. Days later, while on my knees planting bulbs in the grounds of the village church, my spade made a metallic sound as it struck something, I knew it would be a wheel. And so it was—a perfect double-rimmed wheel with one spoke missing, the size of a child's toy train. At this time, I was reading about mandalas and Jung's conversations with the scientist Pauli about synchronicity. Such dreams reflected bursts of revelation in the mind's firmament. They were 'archetypal', Cara explained, with an energising and animating affect. Such archetypal dreams are 'big dreams'. They stay in memory all of one's life, continuing to inform well beyond the personal. In one, parts of a male skeleton were laid on the ground in a pattern. This could suggest a dynamic was being restored. Some parts were missing. While drawing a sketch of the pattern of these bones, thoughts came to mind as to what the missing parts stood for, what was missing in me, and how I was to go about finding it. Cara would amplify this with stories and ancient tales about the dis-membered and re-membered gods. She told the story of the Egyptian mystery of the missing Phallus, and the goddess Isis putting back together the fourteen missing bones of her husband Osiris, who was also her brother. A whole new world opened, an education that thrilled me. I began to feel I was, after all, a part of the universe. 'I exist!' I would whisper to myself, addressing the ghost of my uncle who at the lunch table more than twenty-five years ago had challenged me to prove existence. At the end of a session, laughing and humming part of a *My Fair Lady* song, 'She Did It!' Cara would talk of ancestry and the broken human being in all of us. It gave me a sense of belonging. My life mattered. The chaos of my childhood was being put in place, even to have meaning, even to make sense.

In another dream, I stood beside a turbaned Indian gentleman. We were on a balcony overlooking a quarry. Hundreds of workers below were working at the unearthing of an immense statue of a goddess. These images were extraordinary and became all the more real when I wrote them or painted them, bringing them to Cara as she asked me to. One drawing of a lion at a stream, lapping up the water, made her smile. "At last," she said, "the animal instinct slakes its thirst." I smiled too, sensing a deep nurturing inside. How hungry and thirsty I was.

Cara read me something from the writer of *Little Women*. "Pain," she read out, "travels through family lines until someone is ready to heal it in themselves. By going through the agony of healing," she looked up at me, she was reading slowly, "you no longer pass the poison chalice onto the generations that follow. It is incredibly important and sacred work."

Bitterness

One weekday morning, the day before my fifty-third birthday, I was at home in the country, in the middle of baking a cake, when Julius called. Rosie had attempted suicide; she was in hospital. This was the beginning of a nine year period when Rose would try to take her life once or twice each year, and one year, six or seven times. I lost count. Rose—my wild daughter, full of poetry, pain, light, darkness, and such dark humour—was eventually diagnosed, in the clinical language of today, as bipolar and borderline with perhaps a so-called multiple personality disorder. Uneasy with clinical labels, I prefer the poet's phrase—I am a multitude. Useful, perhaps, sometimes, but then they change. What I did know, and experience, and suffer, was my daughters' suffering. Both. Kate and Rose. Julius, and me. Another both. Separate boths.

After that first attempt---on the day before my birthday (August)—and three months later a second time, on the day of her father's birthday (December) which was also her own—I dreamed I was running down the streets of Manhattan, buildings were collapsing, people jumping out of windows. In the dream Cara held my hand, but then I let go. I'm running. I hide in an underground shelter. Later in session, Cara remarked it was a shame I'd let go of her hand, but at least the dream showed I could find my way to shelter while the inner structures of my homeland broke down. For a few days after, or was it a few weeks, I remember sitting in the garden by the stream where the kingfishers came, unable and unwilling to speak. Julius looked so worried and unhappy and lost, sitting beside me on the bench, our backs to the box hedge, now six feet tall since we'd planted it when moving to Oxfordshire.

"I don't understand, dearest," Julius said. "Take me through it, what's going on in you? I don't know if you're having a nervous breakdown or if it's just shock, or what."

I couldn't help him. He called Cara. "Let her be," she said. "Something is working itself out. There are no words for where she is."

Cara had called me that first time, when she was away on a month long break in August. How could she be asking how I was doing? I didn't know how to answer her. All the attention was on Rose—yet Cara asked about her last of all.

"Go slow," she said with an authority more powerful for being so quietly spoken. "The mother takes the brunt of it. She cannot collapse, cannot give in to the hysteria. Let your family work it out," she said. "They must each face themselves." She even advised I take valium (she, who said avoid medication until you no longer can). "Rest. Let the waves come. Fill that lake with your tears."

Meanwhile I took refuge in silence, alongside the small comforting everyday moments of shopping, preparing meals, and cutting flowers for little vases for a bedside, the kitchen table, or Julius's desk. Sometimes Rose and I wordlessly held each other in a booby hug, her term for being breast to breast.

Another day, another month—it was Kate who called this

time. She said Rose was drinking again, and she'd taken pills, paracetamol, whatever there was in the little cupboard under the bathroom basin. There was sick everywhere, on Kate's clothes, on Kate's cabin bed.

"Mom, the mess was horrific. I've tidied up the worst."

Julius arrived and cleaned some more and drove Rosie to hospital. The doctors said her liver was damaged, but she'd make it, though what damage there might be they couldn't say. I drove down from the country and cleaned some more. Julius was compassionate, but exhausted. Kate was furious, and sensible, whilst I couldn't find the words to say, with angry love, how tired I was of *drama*.

Years later, I was driving back to England from France from my little house in the hills above Nice. Though London was home, and I felt gratitude for that, it was here, within sight of the Mediterranean, I felt a belonging. I lived alone, now divorced for many years. I was listening on *Radio Culture* to an interview with the writer Simenon, "...bourgeois ordinaire, un homme avec sa pipe," as the French journalist Bernard Pivot described him. Simenon was saying: "Je préfère être critiqué et détesté pour ce que je suis que d'être aimé et admiré pour ce que je ne suis pas." He spoke of his daughter, twenty-five, and her suicide. "Une balle dans le coeur." She'd used her father's revolver. I listened to the straight-shooting of his words. He considered his daughter's death a betrayal—she had rejected the life *he had given her*. This did not occur to me—the giving of life as something personal—though I did feel slapped in the face by the Universe, if not by God himself. Simenon said he was embittered by his daughter's act for several years. "Why am

I bitter?" I asked myself, while driving on to the North, passing signs indicating Aix-en-Provence, Avignon, Valence, Lyon. Although I am writing this nearly twenty years later, I think out loud as I drive, foot on the accelerator. "Yes, it never ends, the pain, the stain, the stigma. I can be bitter about that." Thank you, Cara. The stories. Through them I find my life. Medea, Electra. Demeter, Persephone. And Hades, oh, so handsome. My foot pushes harder. "I know them. They are in me. I'm sorry sorry angry."

One day in Amsterdam, on one of our weekend escapes abroad, we were making our way through endless rooms in the Rijksmuseum, when a small painting in a doorway caught my eye. Like a fish swimming after the shimmering lure, I veered away from Julius and stood in front of a young man, his face half in shadow, curly copper-red hair like flame around the wick, eyes barely discernible, gaze intense. A rough, fierce brush-mark of white reflected on a cheek and this small touch of light, I now saw, was what had caught my eye two rooms away. I stared at Rembrandt's self-portrait, the light on the tip of the nose, the one red-tipped earlobe, lips slightly parted, wet-looking, alive. Superimposed onto the painting and melting into each other, in turn, appeared the faces of my mother, my half-brother Stefan, my husband, my uncle Edred, even Orlando—the marmalade kitten that my father put out of his agony with a gunshot. The colour of fox—there it was, saying something, but I knew not what. Only that this painting was more real to me than anything, more real than myself, more real than what I was feeling (which, awkward to say, was love). Love—the extravagance of such a feeling. Love in, of, and for, the artist's work. It made me think of the artist who gave me my name, whose portrait of my mother was more real than my mother. I felt an exhilarating gratitude for this moment, for life, for being, for the colour red.

At home, at the house with the stream where the kingfishers came, while Rose was living there between bouts of rehabilitation and halfway house, she and I had a weekend routine. In the afternoons, we would sit at the big square kitchen table looking over the garden for an hour or two and played a game of cards. Normally Patience, then Racing Demon. The rhythm of play kept us from going too deep, and in this way, with cautious hearts, we talked. There was music from Fats Waller—'Hold Tight, Hold Tight (Want Some Seafood Mama)'—one of Rose's favourites, or Verdi's *Requiem*, another favourite, both of us stroking the gooseflesh on our forearms when it came to 'Dies Irae'. We shared a mental playground, imagining physics and science and the mystical and inexplicable and ineffable. Rose and I could be 'weird' together. I asked once why she said or how could she say the horrible mean and nasty things she sometimes threw out at a person. She replied she liked to provoke, she wanted to see me cry, she wanted to hurt, and no, she didn't feel or want to feel compassion. Rose could look you straight in the eye and lie. In that moment she was a frightening and unknowable entity of her own—but an entity I recognised for being inside me too, the difference being I held mine in while Rose was more honest and let it out. Sometimes she could make the sting deadpan funny, spoken with affection for any one of us.

The Upper Air, There The Labour Lies

I'm remembering a November day, three months after Rose's first attempt at ending her life, when a nineteenth century fog descended on the southwest of England. Visibility stopped at fifty paces. Things froze at night, things dripped during the day. An owl hooted, and the occasional passing car whispered through the milky, icy air. It thinned in the afternoon, just a little, as I would set off for my daily walk up the hill. The sun appeared, a precise white disc with a dark grey outline, whiter than the moon. Kate was married, living in London. Rosie had moved to live and work in a halfway house.

I wanted to take Rose to Paris, but Julius was against it. I listened to his reasoning. He was right, going to Paris didn't make sense, but the heart doesn't, nor does an attempt to end your own life—until it does. I felt a near desperate need to 'go home', to take my daughter to France. Chez Tata. Julius didn't understand. I didn't either. The need had no words.

"Listen to your husband," Cara advised. "Don't contradict him, not even in your head, but stand up for your motherly instinct however it manifests. Don't try to explain. Explanations are the germs of misunderstanding." Where did my motherly instinct come from? How could I trust it?

In the end we went for four days in the autumn. The

Eurostar was on its beginning runs—just two hours to Paris! We walked along the Quai du Louvre, across the Pont des Arts, the pedestrian passerelle. We sat down on a bench, halfway looking out over the river Seine at the Île de la Cité and Nôtre Dame. Up the Rue Bonaparte to St Germain. Rosie beamed at the watery image of herself reflected in the street windows. "Look. I'm a mermaid! See? I'm swimming."

We sat amongst a crowd of young people wrapped in long scarves, long coats, faces lifting to the sun, smoking, sipping café crème. A young African man was poised on the back of a bench, his feet parallel on the seat, stroking and thumping a Bongo drum. Rosie ordered a citron pressé, we shared a croque-monsieur, and we spoke French. I was chez moi avec ma fille.

Chez Tata, supper at the round table, candle flames flickered in the windows. Beyond the Tuileries, and the chandelle of the Tour Eiffel. We had caviare and baked potato, lapin à la moutarde with tiny onions and mushrooms prepared by Tata in her usual haphazard, effortless way. After supper we sat in the Aladdin's cave of a drawing room, with its multitude of cushions, throws of silk and cashmere over the backs of chairs and sofas, silver candelabra, marbled turquoise eggs, semi-precious stones of quartz and amethyst scattered across the glass coffee table—all reminders of a life once upon a time in Brazil.

On the last afternoon, while Rose was being soignée by Tata's at-home beauty technician, I made my way to the Left Bank to the Boulevard St Germain, number 224 on a small blue plaque, to where my mother had lived when I was fostered in Strasbourg by Agatha and Edred. I walked through the big porte cochère to a wide cobbled courtyard—no tree, no pots of flowers, nothing but greyness and stone. A little shock went through me, how lonely the courtyard was, how lonely we both were then. I stood by, looking at the two windows of her one-room apartment, noticing what I had not noticed before, hearing her voice in my ear: "Monkey, as long as there's a tree outside the window, you're safe." I stood there, quiet, alone without her, remembering more. There was always a guitar, standing in the corner by the fireplace. Bookshelves either side. A bed covered in cushions acting as sofa. Two open armchairs with caned seats. Round a corner, a space for cooking, a small sink. At the other end, a curved wall which she had papered with a blown-up black and white photograph of Spain. No room for chairs, so a banquette was cut into the wall for seating. Anything to do with Spain brought magic. She'd pick up the guitar, strum an alegria, or a blues-y song. Just outside her flat door was a storage space with a mattress on the floor. This is where I slept when I came for a visit. There would be a candle and a torch on the floor for me. I stared through the two dirty windows at memories of things no longer there. I turned around, crossed the threshold of the porte cochère out into the Boulevard St Germain.

Thea was in hospital, the cancer ward. The end was near according to Sofya, my (half) sister, who'd seen her earlier that day when the hospital was having a fire alarm practice. In less than a second, Thea was up, Humphrey Bogart raincoat over her hospital gown, kilim tapestry handbag over the arm, as if it were 1941 and the Germans were around the corner. Listening to Sofya's description, I visualised the cover of Thea's last novel, a black and white photograph of a small leather suitcase covered in stickers, sitting on rough decking over a body of water, a raincoat folded over the suitcase. The first time I saw the cover, I drew breath. An emotion moved inside me---violent, a tide, a rush of sea towards the shore. I propped the book up on the mantelpiece. The title was in pink letters which jarred, so I painted over it black and white swirls and waves. It stayed there for months, maybe years, its symbolic power undying: suitcase for one, raincoat folded over, imminent departure.

I went to the hospital the next day. Thea was sitting up in bed, head wrapped in one of her silk chiffon scarves, shielding scarred tissue. Cancer had ravaged her face, robbing her of beauty, yet there she was, ever more beautiful. Our conversation was a little stilted. We'd left behind true conversation in Spain many years ago. After a moment, I moved closer, half whispered in her right ear, afraid to ask what I was about to ask, not knowing what it was I needed to ask.

"Mummy. If you can. Send me a message?"

Head on the pillow, looking at me, she nodded. Did her lips move, did they draw the line of a smile? I want there to be one to remember, but I don't know except that we were back in Spain, once more the sisters we had pretended to be—we were young, we were together, back in the days of talking of the impossible.

Thea died later that night at one in the morning. Sofya called to tell me. Again and again, the lights in the house fused. Again and again, I reset the switch. The house electrics went on and off like this until mid-morning. Weeks later, I filled a shopping bag with old letters, photographs, newspaper articles, bits of manuscripts, any stuff to do with

Thea, and took it all to the yard area behind the house. Feeling empty, blank, I struck a match. The little bonfire flamed up. I walked around clockwise, anti-clockwise. I wanted to feel, but there was nothing.

Near Christmas, almost two months after Thea died, my cousin Jas and I were walking down the Fulham Road. We stopped at the florist's stand in the Michelin building. I put together a large bouquet, the florist asked if I would like some wet newspaper to wrap around the flowers. It would be two hours before I put them in a vase at home, so I said yes. I walked up to the counter, where a stack of newspapers lay open for wrapping—facing me was the page of my mother's obituary, October 16, 1992. I stared at the photograph of the Moïse Kisling portrait which both *The Observer* and *The Independent* newspapers had used.

I tugged at Jas's coat sleeve, gesturing at the newspaper.

"Mais oui, Cus," she said. "You asked for a message, remember?"

"So she heard you," Cara said when I related the moment later.

Maybe there *was* a bond, but why do I not feel her?

I brought Cara a copy of Thea's autobiography, *Mad Mosaic*, with the list of my life's main events—just the headlines as she had asked for, no details—to help me, and her, make sense of things. She looked at it slowly, in a silence reassuring perhaps because she was giving it time, an attention unknown to me. I could have sat in that silence as in a warm bath for hours.

It had taken me two years to draw up the list. At times,

the effort triggered dizziness, even waves of seasickness. "Mal de terre," Tata called it. I had called on Tata, and on my father to help me with the list. Tata remembered things, while my father would sound surprised at questions such as 'Where was I this or that year?' as if he'd not noticed, nor even stopped to wonder. Cara spoke of neglect, abandonment. Her words shocked me. I'd not thought of any of the family events, and stories, as being about abandonment, neglect, kidnapping, damnation (by the priest in Strasbourg), sexual abuse, foster care—such terms didn't exist. I'd had to look up the words 'waif' and 'fostered'. This is what it means to examine a life—not the ego; Life. The events, the patterns, and how we poor humans relate to the forces. Cara would give the examples in literature across the ages, such as Augustine, Virginia Woolf, Proust.

The list:

August 1944 Birth, Manhattan

December 1944 Atlantic crossing to England on troop ship with mother to meet with father on special leave

March 1945 Paris, South of France—father/allies St. Tropez landing: 'Operation Dragoon'

Dec 1945-Jan 1946 Manhattan & Paris (apartment in Passy courtesy of US Army)

August-Autumn 1948 Parents separate. Father in Paris, mother Manhattan

April 1949 Paris. Parents together for a few months

June 1949 London, with Thea (parents separated again)

July 1949 London / father / kidnap / Paris

Aug/Dec 1949 Spain, Brazil, Paris (or the other way round, Leïla not sure)

Jan/July/August 1950   With father to Spain, France, Switzerland—Antibes in the summer with Leila, Ninin and Miguel, where we 'jouer con sand'—school somewhere, Leila can't remember

September 1950 *Manhattan, father*

January 1951 *Manhattan, Ninin (grandmother)*

April 1951 *Manhattan, father, Park Avenue, Orlando & Jo*

July 1951 *Manhattan, mother*

June 1952 *Madrid, mother*

Aug 1953 /Aug 1959 *Strasbourg, Aunt Agatha and Uncle Edred*

Sept 1959/Aug 1960 *Paris, mother and stepfather*

Sept 1960/July 1960 *Finishing school, Maidenhead, England*

Aug 1961/Spring 1966 *Manhattan, father—told to leave— live with Ninin, grandmother. Decide against university. Start job.*

"Too much," Cara said. "Not possible to take in such madness—a mad mosaic indeed," she added, paraphrasing the title of my mother's autobiography. "It is a miracle you are sane, but at what cost?" she wondered aloud. "You are a very talented woman, but you are slow. You must be slow to integrate the mass of material and what it has done to you. It grounds you, and we need you grounded. Your children need you to be grounded. To be here. *Here*," she gestured sternly to the space between us.

Then she asked, "What is 'jouer con sand'?" I told her about the little sentence, one of many, that it was a passe-partout phrase in the Vincent family. Miguel and I—all of us, spoke a mishmash, macaronic language, bits of made-up, pretend Russian, German, Chinese. She liked the phrase. Play in the sand. "A sense of humour puts things in proportion, especially about one's self."

I didn't know I'd attended thirteen schools. Later, Tata added one more. I was ashamed of the unknowing, of the excess of my childhood. Cara opened her dictionary of etymology, a much-consulted and loved reference book. She read out: *sufferre*—from *ferre*—to carry across, to bear up from below, *su*. I was not to be shamed, she said. We questioned Aunt Agatha—had she been aware of what her husband was doing to me? Cara read out another word: respect, *re spectare*—to look again.

"You have your life's work ahead of you," she said at the end of that session. She read from a book taken from the little table at her side. She added, as ever, part of a story ages old, to do with Aeneas after many battles and losses, lands in Italy as the prophetic priestess, the Sibyl, addresses him: Man of Troy.... To me, Cara passes on the Sibyl's wisdom - that I know of the gates of hell, always open, so easy to fall through them; now the task, the struggle is to 'retrace your steps (remarrying your husband, for instance?), and *to climb back up to the upper air*; she finishes looking not at but straight into my eyes: there, *there the labour lies*. My analyst is quoting from a small book on her lap, while my memory (and education) for the great minds and their words is poor but there's always a little, like the lizard's tail that I catch and that comes to me when needed. This time it was to do with the climbing back to 'the upper air'. When in a hellish moment I look up at the skies for those blessed words to come to me. Oh, the longing for that upper air.

Myth Lends A Hand

A note slipped through the front door letterbox.

"Dear Mrs. Gallagher," in an old-fashioned curly scrawl, "I'm writing to you because of the wonderful display of daffodils around the church at present. I am a church warden and the comments from everyone make it clear how much pleasure they have given."

I took the letter to the kitchen, made myself a cup of tea, and read it again, slowly. I had been planting bulbs around the church in the village for three years, almost completing the circle, not aware that this exercise was a meditation—a mandala of the sort Cara had been talking about.

I woke that morning to see snow on the ground. It was April. I felt low, heavy, peculiar. I went back to bed and lay there, warm and comfortable. I read and wrote a little. Kimbers, the cat, came round the doorway, jumped up onto the bed. "This is splendid," he said, the purring in my ear a mini avalanche rumble. Then it was one o'clock, it stopped snowing, and I felt well again. The house was quiet, no demands, everyone away.

'Something inside is changing,' I thought to myself. 'I can read Wodehouse.' I can't believe I ever found him boring, that I couldn't read even a paragraph. What a master of structure. The reader is led from dialogue to place without ever having to cross the street. His people arrive, leave, walk in the park, sit in cafés without having to get there in so many words. I took the book to London and there, woken in the middle of the night by a songbird, I heard myself saying, "I say, old prune, bit much this. Do you have to?" Cara was right, humour lent proportion to drama of all sorts, even ours.

Cara invited me to attend a seminar she was leading on the subject of the feminine and the insights of her nature. I kept notes which though I didn't understand would serve me for years. The title of the seminar was *The Three Faces of the Great Goddess: Hecate/Demeter/Persephone.* Cara's story explored and circumambulated the Eleusinian Mysteries— the secret rites that male scholars and historians, with disguised envy, have never been fully able to uncover let alone understand. We do know that these mysterious rites began by the sea, the mother of us all, and as Cara put it, the mystery not that 'it must not be told', but that 'it *could not* be told'. Throughout my studies and Cara's telling of stories I was included in the family secrets of ancient literature, the kind of poetry whose written words evoke what cannot be openly spoken of.

And that is how my daughter's absence still feels to me today, after so many years. She is not dead, and yet she is. She is gone from my days yet fills my living space. I have put away all photographs, they only show me the physical. Through the story of Persephone—I could be with my daughter so long as I followed the myth's rule: we would be together invisibly half in darkness, half in the light, half below and half above. Rose connects me to the universal, she is where Hopkins said dwells, 'the dearest freshness deep down things'.

And, but, no and no...

Echoes Across The Divide

What is it like to take a leap into the void? First, you walk into the shadow of an idea. Later—so many years later, maybe even decades—light enters in strips and streaks, as though through a shuttered window. I stare through the vertical and horizontal architecture of my memory, the white spaces between these written lines, and something awakens. The ancient snake brain stirs itself, and rises up the spine in an electric shiver. Nostalgia gone. I see the patterns, the forces at work and how I relate to them - fighting, running away, denying.

A nameless dread since the death of my daughter would approach me as I drove home in winter, darkness falling, horizon melting into night. I learn to ask, politely: oh, my soul, wait, hold there, hold, almost home. Arriving at the house, I take off my coat, and out it comes, rivers of it, rolls and swells of it. Then, perhaps quenched, it leaves, only a tinnitus hissing in my ears and behind it a silent house.

A toothache raged through my night.

Another time in time forgotten, time not wanted, the time of suicide attempts. I dreamed about a problem child. "The problem is yours," Cara said. "The problem child in your dream is you," she reiterated. "The *child-you* that didn't know what to do, helpless, hopeless, homeless, loveless. The *you* staring at defeat, the *you* who wanted to give up. The *child-you* which didn't, and still doesn't, want to live—until you give it attention of the loving kind. The child that is the soul you have denied—aborted, sacrificed. Accept her, that difficult moody self that is *you,* lovingly, with compassion for the times you have hated her. It will change your relationship with your wild Rose whose moody self will seem less difficult, lovable in your truth to self. When we know we love someone, only then are we able to say No with Love." That day came to be. If Rose truly needed to act against life, I could no longer run to rescue. Rose, I said, no more. I love you. But I can no longer bear it, I can no longer rescue. Do what you must do. I will love you in the beyond. You will teach me from the other side.

Perhaps it was around that time Cara described a Pietà driftwood carving in the Lady Chapel in Winchester Cathedral. She spoke of it in such a way I knew I had to see for myself what she was talking about. The following week I drove to Winchester. The Virgin looked so *old*. Not what I had imagined—not kind, not gentle. Her face was sour, angry, even bitter. The way the corpse of her son dangled across her lap, the head so loose. The kitten body flopping over my hands like an empty glove—Orlando, my father, the gunshot, Jo, all there as I looked upon the Virgin, her eyes cast down at the dead weight across her lap. Her big knees. My big knees. Rose. Please, dear Lord, not Rose.

I had expected beauty. Cara's heartfelt description spoke of beauty. This Virgin, so exquisitely carved, ravished and hideous—magnetic. Her right arm held outwards, her hand wide as a paddle, seemed to be confronting the viewer. "Your daughter is nailing you to the cross," Cara said. "Know it or not, she is carving you into motherhood."

Rosie moved to Los Angeles and there she met and wedded a solid, kind young man. They wrote a story together about a tree and a bird. The tree loved the bird, the bird loved the tree. Time passed and one day the bird had to fly—that is what birds do. The tree stretched to the sky and held out its arms to the bird, but it could not follow. The bird had to go. And so they separated.

I had moved house the previous December to a tiny thatched cottage in a village five miles away from the family house. It had taken me, plus eleven packers, almost two weeks to move out. Julius had fled back to London, Kate was married and was busy with her own life in London, while Rose lived a world away. I had spent a year in the cottage of my cousin—a godsend, barely two hundred yards from the old family manor house, giving me time to digest the breakdown of family life. It was during that time that I sold the seven containers of furniture that I knew I'd no longer have space for. I was settling in by that summer and I was, at the same time, deeply engaged in, and held together by, my Jungian training.

A year passed without suicide attempts. Julius and I, on a knife-edge, counted the months. We confessed to each other the relief and the hope. Another year passed. It began again. Seven, or eight, or nine attempts. We took it in turns to fly to Los Angeles. I found Rosie in the hospital, sitting on the floor in the corridor of the psychiatric wing, legs straight out like a doll's. They'd taken away her pencils, paints, and brushes.

She looked up. "Mom," she said, eyes empty.

Back home, to find Kate overwhelmed, her needs pushed aside by her sister's needs. My heart ached for her, but she no longer lived at home and I didn't know what to do. I woke with it every morning. The ring of the telephone anywhere anytime became unbearable to me. Shooting pains in my head turned into cluster headaches. I couldn't listen to a friend talking from across the table. Days passed, weeks, months. My terror of flying became phobic, mixed with the terror of losing my daughter, of not arriving in time.

There would be one more visit—though I didn't know that then. It was Easter. I was alone, without Julius. Rosie seemed strange—while affectionate, she insisted on remaining on the surface of things. I couldn't get past the façade. I was touched by the friendships she'd made and the life she had built for herself in Los Angeles. I was intrigued, also, at how she made her way in a city famous for not having a centre. She drove with such confidence. I didn't insist, careful to respect her need for private space. I flew home.

One evening in the month of July I was in a friend's garden at a summer circle dance. There were a dozen of us, all women. Each was to call out a name. I called out, "Rose," which was unusual for me, normally shy about extroverting. I looked up. There was a fine sharp-edged crescent moon lying halfway up the evening's summer sky, deepening into a dark lapis lazuli blue. This image would implant itself in my brain evermore.

I drove home feeling odd.

"What's the matter?" I asked the road.

There wasn't a phone in my bedroom so I didn't hear the one downstairs ringing and ringing. A voice called my name. It was the middle of the night. I got up, peered out of the bedroom window which looked over the front door of my new home. There stood Julius, gesturing to be let in. What's he doing here? I thought a little wildly. All the way from London. I let him in. He held me. "She's gone," he said. I screamed the scream of an animal, almost the same noise as when I gave birth to Rose. Julius had told me that the day after her birth, standing at the station on his daily commute to New York, he had heard the locals gossiping about the screams coming from the local hospital. "You're talking about my wife," he'd said. I don't remember screaming. I asked about it: who is making that noise, I asked. What I felt was my body being torn apart. What I saw was the line of ice cracking and running across the pond at the end of the garden. It was December, the ice thick.

Julius drove back to London. By then it was two in the morning. He would arrange for the three of us to fly to Los Angeles later that day. The five-page suicide note Rose wrote was addressed to each and all of us, one at a time, family and friends. She wanted her ashes scattered in Joshua Tree Desert, where she had been married to Tree. We took her wedding dress, a silk chiffon of deep pinks and mandarin orange on a creamy-whiteness and hung it on the prickly arm of a Joshua Tree. It drifted lightly, rising in the hot heat breeze like a bird in slow quivering flight.

Later, driving back to L.A., Julius at the wheel, both of us in silence, something made me turn around. There she was. Rose. On the back seat behind her father. A solid human being, in full colour, without expression. An out-of-time moment passed. The ghost, the spirit, the apparition—whatever it was—faded into nothing. I stared at the now empty leather seat, the window, the door handle.

Two weeks after Rose died, I was in a small aeroplane, a four-seater Cessna, with two friends I was staying with in Maine. I was in front, beside the pilot, behind us Tony and Roxana. The pilot gave me a pair of large headphones. I was to keep my eye on a particular dial and tell him when the needle dropped below zero. He explained that if we flew at too high an altitude, the wings of a small plane like this could crack. They were not made for temperatures below freezing. "It gets very cold up there in the upper air," he remarked.

The skies were metal grey. Storm clouds ahead. "Anvils," the pilot said, pointing to the v-shaped space between the two massive shapes. He shouted above the noise of the engine, and crackling radio talk, "Have to warn you. Turbulence ahead. We might not make it through before they close in on each other."

Do we have to go there? I asked in my head, my feet in braking position. The radio came on and off, making scratchy spitting noises. The pilot informed the airfield tower we were heading towards the storm. The plane bucked. We entered thick cloud, blanketing the windscreen like a hand on the face. No up, no down. No colour, no shape. No horizon. We dropped like a stone, forty, fifty feet at a time. Again. Again. A sensation of being squeezed, being unable to breathe, a kind of strangulation enveloped me. At any minute I felt I would scream. An impression-sensate-memory burst through my brain of being squashed, stuffed down a tube. I knew, without doubt or verbal thought, that this was a cellular memory of going down the birth canal. A fierce concentration on body, breath, the contraction of muscles in my neck like a vice, my back, my jaw, hips, shoulders. I guided myself over and over again to let go, let go, get through. And then we emerged from the tempest and all was still. We were floating gently over the Maine coast, little lace-like islands spread out beneath us. Blue sky, open sea, sun. "Whatever the tragedy, life walks on by," I remember somebody saying—or I thought, feeling furious. Did that have to happen—now?

Echoes and repetitions, patterns weave themselves through time and space, like a spider, its web across the divide. Cara and I do the counting: my (half) brother Stefan, four years old, left in an orphanage (with me inside Thea, our mother's belly); my mother and her sister (Aunt Agatha), eight and twelve, abandoned to live with cousins; from birth I am a package dropped off here and there, and fostered aged nine to live with an unknown aunt and uncle (Agatha and Edred); on the patrilineal side the foundling (great grandfather) without memory of name or age rescued from massacre in Damascus; my three abortions; my own two daughters, one lives, one dies.

I hear Rose's voice in the rustling of leaves, in the tinnitus in my ears. I close my eyes, bring to mind the stream at the bottom of the garden of our once-upon-a-time family house, the day that not one, but two kingfishers stopped for a moment, and I held my breath (I'd waited four years) and let it out very, very, very slowly.

The Thing About Trees

It was sometime during the walk across France with Julius that I dreamed of my mother. She was in one of her states, be it anxiety, wild enthusiasm, or an urgent eagerness, I could never quite tell—we must talk about healing, she was saying, and lay me down under a canopy of trees.

"Look up at the sky, look through the spaces between leaves, keep looking," she said, "and wait."

I took little heed of the dream. Too strange. Beside the point. Anyway, how would my mother know about healing—she who had abandoned a son, a daughter, cats, houses, husbands. At this time I was reading Gerard Manley Hopkins' letters to his brother where he described the 'crown of the oak' and the different shapes of sky between the different shapes of leaves of this or that tree. Later, looking back on this dream, which Cara said was important, a little more of the healing worked itself in me. I was learning to read a dream symbolically instead of literally, coded language. Something in me—but not me, I was to understand (not the egoic side)—was in the process of change, and perhaps transformation within my person with my wobbly ego cooperating.

Maybe we are like trees, rooted in the two elements—sky and earth, spirit and soul. A storm was blowing the trees outside my study window. Branches were swaying, I felt anxious watching their movements. It can come upon me suddenly: the need to stand by a tree, lie under its canopy, stare at the space between the leaves. This enchantment for the tree began with the sight of felled trees on a beach, by a cemetery on the French Caribbean island, St. Barth. I photographed these felled trees and wrote about them. It was much later that the need came to draw live trees while on my travels en famille.

In India, it was a palm tree which had fascinated me. Or maybe it was the uprightness of such a trunk, a tree made of one trunk without branches, and a burst at the top, like fireworks—energy, or something of spirit returning, made of joy, even happiness. Dead tree trunks—the felled, no longer resonated inside me. Instead, trees—alive upstanding rooted trees to which my body responded with shivers of pleasure, alongside their transformations, the changing of the seasons. When a strong emotion comes, do not look at it, the Zen masters say, just as you do not look at the branches being tossed by the wind. Imagine a tree, focus on the trunk, solid, rooted, grounded—focus on your belly and stay there until the storm passes and it will.

Drawing that first tree—I was using pen and ink—began a process that took three months. Morning after morning, hour after hour, painstakingly drawing leaf after leaf, losing myself in the canopy of the tree and feeling somewhat at peace each time. One drawing took several weeks, each star-shaped leaf like a tapestry stitch, each stroke sinking into a system from the pen to my fingers and up my arm and down through the entire being I inhabited, the very bone of self. My Arbor Vitae—the Tree of Life. I read later that neuroscience uses this term for the cerebellum.

*

All this was the dream reaching out from the night into my days, during a time of family storm, both girls in trouble wrestling with addiction, Julius and I desperate and not knowing what to do next. I remember how Rose used to spend hours working on stringing minute beads together while sitting in a bath, and I sketched leaf after leaf sitting at my desk, And I think of Kate, so true to her feeling, how she paints trees, their leaves, every line and canker and shadow in a kind of loving trance, free in that moment, of stress.

Those were the nights when I sat up in the dark hours knitting until the edges of dawn paled the window and I felt safe from the darkness. I knitted long rectangles of different colours and sewed them together to wear as woolly hats. A collection of different colours for every day of the month sat in a basket by the front door.

On The Road To Damascus

One day an idea came to me to do volunteer work in a hospice. Not something I exactly *wanted* to do—it was something I had to do. Perhaps like the time long ago, newly married living in Westchester County, when I volunteered as visitor of women in the maximum security prison, Bedford Hills Correctional Facility. That, I now consider, to have been a need for freedom from the unconscious fear and anxiety that ruled in my bones, and still does. While the pull to the hospice, I want to say, came from the death cry of the soul in the stone matter of my panther sculpture. Only by following such impulse that does not make sense, starting with marrying (twice) an Englishman with no eyebrows (and hair the colour of fox), did I learn to differentiate between what comes from the ego, and what comes from the angels who I know don't exist.

And so, after a little hunting, I found a hospice in Oxford and was accepted. I had also been planning a trip to Syria (another contradictory impulse, surely) to research the paternal side of my family such as evidence of the great grandfather's existence.

After a few months at the hospice, I met a woman whose first name was the same as mine, including the umlaut on the ï. But more than that, after exchanging a little history with this other Loïse, speaking of my quest she said that she

244   On The Road To Damascus

had just returned from Damascus where a good friend lived who would help me.

Fate, the predetermined, that which is spoken for by the oracle, comes from the Latin *fatum*. In French this becomes *fée*, fairy—the first fairy, the one who stands by the cradle endowing the new life with gifts. There is no word in French for fate. The language has *destin*, and *sort*—a spell. Jung once said either you go with fate, unconscious and screaming like a pig to the slaughterhouse, or you go consciously, eyes open. In taking on the training to be a Jungian analyst, in working in a hospice, on traveling to Syria, I was going with fate, with a sense of duty, taking on what felt like the unfinished business of ancestors Jung wrote about, the karma within a family passed on from parents to children and grandchildren.

The family story, told and retold down the generations, becomes a family's map—a narrative landscape bringing a sense of place and belonging with recognition. Bit by bit, I imagine how each telling and retelling leaves a deposit, each life span thickens the sediment, and fate thus evolves.

So who was Alfred Vincent de Damas, the mythical great grandfather? Might we have Persian blood running through our veins? How come the family never spoke of the foundling it descended from, or, at least, only as myth? There was one person who could answer these questions. I called my great uncle, Yves Vincent, his son—therefore the person of Alfred Vincent de Damas existed in living memory. This revelation happened as my cousin Jas and I talked about the family trying to unfathom a secret or two.

*

Yves lived at the edge of a hamlet near Sens, south east of Paris. A date was arranged. I would drive on my way to the South of France. I arrived at the house, almost hidden behind a copse of trees, a little oasis in the middle of a flat, nondescript landscape. It was late morning. Stepping out of the car, I found myself nose to nose with a cat balancing inside the V of a lime tree.

"Marmalade! Hullo pussycat," I said, an image of Orlando in Manhattan dancing between the branches.

"Ah. Tu parles comme ton père."

I turned around. There he was. A big man, big hands, standing well over six feet. He had splendid white hair, white-white, as once upon a time I recalled it black-black like my father's, and my own.

"I thought you and Daddy hadn't seen each other in years." I spoke French as Yves spoke not a word of English.

"My cat is seventeen years old," Yves answered, his embrace warm as the Mediterranean lands he came from. "What interests me is that your father would speak to women, and cats, in English, and you do too—at least to cats."

The last time we'd met, I was fourteen years old, living in Strasbourg. Yves was touring with the theatre, playing the lead in Tennessee Williams's *Un Tramway Nommé Désir*, and afterwards he had come to see me. He looked so much like my father, it had left me trembling with longing. During the entire six years that I lived in Strasbourg, my father had never come to visit.

I followed my great-uncle into his small mill house. Some thirty years ago, when his stage acting career was nearing an end, Yves had just enough money to buy the moulin and, with his own hands, wire in electricity and install water pipes. Walls the colour of parchment showed trembly, zigzaggy hairline cracks, and fading paintwork in uneven patches. It was modest, dignified, comfortable. A short passage led to a bedroom where my great uncle put down my bag and pointed to a large manilla envelope on the bedside table.

"These are the only documents I have," he said. "They are copies. You may keep them. There is a photograph of my father, the birth document drawn up by the French consul in Alexandria, and the first few pages of an account of his early life, unfortunately unfinished. You'll see…"

We returned to the central room of the house. There was a refectory table, two benches at either side. On the table, a pile of scripts Yves was working on, and his reading glasses. Cha-chaouine, the marmalade cat, jumped up onto my lap and stayed there for the next two hours. Yves began.

"As you know, my father was first married to Rose Inès Schaefer."

I shivered a little as the ghosts of family lore seemed to gather around us. Something Thea said about my grandfather, Yves' half-brother, came to mind. It was the summer of 1944. Hot. I knew very little about my grandfather other than how his presence always left me uneasy—his elegance, coldness, the way he would stand behind after lunch to hold my coat in an almost ballet-like posture that was strange and disturbing. Thea told me a story about him. "I was in my ninth month, with you," she had said. "I was staying with Papa and Marguerite, your grandmother. Your father was away—the war in Italy. No air conditioning in those days. New York in August—God, that heat wasn't human. There was one tiny, tiny finger of a breeze. You could feel it as long as you didn't move. I opened the window in Maman's room—the correct form of address for my mother-in-law—pushed a table up to the window and lay there, on my back, concentrating on the breeze as it brushed my big tummy. Oh, it was something! Suddenly the door opened. I turned my head sideways. Papa—as he was known by all—just stood there, in the doorway. Not a word. I don't know what it was, but something thick and dark remained in the room after he left. Without thinking, I crossed myself."

The atmosphere my mother had described was familiar to me. It had a shape, a movement I recognised, the serpentine quality circumambulating the family—my father, Tata, the cousins, myself. It felt different with Yves, though, perhaps because he was more aware and he had learnt to befriend, even tame it on the stage.

"My father, Alfred, was a widower when he met the woman who would be his second wife, my mother."

"Do you know how Rose Inès died?" I said, interested in what happened to his first wife, this being my grandfather Arnold's mother. He never forgave his father for divorcing her, and then she died mysteriously. That may be when the suspicious rumours began about her being poisoned. And there the broken relationships began: my grandfather Arnold did not speak to his father Alfred; my father Louis, years later, will not speak to his father Arnold. No one speaks about any of this directly. A silence thickens, heavy with ancestral trauma. Secrets held too long emit secretions in the body. And Yves, ignoring my question, continued with the family tree, he too unable or unwilling or wisely refusing to enter the silence.

"My mother was in her mid-twenties when she met Alfred, who was then in his mid-fifties. He already had two sons from his first wife, one of whom was killed in action during the First World War. You know, my father—he who never showed emotion—is said to have fallen on the floor in a dead faint when he received this news. So, later, when my mother became pregnant, he sent her to the Haute Savoie in France so that she could have the baby—that was me—in peace, *sans scandale*. They were married five months later, back in Algiers."

Cha-chaouine emitted rhythmic little purrings. I nestled ever deeper into my leather armchair by the fireplace as Yves continued. "Can you imagine what it must have been like to have had a son who died '*que pour du panache*'. Those young men, obediently charging straight into German fire with no more than their *épées de gala* to protect them, dressed in the ceremonial uniform of the École Militaire Spéciale de St. Cyr. Ah, the treachery, the cruelty of it."

The force of emotion in Yves's eyes and voice took me across a threshold. I was seeing emerge an entity of what was my great-grandfather, standing there in the ephemeral space of myth. I became aware of a tingling running up and down my legs. Yves addressed his father as Père, and Mon Père, and his mother as *Mozeur*—'mother' with a French accent.

I could feel myself settling into a storytelling place, beyond time, where the personal meets with the universal. Alfred had never told his story. I imagined his silence simmering alongside the lives of three generations—all the way to us, his family in the making. Perhaps it took my father's storytelling gift to bring it out into the open, to resonate in one of us strongly enough to break the silence.

My great-grandfather's story and my own lost childhood overlapped in a way that could rescue the both of us from the non-existence of myth. I didn't understand my own life importance---the saying is not 'an ego unexamined' but 'a life unexamined is not lived'—that a never-known person could matter so much… could matter beyond death, even given a voice.

Yves continued, "Mozeur was a scribe. She read and wrote letters for her illiterate neighbours. She loved to go to the theatre, to cabarets. She was a coquette, and a great mimic."

We talked about origins. "You must understand," Yves explained, "that Syria, as it is known today, is barely fifty years old. Alfred's time goes back to a country that does not exist today, a country that included Egypt, Alexandria, and what is known today as Lebanon and Jordan."

"Describe your father," I asked.

Yves replied, "Very much the Middle-Eastern type. Not Arab. Perhaps Armenian. Or Persian. Ferocious," he said, "And triste, solide," and a little later, "*froid*."

I asked Yves about religion—he said he hadn't been baptised. Although an atheist, he was interested in the *idea* of the Trinity. I liked that. It mattered to me to find someone in the family with a moral code if not at least faith in the mystery of the universe.

"Dieu, Jésus, Marie," he began oddly—with father, son, mother, evoked as a family unit of his own experience—relating the story of a visit to the Lascaux caves before the site had been closed to visitors. He described a small entrance leading to a vestibule. Crouching low, you passed into a long, narrow tunnel.

"Finally you arrived in an immense hall. Like a cathedral,

but more impressive. The guide held a very small pin-point reddish light. You were told not to open your mouth, not talk, not exclaim—no toxic exhaust of human breath allowed. Pitch blackness all around. Imperceptibly, emerging through the dark red glow, drawings on the walls of animal figures came into focus as if of their own accord."

Yves looked out of the window. "Yes. There, I sensed that there could be a spiritual dimension to life."

Cha-chaouine stirred, pulled herself up, stretched and left my lap. Yves went to the kitchen and called out instructions. I laid the table. We had dinner and the fire burned down to embers.

"Well. My father idealised women," Yves said, the next morning, "which of course created a distance between him and them. He had a natural grace. He was skilled at fencing."

Recalling my father's stories about his own fencing prowess, I extended my right arm, raised my left arm, mimicking his gesture of the flick and twist of the wrist.

"*En garde à vous!*"

"Ah, Louis. My nephew, his great charm," Yves said, with both affection and regret. "*Quel dommage* to have used charm for gain. To become *brigand des grands chemins*. It is the problem of becoming entirely material about life."

Yves continued, "As for my father—well, he fought two duels. And you know, my mother loved to flirt. *À propos*, I will tell you a little about *mon éducation sentimentale*. It started early."

It was on a Thursday afternoon, the Lycee's half day, that Yves's mother took him to tea at a friend's house while she had errands. The lady said she would be happy to have the handsome little boy at her house any time that Madame Vincent was busy. Soon Yves, eight years old, was there every week. The first time he arrived in Madame's apartment, she was standing naked in the kitchen, leaning against the table, legs akimbo.

As Yves told this story, my mind drifted, picking up eerie coincidences, like crumbs in the forest leading back through three generations. "All I saw was this '*pubis énorme*'," Yves was saying, in a tone of respect tinged with delight. "Of course it wasn't really so big, but I had never seen anything like *cette chose noire, ce triangle bouclé, étrange, très interessant…*"

The ease of his manner disconcerted me. Only in a Latin country could such a sensual point of view be voiced, and with such pleasure.

"Were you afraid?" I asked.

"No, not really," Yves replied. "I was too small to have an erection. All she could do was rub me against her. It was quite nice. Soon I was going there readily and punctually, but, after a month or two, Mozeur found my eagerness suspicious. She realised what was going on. It was quite a scene."

The next morning, after breakfast, chunks of fresh baguette dunked in our café au lait, we returned to our armchairs.

"You know, I had a job broadcasting on Algiers radio. When France fell, I thought I might have to desert as I didn't want to join Pétain. There was a new movement, the Free French, but that was no good either. I was told to wait, in Cairo, until notified by the FF. 1941, 1942 passed with Glenn Miller on the air waves—'String of Pearls', 'Chatta-

Nooga-Choo-Choo', 'Knit One, Purl Two'. The French were depleted—very, very poor. No one had decent uniforms. They wore what there was—English, Russian, anybody's. And then, at last, I received orders and returned to Algeria. Who should I run into but your father who was with the Americans finishing the war in North Africa. Looking splendid, bristling with energy and, of course, in a spotless grand uniform—American. *Where* did you get that uniform from? I asked him. You see, I was envious. Louis said, 'Don't move. Be right back'."

Louis reappeared half a day later, Yves recounted, beaming, "With socks, trousers, jacket, cap, the whole *trousseau*. I didn't ask, but I knew perfectly well that my new wardrobe could only have come from the PX—stolen." I was delighted to see Louis, but then we lost track of each other until after the Libération. Once again, we meet by accident. This time, Paris. It was 1948 when we all danced in the streets. I was back at work, married, with one young child. One morning—in fact to be precise it was six in the morning—the doorbell rang. It was Louis.

"Hello Yves," he said, as though we'd seen each other yesterday. "Can I come in and have a bath? And can you lend me a suit?"

"Well yes," I said, "What else?"

I showed my dear nephew, whom I was very fond of, to the bathroom. A little later, my wife bumped into a smart young man she'd never seen before in the corridor. She was somewhat surprised. Louis said hello in his usual charming, deadpan way. He left just before nine and just as he was stepping out, he asked if I could give him a loan, just temporary. I did, suggesting that we have lunch that day and catch up on our lives.

"Of course," he said. Midi, one o'clock, two o'clock, no sign of Louis. He never appeared. A year later, I ran into a mutual friend and asked after Louis. I was worried about him.

"Louis?" said Emile, looking amused. "Don't you know? He's made a fortune for himself. He's very well, living in New York, driving a Bugatti."

Shortly after this, I received a package in the post: my suit neatly folded and in each pocket a bunch of U.S. one hundred dollar bill notes.

"Where did this joie de vivre and insouciance come from—your father?" I wondered.

"No. Not from him," Yves said, "I don't know where it came from. Maybe his grandfather, but we still don't know where he came from. How could he remember? He was stripped of memory—orphaned, growing up under the monstrously strict religious orders in Alexandria where he was taught nothing, neither to read nor to write. Aucune tendresse. Treated as a street ruffian, used as a child labourer, worked to the point of exhaustion. Every day he had to carry one hundred kilo sacks of flour on his back for the kitchens to make the daily bread. All this in a monastery in the middle of the desert. Imagine the heat!"

At sixteen, Alfred rebelled. He ran away. He aspired to join the French navy, but orphaned in Ottoman territory, presumed Turkish by his looks, it was inadmissible. He was a survivor though. Determined, tough, resourceful, he made his way to the Austrian consul and was given passage on a ship to France. His intention was to find reports on the massacre that might lead to traces of his family. By some fluke or miracle, he could recall the street address in Damascus—a well-to-do residential quarter of town—

where he had lived as a child.

Alfred sailed on a frigate, spending three months at sea—most of it seasick and miserable. This is all that we know of his past from the brief account he wrote in the last year of his life. He describes a moment: he recalls standing on a balcony overlooking a typical Damascene courtyard. There is a tree, a fountain, birdsong. A boy stands beside him, also a man and a woman—mother, father, and brother he surmised, but couldn't be sure as he remembered no names, nor even the language they spoke. The slate of his young mind had been rubbed out, leaving only a memory of the large, wide double doors of the courtyard thrown open, a riot of men shouting, being shoved into a large packing chest. And then walking, running through streets, into the hills, pulling up weeds, feeding himself on their roots. He thought he might have been five or six years old and may have spent two years like this until the next part of the story when a French officer on horseback took him off to the monastery of the White Fathers, St. Vincent de Paul, in Alexandria. That is where he was given a name, being of the monastery.

During the months in France, Alfred taught himself to read and write, studied grammar and arithmetic, and bought himself a mandolin. So that is what and how the autodidact works, I thought to myself, not quite making a personal identification. Yves remembered his father plucking the strings with a little piece of bone, playing quite merry unfamiliar little tunes, tunes without names. Eventually Alfred returned to North Africa, settling In Algiers. He never went back to Syria, refusing to speak any other language but French.

"You know, my greatest regret," Yves said, "is that I never

told my father how much I admired him. I gave no thought to his traumatic history because he never spoke of it. Not one word. The daily effort of his silence must have cost him. I remember him one day, suddenly peering at me so intensely with his oyster-grey eyes, like this…" Yves looked straight at me. A hair-raising tremor ran up my spine. Yves remembered his father's temper too. One day he accused him of rimming his eyes with Kohl. Yves had been swimming in water full of mazout, the oil from ships that thickened the seas on that coast. Yves scrubbed his eyes and the skin around his eyes over and over, but it was of no use.

"Perhaps a flash-memory of the massacre was stirring in him, as if he were looking into the eyes of the rioting Muslim men who had massacred his family. He wouldn't believe me when I insisted it was only mazout. Menteur, he kept repeating."

The physiognomy of my family on the Vincent side is Mediterranean: the cliff-edged cheek bones; amber eyes as if, yes, rimmed with Kohl; the near-dark olive skin; the thick lion-mane head of hair; the animal grace, the cross-legged position held with ease and for hours.

"You asked about my father and *joie de vivre*. Well, I'll tell you something. There was a love of mischief and disguise in him, as in all of us. One day when my mother was old, and I was almost sixty, I asked how my father died. They had separated and divorced but later my mother returned to him. My mother said, 'Well, you know, I will tell you. It was another time when the *Chansonniers* were performing. At home, I danced and performed, as he liked me to do. Propped up in our bed, laughing so much, he asked me to stop. You see, your father died laughing, right there in front of me. A heart attack, I suppose, brought on by laughter'."

Six o'clock came around. No more storytelling. We stood up, stretched. Yves picked up a bag of crumbs from his turquoise painted kitchen. We walked to the pond below the little house and sprinkled the fishes' evening meal. A blackbird sang overhead.

"*Le merle chante*," Yves said, looking up into the tree.

Le merle blanc is an exceptional person—for good or bad. S*iffler comme un merle* is to sing with twists and turns and acrobatic swings. The men in the family, like my father Louis, and my cousin Miguel, they whistle and bend the air finer than the reed. *Un fin merle* is an uncatchable figure, an Hermes, an angel, a turbulence in the air around you. *Un villain merle* is a cunning trickster.

Yes, that's all of us.

We strolled further down to the riverbank at the bottom of the garden. Across the way, stood a line of seven poplars. "I planted them all at the same time," Yves said, "shortly after buying the moulin. Look how different they are from one another. Yet they stand in the same soil and have received the same rain." He pointed out a small tree standing beside the taller tree at the end of the row, "*Père et fils*," he said.

I thought of my mother's painting of the *Place Furstenberg*—the winterness, the two slim trees, one tall, one little, standing together on an oval—*mère et fille*.

"L'acte d'observation est une tendresse," I said.

"Oui. Flaubert." Yves nodded.

We stood side by side. The reflection of the trees trembled in the water. We turned and went back into the house.

Home from my visit to Yves I decided: Yes, I am going to

Syria. We'd explored the idea together. Yves gave me his blessing, and this gave me the courage to do it. He asked that I bring back some evidence of his father's existence, whatever it might be. Julius helped and I chose a date in September. I did not want to stay in a hotel behind the tourist curtain and liked the idea of a St. Vincent de Paul monastery in Damascus that took in visitors. I wrote the letters and arranged for a driver. I had a collection of names and addresses gathered from friends, and friends of friends. Beside each name and address, the equivalent in Arabic script so I could ask and find my way. There would be no signs in Western writing, though I was advised that one or two people might speak French.

Professor Nazih Kawkabi at the University of Damascus—
الأستاذ نزيه كوكبي في جامعة دمشق
*Sarab Atassi, Science Secretary at IFEAD—*سراب أتاسي،
أمين العلوم في IFEAD
*Jupiter's Temple, and the café next to Zeus' Gate—*معبد
جوبيتر، والمقهى المجاور لبوابة زيوس
The 'Abouromani', the pomegranate tree beside the café—
«الأبورماني"شجرة الرمان التي بجانب المقهى
*Restaurant Zeitouni and Restaurant Elissar—*مطعم زيتومة
ومطعم اليسار
*Dr Bashir Zohdy, Conservationist, Islamic Department at
the Museum of Syria—*الدكتور بشير زهدي، خبير
الترميم، القسم الإسلامي في متحف سوريا
*Kamar, driver—*قمر، سائق
*Père Bulos at La Terre des Hommes on the coast who would
know about orphans—*الأب بولس في
على الساحل والذي يعرف شيئا عن
الأيتام *La Terre des Hommes*

The Familiar Unknown

The aeroplane began its descent into pitch-black darkness. Then, far ahead, a runway marked with lights, mirroring a sky full of stars, and beyond that the city lights of Damascus. I thought about a book on my French grandmother's bedside table—for years, always there, like a favoured object. It was titled *Une Femme au Nom d'Étoile*. It was not about a woman, though, but a country: Algeria— Al-Djazair. It only occurred to me now, as I walked off the aeroplane, how fiercely my grandmother had loved and missed her country, and Mostaganem, Morocco, where she was born. Lying in her pale pink bedroom—the frou-frou pink dressing gown, the white-white hair in startled corkscrew style and me, stretched out on the end of her bed—she would recount stories of playing tennis in a long white dress in the light of a full moon. Stories always set in the most delicious climates. The way she padded about her apartment on 52nd Street, little whistlings under her breath. Memories of all this rung in my ears as I handed my passport to the custom official. *Quand Il Me Parle Tout Bas, Je Vois La Vie En Ro-se.*

I stood by the carrousel waiting for my bags, silently repeating to myself: *You are in the homeland of your ancestors.* The automatic glass doors slid open and outside, standing on the pavement, the night air was gentle, warm. No moon.

Then came my tears. I licked the saltiness. Beside me, around me, that presence.

My driver, Kamar, had a schedule. Tomorrow, *La Terre des Hommes*, on the coast near the border of Lebanon. It was a day's journey. Then back to Damascus, to the monastery of St. Vincent de Paul, where I'd spend the rest of the week. Kamar started his sentences with, "To speak frankly, Madame," and assured me that he knew his country like the back of his hand, that the drive would be pleasant, and not too long.

For the first two hours we drove through a landscape of fruit orchards, olive trees, and fields of grain. Passing a well-tended field, Kamar remarked with pride, "You see, Madame, we work our land very hard." He talked of war and asked me if I knew that, according to the ancestral code, war is only waged to protect the home where a woman dwells. It is her domain, her sanctuary, and a man's honour is measured by his ability to protect home and wife from outsiders. Nature is land, woman is nature. He told me that the Iraqis were tough, and not so charming.

"They are the officers. We are their soldiers. Arabs do not care for the intellect or for history—all they want is food and drink and entertainment. The Iranians come for religious reasons and some are charming, yes." He pronounced 'Sahara', the word for the desert, in a way that sounded like the wind on the sand: Dza-hha-rra. The desert was the dark pink colour of skin under the eyes. He told me that 'Zarab' was the word for mirage.

We drove along the Alaouite Mountains, the Orontes Valley, along a wide plain of dark red soil rich with iron, past round-shouldered mountains at whose feet olive and fig trees grew. Some were bald, crusty with limestone, flanked with grey rock, others the soft brown of animal hide. Fields were cleared of stones, collected to make walls, bigger stones used to build one-storied houses. Every man, Kamar said, was to have his patch of land. "You are not a man if you do not have land and your own house."

We stopped at Palmyra. The city melted in the sunset light like a sandcastle in the sea. In the distance, columns seemed as small and as thin as pencils, whereas up close, they stood monumental. We had dinner facing the ruins. A black night, without moon. Venus was there, the one light above a temple column. The wind lifted and I turned my chair to face away. Like a squall it twirled and swirled around me, blowing sand and grit in my eyes. Then it was gone, like the djinn. Palm tree fronds stilled.

In the morning the ruins stood like bleached bones under a pale sky.

"It is so nice and quiet. I like that. You drive slow and quiet, like the land."

"Madame, silence is where life happens, between the lines, where our fables are born," Kamar said.

Our conversation turned. I wondered why every man in every street had a moustache. There was a manly chuckle. "Well," Kamar said, "Of course, it is to say that we are not women," and, both hands off the wheel, he polished the ends of the whiskers under his nose, with a little twist at the end. "Women do not have *this*. Some men, when they go to Europe, shave it off, but at home it continues. If you are a man, you wear your moustache."

Kamar had much to say. People with blue eyes were the children of the Crusaders. "When they came here, many did not return. They stayed, they married, they became Arabic. If you say 'your grandfather was a Crusader', it is a very big insult. As if it was yesterday, fists are made and a fight breaks out. You should hear our women talk about it."

"Is this not the storytelling country of all countries?" I asked. Kamar, delighted, continued. Tamburlaine killed more than 25,000 men, ordered a tower to be made of their heads. For years, people refused to go to the mosque because of the smell—the river of blood was thirty centimetres thick. Kamar's eyes, brimming with emotion, filled the rearview mirror. I told him I was here to meet my great-grandfather's spirit.

La Terre des Hommes was a mix of houses and villas scattered on a piece of land by the sea. Rocks, sand, columns, stone floors. Solid, basic, one-storied, airy little dwellings. No shops, but everybody had a task and everybody was busy. It was its own kind of village. The foundation was built by Paul Sleimann, the Lazarist Father of the charity of St. Vincent de Paul, and had been established with a handful of American dollars barely ten years ago. We found Père Bulos (his working name) in a little, white-washed chapel. He wore a long white robe. As he took it off outside, he introduced himself as Paul. Standing in a t-shirt and faded floppy blue trousers washed by sea, he told us his foundation cared for adults and orphaned children who had been left wounded, mutilated and starving.

Paul, a man in his fifties, once one of them, had been left in an orphanage by his mother when he was five years old. The rule then was one child per family. She had deemed Paul, her youngest, to be the strongest. Many years later his mother's sister, and a brother—the two members of the family who remained—informed him that the rest of the family had been massacred in one of the many uprisings. It took him a long time to understand that his mother had, in fact, saved him, and that he owed her a gratitude.

"They called me 'Le Briseur'—The Destroyer. I was bitter, angry," he said. "I resented life." Paul continued, relating how he'd come face to face with his sadism, recognising it in the eyes of the children in his care. "It starts very quickly when you live with fear every day. Touched by the negative, you take it out on the world." He added later that, as a survivor, you take more than you can give, wrenching yourself from your own history. Only later can you give—maybe. How you survived your childhood, I don't know, Cara once said. How much did I take, to do so, I now asked myself.

I spoke to Father Bulos about the violent feelings running through my father, through myself, all the way down the Vincent family line of aunts and cousins.

"There are two movements in a human being that direct them from birth into their own way of life," Paul said. "One positive, one negative. To me it is simple: a person will pursue whichever is first impressed upon him. It is to do with love. This understanding came to me when I accepted my mother's decision of choosing me to be 'saved'. Left in the care of the Fathers, I felt abandoned. But I was not abandoned, I was loved."

When it was time to go one of the Sisters working at the foundation placed eight jasmine florets on the palm of my right hand, blessing each one with a little prayer.

Kamar and I were silent on the drive back to Damascus. I needed that silence. It was good to be left alone, to get to know the silence.

The monastery of St. Vincent de Paul had once stood outside the city of Damascus on its own grounds. Today it stood on a traffic island on a three-lane highway to the airport. Honking vehicles, wailing sirens, metallic coughings and wheezings of lorries and buses, and motorbikes changing gears, revving up to the roundabout. My room, overlooking the road, was functional, cell-like. Numbered 54, it smelled of dust and stone. Mosquitoes bounced against the walls and whined through the night. Loo, shower, a basin in a corner. All impeccably clean, with a fan on the ceiling swirling the stifling heat.

Visitors were not invited to share meals. After Kamar dropped me off at the monastery, I went in search of something to eat, looking back every so often to note landmarks for my return to the monastery's gates. Every street was crowded and looked the same. Little shacks, one-storied square dwellings and buildings, weak flickering lights coming from the doorways of little shops. The atmosphere was open, courteous, now and then a smile in the eye exchanged as I made my way past. There was very little fresh food, mostly things in plastic or foil packets, glass jars, tins. I brought a tin of sardines, a bag of Aleppo pistachios, a handful of apricots, and one banana back to my room. Also water and plastic cups. While feeling somewhat *dépaysée*, it was, at the same time, eerily familiar.

I propped up the icon of the Virgin and Child Père Bulos had given me on the metal side table, with my books and watercolour travel kit. I read a passage from Isabel Burton's book, *The Inner Life of Syria*. She'd hated Damascus, but the desert grew on her, and she wrote that the emptiness and silence brought her solace. Back in England, hungering and thirsting for Damascus, she mourned what she described as the cab-shafts of civilization, the contamination of cities, yearning for the desert to recover the purity of mind and the dignity of human nature. Yes, that is right, I thought to myself, reading on.

The Sisters at the monastery were Italian. Père Fernandez, their director, was Spanish. During our interviews he spoke in fluent Italian when speaking on the telephone (which often rang). He was a very small man, with a tonsure, and wore a brown robe tied with a rope around his middle and brown leather sandals. When he got up from his desk his height didn't change. *Mister Five by Five*, I hummed to myself later, thinking about our conversation. Père Fernandez confirmed many things in the story of my great grandfather. At first, he had been upset, offended even, by my report. It was not possible, he insisted, that Alfred had not been taught to read or write while in the care of the Sisters of Charity in the monastery in Alexandria.

He looked upon me with reproach. "No," he said. "It is a lie."

My image of Alfred shrank and turned into a small child, traumatised, difficult, of ill will, mute. But then the next day, when we met again, Père Fernandez said, with some equanimity,

"It is important to view such events in the context of their time. Your story has made me think. It was all so new. The work for the Sisters to establish their order in the middle of nowhere was enormous. No assistance, no culture, no education—there was nothing there. Life was harsh, and the Sisters in turn were harsh. How else could they surmount their tasks? Of course, they would have demanded assistance from their orphans, engaged the child-foundlings—like the boy, your great-grandfather—in hard labour. Carrying 100 kg sacks of flour, as described in his written account, was no doubt true. Indeed, times were very hard, and it was the accepted custom to discipline the children by beating them." He smiled ruefully. "Up until not so long ago… On reflection, I can see that it is possible that a child might not have been educated—especially if the child was difficult and near-mute from the shock of his experience."

My father, his father, my great-grandfather—there they were, and there it was: the task Cara spoke of, to look back without blame—of others, events, self. See what is.   No excuses. The act of looking back with the splinter of ice in the heart. I spoke of my childhood rages, how they had re-emerged when I gave birth to my own two children. I described the movements of the Vincent family—England, South America, North America, Spain, forever on the move. Father Fernandez smiled, lips drawing a crooked line.

"Typical," he said. "Seekers. Never in one place. That is the Syrian."

The next day Father Fernandez spoke about the character of orphaned children—the insecurity, the loss of identity, the restlessness, each forming itself into a mosaic of all the broken pieces handed down, generation after generation. The way they survive is by being tough with themselves, which means tough on others—no time for compassion. Meanwhile, the deep rage within grows, and that too is passed on. In my case, yes, I was abandoned, repeatedly abandoned, sexually abused, and none of these things came into my consciousness, let alone moved my heart, for a very long time. My childhood became, for me, shameful, grotesque and, worst of all perhaps, too much to live with. Hence the disbelief. Yes, 'too much', as a family therapist once said to me in private, asking me to not speak of it in the group circle. I was to remain silent. It would take Cara's shocked expression for me to feel able to share—at last someone to help contain it and carry me over the abysm. Teach me to mend, and amend.

I spent the next few days in Damascus at *The Librairie de France* going through the archives around the time of the massacre of the Christians in the latter half of the nineteenth century. Some sixty villages outside Damascus were destroyed while, within the Christian quarter of the city, it is said over twenty-thousand men, women, and children were killed. Hate raged through the streets. I read the official account of the mounted officers who had been sent from France to round up any children sheltering in the camps set up in the surrounding hills and take them to the newly founded monasteries outside Syria.

I immersed myself in the history and politics and culture of North Africa, falling under the spell of *Ibn el Arabi's* mystical Arab poetry. Though a direct connection to my great-grandfather did not happen, almost everything that was written around his time of life assembled itself into a living, breathing presence of the human being. I walked through the streets of Damascus, sat in cafés observing the physiognomy of people around me, struck by a resemblance to my family. I saw them all—my father, Tata Leïla, brothers and sisters and cousins. I don't walk around France and see my family in every face. I did not feel foreign; I was at home, even though I got lost at every street corner and had to ask my way. And yes, so familiar - home to me was like that.

On my last day, there was a demonstration by the Palestinians. I stood in a doorway with history at my side. Angry men passed in a wave, roaring like the ocean, lifting and swelling. Shiny metallic helmets, silver-sharp in the sun. A glint of knives, policemen with batons.

Back home, as promised, I wrote to Yves (in French). A few days later he called. I had returned his father to him, he said, my pages made him real. He could believe in him. He thanked me from the bottom of his heart.

"Tu m'as rendu mon père."

Cher Yves—

Par où commencer. Damas.

Nous sommes arrivés la nuit. En sortant de l'aéroport des larmes me montent aux yeux. Pas de lune. Il fait bon. Le lendemain nous quittons Damas vers dix heures pour commencer notre vol d'oiseau de Syrie—voir Palmyre*, Hama, Alep. Ville* morte dans le désert—impressionante mais me laisse le coeur froid. Mais le désert, paysage nu, couleur de peau, vide mais d'une pureté, tranquille, ouvert, ombres couleur de cernes sous les yeux. Vers Alep, terrain arrosé, agricole—arbres fruitiers, olives, graines, mais—terrain si pierreux; comme les Syriens travaillent dur. Dimanche (donc une semaine après) je quitte Jules qui a des affaires au Liban, à Muscat, à Abu Dhabi, et je repars pour Damas. Six heures de route. Je suis en bonnes mains, je le sais maintenant après une semaine avec *notre chauffeur, Saïd; je ne me sens pas du tout menacée seule en Syrie.*

Première étape de mes recherches est de rencontrer Père Paul—Père Blanc, Libanais, Catholique, en charge d'un programme nommé Terre des Hommes, qui soigne les invalides, mutilés, surtout enfants. Je lui raconte l'histoire de mon cher arrière grand père, cet enfant trouvé. Père Paul était mis à l'orphelinat par sa mère qui, si pauvre, espérait qu'il aurait là une éducation, et nourriture. "J'en ai voulu au monde," me dit-il, "on m'appelait 'Le Briseur'." Puis il m'explique qu'il a vu le sadisme—en lui même, dans les enfants dont il s'occupe, qu'il guérit comme il peut, que cela vient de la peur, du mal au coeur, et à la fin de mon histoire, ou plutôt de celle d'Alfred: deux foyers, toute une vie, une famille, trois fils dont un qui en parle avec tendresse, mais dont la réputation est de froideur et distance, il dit, "cet homme a été aimé. Quelqu'un l'a touché." Il m'explique ce que sa tante lui a dit un jour: il y a deux forces dans un être humain, une force positive, et une force négative— et la direction que l'être humain choisira, et suivera, dépend de laquelle est touchée. Même si ce n'est qu'un geste, un moment d'amour, le vrai, cela est suffisant pour que dorénavant cela soit la force positive qui sera poursuivie—quoique en lutte. Je venais de lui faire part des Soeurs de St. Vincent de Paul, si dûres, qu'Alfred n'avait pas été instruit, ni à lire, ni à écrire, qu'il était battu. Mais lorsque Père Paul me dit cela je sentis un soulagement, une caresse sur la joue, un petit courant d'air. Moi aussi j'en ai voulu au monde. Espoir.

Puis une semaine à Damas, à trouver des livres, lire des récits de l'époque 1860, parler avec le Directeur du Monastère où je logeais qui me parle de Abd del Qadir—émir Algérien, homme extraordinaire, un Sufi, exilé par les Français (qui, bien plus tard, après éclaircissement, lui donnerait la Légion d'Honneur) qui éventuellement quitte l'Algérie pour vivre à Damas et au moment des massacres sauve des centaines (et héberge) de Chrétiens.

Bon. Je lis, je lis, et, petit à petit, les morceaux d'une mosaïque se joignent. La dizaine d'années entre 1860 et 1870 en Syrie est tourmentée, terrible. Je vois Alfredus Vincentus— l'enfant—né à Damas en 1860, sa mère accouchant en cette époque si difficile, son enfant est mis au monde parmi violence. Néanmoins, il vit. Elle l'aime. Il est entouré. Il a quatre ans où son petit corps est soutenu, habillé, enveloppé. Puis le rideau se déchire. A nouveau, massacres. Pourquoi ses parents n'ont pas écouté les premiers conseils des autorités locales, de quitter la ville, qu'il était dangereux de rester à Damas. Cette fois-ci ils n'échappent pas au désastre, la famille est massacrée. Mais pas lui—le Destin le béni; la vie lui est donné. Je le vois sauvé, un parmi mille autres enfants, réfugiés dans les collines dans un camp organisé par l'armée Française, et Ab del Qadir. Enfin, après deux années, on l'emmène à Alexandrie, probablement faisant partie d'un convoi d'enfants.

Le Directeur du Monastère St. Vincent de Paul à Damas m'explique que oui il y avait des Soeurs de Charité à Alexandrie (seulement depuis 1845), à côté du Monastère des Pères Blancs. Donc voilà pourquoi il aurait été baptisé par eux, c'était la coutume, l'organisation des Pères Blancs, leur responsabilité. La première fois lorsque je lui parle de la dûreté des soeurs, du manque d'instruction, il me regarde avec reproche, "Non. Cela n'est pas possible. Mensonge." Les deux jours suivants je vois un autre côté de l'enfant trouvé—traumatisé, difficile, de mauvaise volonté, silencieux. "La vie était très dûre pour les Soeurs," me dit le Directeur la deuxième fois que je le vois, "surement elles employaient les enfants à les aider," il parle plus doucement, je vois qu'il a beaucoup réfléchi mais qu'il ne veut pas trahir son ordre religieux, sujet délicat. "Il est important de regarder ces choses à travers les yeux de l'époque, et non avec les yeux d'une centaine d'années plus tard. Mais il est vrai que les temps étaient dûrs, que la discipline était de battre, cela était accepté—" il sourit, "et jusqu'à il n'y a pas si longtemps..." Il rajoute, "Oui. Il est possible qu'un enfant n'aurait pas été instruit, surtout s'il était d'un comportement peiné et difficile a comprendre."

J'ai hâte de te faire parvenir mes impressions, Yves. Tout ceci mes pensées dans l'ordre qu'elles viennent, dans mon Français des îles. Il me faudra beaucoup de temps pour tout digérer, intégrer, mesurer, et bien écrire.

J'ai quitté la France à l'age de quinze ans. Mon côté Anglais dorénavant est devenu mon monde, un monde où je me sentais plus sûre. Je n'ai plus employé la plume de ma langue paternelle. Ni lecture. Toute une vie en Anglais se passe. Petit à petit je sens en moi un creux.

Je m'égare.

Comme je t'ai dit au téléphone j'ai vu passer Guy, et toi, et Papa—Arnold—que de fois dans la rue, dans un magasin, dans le souk, dans une mosquée, dans le restaurant où je déjeunais à côté de l'Institut Français des Etudes Arabes (IFEAD). Pourtant je ne passe pas mon temps a les voir en France—Arlette aussi, même un côté de mon frère Glyn, et Miguel, et Dariane, Claudia, Fabien. Quelque chose dans la physiognomie, un comportement, un regard dans les yeux, la qualité des cheveux blancs chez les hommes après un certain age, une détermination et indépendance. Je ne sais pas. Mais il est sans aucun doute maintenant, dans mon esprit, que nous avons un héritage Syrien. Je me sens fière d'avoir une part de ce pays en moi, dans ma famille, je lui suis reconnaissante.

Bon. D'autres images. Un pays magnifique, une race un

peuple qui ne perd jamais son but, pourtant envahi de tous les côtés, presque impossible à le définir: Maronites, Kurds, Musulman, Catholiques, Grecs, Turcs, Bédouins, Arméniens. Je me suis rappelée de l'Alsace—où j'ai passé une partie majeure de mon enfance—ni Française ni Allemande; identité à elle: Alsacienne. Maintenant, en Syrie, ce régime Police-communiste, mais on sent partout un esprit vif, pas esclave, pas brisé—travailleur, cultivé—et quelle culture.

Typique de Syrie, me disent Père Paul, et Père Fernandez (Monastère), sont les origines mosaïques de ses habitants. Je décrit les mouvements de mon côté de la famille Vincent—vies en Angleterre, en Amérique de Sud, en Amérique du Nord, en Espagne; vies tout le temps en marche. "Typique Syrien," me dit Père Fernandez, doucement. Des chercheurs; ne peuvent jamais rester sur place. "Oui. Enfants sans pères," me dit Père Paul.

Une maison dans le souk. Rues étroites comme dans la Bible. En haut vers le ciel les maisons si proches qu'elles se touchent. Sombre. Petite porte insignifiante. Je me trouve dans une cour intérieure. Deux citronniers. Chant d'oiseau. Le murmure d'un fil d'eau. Balcon. Si calme, tranquille, frais. J'imagine ceci serait la forme de la maison de notre ancienne famille.

Père Fernandez me parle du caractère des enfants orphelins. "Insécurité; manque d'identité; aventuriers; différents: quoique l'éducation, quoiqu'ils reçoivent—ils ne finissent jamais comme les autres."

Le monde dans lequel Alfred est né—je lis que l'ancienne organisation du Liban étant détruite par les Turcs. Le pays se trouve sans chefs, sans autorités, et la population jusque là très unie fût profondément divisée par les passions politiques... ce qui mène aux douloureux évènements de 1860... Tout ceci fait partie de l'atmosphère, sera une partie de lui. En Mai 1860, soixante villages aux alentours de Beyrouth réduits à l'état de

*ruines. Juillet 1860, population de Damas 130 à 150,000
dont 18 à 20,000 chrétiens. Quartier chrétien: rien ne
manquait à cette petite ville dans la grande ville: églises,
couvents, vastes habitations, belles fontaines. En trois jours,
trois cent maisons en ruines, trois couvents détruits, onze églises
brûlées; 10,000 chrétiens assassinés.*

*Je t'envoie les passages suivants—des livres trouvés à
l'IFEAD –*

*Dans Le Voyage de Monsieur d'Aramon c'est la "Lettre
adressée à François 1er par Sultan Suleyman" qui m'intéresse—
le langage fleuri, décoré, emporté—qui me met dans cette
atmosphère Arabe, de culte et de rite—qui doit si influencer
autour de soi lorsqu'on y vit—*

*Abd el-Kader (son nom est écrit de toutes sortes de façon dans
les textes), 'Lettre aux Francais' pour sa vision et compréhension
de la nature humaine, sa poésie et générosité. Qui sait, aurait
notre enfant trouvé été touché par cet homme mystique; bien
plus tard aurait-ce pu l'influencer (inconsciemment—) de se
décider à vivre en Algérie?*

*Puis, 'Le Liban et L'Expédition Française' du Général
Ducrot qui décrit lucidement mais avec du coeur les
évènements, le déroulement.*

*Et maintenant dans un livre Anglais je viens de trouver
référence au seul récit d'une personne sur place en Juillet
1860—mais la traduction est en Anglais. J'ai commandé le
livre et pense le recevoir d'ici quinze jours.*

*Après ces jours de recherche et lecture, sur place, après la
visite du pays, et de la vieille ville de Damas, de la montagne et
des collines derrière la ville où les camps des refugiés auraient
put être—la présence de mon arrière grand-père a pris forme de
plus en plus. Je me suis sentie accompagnée et soutenue, et une*

portion du creux se remplit.

Mais pour toi cela doit être différent, je ne sais pas si c'est utile ou rassurant ou éclairant.

Tout ceci est un peu confus—je vais mettre beaucoup de temps a pouvoir y mettre de l'ordre, et un livre—!

Je t'appellerais dans quelques semaines—te donner le temps de lire et réfléchir—j'aimerais beaucoup savoir tes pensées et impressions.

Je t'envoie toute mon affection et admiration à Celine.

x Loïse

The act of writing the letter in French (by hand) was itself a revelation. Somehow the gesture involving hand, pen and page brought me to a sense of place and root. The whole event connected me to my paternal origins, bringing the lost child back to itself. *La femme propose, l'homme dispose*, Tata Leïla would say. Once again, it was Julius as Hermes with his winged golden sandals who made an idea and a fantasy real. He arranged for himself a business trip to the Middle East and would 'drop me off on the way' as he put it. My husband was at my side and I was safe. I was privileged, and learning.

The nightingale sang all night long.

Endings

Late August. My father drove me around in his beaten Chevrolet, parking sedately. Gone were the days of bumping up on the pavement, abandoning the Bugatti in a swoopy dancing movement, the tap-dancing footsteps, the whistling of a jazzy tune. We walked together through the streets of Paris—his Paris, his streets—speaking of nothing much, and nothing about Rose. Not once did he mention his granddaughter. Not once did I find a way of entering his silence.

Cara was outraged.

"You must find a way," she said. "Call your father. Speak to him about Rose. For the sake of your own soul, for the sake of your daughter, for the sake of womankind."

I said I was drained.

"Who cares about womankind, soul, daughter?" As I spoke like this my voice changed. I heard myself whisper, "Cara, I am angry. Angry." The whisper took me by surprise. I loved that whisper. A rush of energy, such an energy, joie de vivre, *my* joie de vivre.

"The hardest thing," Cara said, "is to let go of meaning. See *what is*. Be there. Hold it, suffer it." Cara would say. "We can't let go of what we don't feel. Without emotion, no transformation."

*

My father had a gift for friendship. He had charisma. He could squeeze fun out of a stone. He had a milieu of friendships, bonded by the experience of war. There was Dédé La Bicyclette, who opened a tiny cabaret restaurant on a cobbled uphill street in Pigalle. Dédé who, with the rest of the gang, rode around La Place des Lilas—the little square in the back of St Tropez—at midnight, in white boxer shorts, drunk as a sailor on leave. And Loulou La Terreur, who went from top boxer to top bounder, standing outside nightclubs with his arms crossed against his cupboard-size chest, then opening his own boite-de-nuit where the louche and the glamorous came for the hell-fun of it. Philippe—Fifi—the little guy, was also there—a cartoonist who trailed around the world with his pad and pencil, drawing himself and his friends for a strip in *The New York Herald Tribune*, because "c'est comme ça qu'on existe." Calling themselves *Le Club St. Trop*, the gang met every morning at the same table, at the same hour, at *Les Deux Magots* in St Germain—"L' heure pour chasser la honte du jour." Claude Terraille, (head of the oldest starred restaurant in Paris, *La Tour d'Argent*), was there too—and writers like Jimmy Jones and Norman Mailer (whom I had met before in my father's apartment in New York. He found me hiding in the bedroom, took the journal I was writing in, had a look, and said "Keep going kid").

There was a fascination in how Louis had a way with the man in the street, the woman behind the market stall, the maître d' of any restaurant—how they all made way for him, his savoir faire. This streak runs in the family—the apparent nonchalance, the deceptive ease, the one finger on the steering wheel. I recall Tata's repartie to the policeman about to write out a ticket, who then changed his mind and waved her on, big smile on his face.

But age creeps up from behind, even on the charming, even on Louis. Flames of anxiety flickered in his eyes when he came to visit me in the little cottage I'd moved to after my divorce. I realised how little I knew him, but slowly true conversation developed between us. We both asked questions of the kind we'd not asked before—about the past, about the present, about him then, and me now.

"Was I a bad father?" he asked, and looked like he was afraid, but really wanted to know. "My ears tell me things."

I couldn't reply to his question. There was too much to say. And I wondered if I would be brave enough to ask such a question? It was not until I began having therapy that I woke up to the fact of how much one's personality, one's fears and insecurities, like bad weather, could influence one's surroundings, even harm..

Looking back at my father, I nodded. And asked, "What things do your ears say?"

"My ears tell me to tell my children what I have done in my life."

"Will you?"

"Jamais," he said, pronouncing the word with a metallic strike.

We spoke more in French and he told me that I should write. "You are the writer, not your mother, not your husband."

The first time my father came to stay, I picked him up from the Eurostar in London. The drive out to the country took a little more than an hour and a half. I had acquired a new gadget for playing music, an iPod. I'd put together songs from all the years of my life into playlists. One, which I named *Daddy's Music*, was two hours long. He didn't know of this new gadget. On came Louis Armstrong—Satch, to my father—'It's A Beautiful World', pronounced 'woild'. The theme from *The Third Man*. Fats Waller. Juliette Greco. Piaf. Strumming of the zither, trumpet, saxophone, accordion, piano. Father and daughter humming. My father's voice was a little breathy, hoarse with age, edges frayed. Mine, girlish. Down London streets I drove, along the Cromwell Road, 'da da di, da daaah', onto the motorway, off the motorway, down the windy roads, down the long hill through Lambourn and up past the barrows and open rolling spaces of the Downs. Sighs of delight. Yves Montand singing 'Ma Gigolette'; 'La Bicyclette'; 'La Chansonnette'. Manhattan in the rain, 52nd Street, London, Paris, Cuba, South America.

"Aah, marvellous," he said, sighing. "C'est si bon."

We arrived in the village. I backed into my tiny driveway.

"Merci, ma Loulouette," my father said. "You don't know what that did for me."

Oh yes I do, I will remember forever. I remember now, writing these lines. You are here, we are together, remembering.

And then Le Vieux Mousquetaire, as he referred to himself, ended up where he swore he never would—in a nursing home in Paris. There were tears in his eyes when he said, "Everyone is so old, they have nothing to say."

"I'm ashamed," he said. "I have known the fears of war, flying aeroplanes, the jungle, mining, the racing track. A man's fear. This... this is something else—a coward's fear. I'm shit-scared. That's what I'm ashamed of."

He looked out of the window.

"Blue skies," I said.

"Shit sky."

"Why do you say the sky is shit when it's blue, Daddy?"

"Because I'm full of shit," he replied.

The room filled with his self-hatred, and the sadness. Later, I would love this moment, I would love my father, his honesty—the manner of his experience gave me a role model for when my turn came. At last I would honour my father. But not yet.

During the two years at the nursing home, Louis slowly made peace with himself. The first few times, the sight of him standing at the door, face near-skeletal, old and shrunken, waving goodbye and saying, "Come back soon," was heart-breaking. Cara pointed out that, unlike my mother, my father was living long enough to give us, his children, and him, time for reconciliation. My mother did not, and I continue to struggle with reconciling myself to her. Freud says it is easier to forgive the father.

When the nursing home called and told us daddy was in hospital, in a coma, they said they thought it was the end. I couldn't help but wonder if this was another yell for rescue, another drama. Once again, the family rallied round. I spent a night wide awake rehearsing my words, cold, angry. My turn came to stand at his bedside, and bid farewell.

"I'll never see you again," I said.

He lay back, eyes closed, breathing heavily, no signs that he was listening or could hear me. I waited to feel something, anything at all.

"It has been difficult having you as a father," I said. I

looked out of the window, asking for a sign, a thought. Nothing came out of the grey sky, the colour of ice.

"Why do you say ice?" I asked myself. "Because I am ice," I answered back.

Louis recovered and was returned to the nursing home. False alarm, once again. The family dispersed. Back home I thought about him every day. The hardness in me wouldn't budge. Three or four or five months passed, when at last my heart gave way. I had to go back to Paris.

We sat at a round table in the dining room of the nursing home, my half-sister Laïsha—his last born—with us. He was forgetting things—perhaps he was done with regret and self-hatred.

"Are you married, do you have children?" he asked.

"No, I'm not married, I'm divorced. I have two daughters," adding, slowing down, "One died seven years ago."

He looked away. Silence. Then, with authority, *"Ah, ça du être dûr pour la mère."*

It was enough. There it was. I felt it. Just as Père Paul said in Syria. Love.

We had a cup of tea with a slice of lemon, the way he and Tata always did, though she would let the lemon float gently on the top, while he crushed it to the bottom of his cup to get everything he could out of it. Both our hands were on the table. His right hand covered my left hand. My right hand covered his left hand. Swift as the dark spirit he was made of, his left hand slipped from under mine and landed with a slap on top.

"Daddy wins!" he said. English now, voice shaky but triumphant.

I walk down familiar streets, past Le Montana Hotel where my father and I stayed that time I was eleven on a visite éclair from Strasbourg. I had not seen him since I left New York when I was eight and wouldn't see him again until I returned to New York for my sixteenth birthday. Across the street, the jazz club down steep stairs where Juliette Gréco—before her nose was fixed—sang 'Je Suis Comme Je Suis'. I see it all. Lunch at *Le Boeuf sur le Toit*. Cocteau and Picasso walking by. Brigitte Bardot, so young, so graceful: 'Je me donne à qui me plait'. On the airwaves Eartha Kitt sings, 'Darling, je vous aime beaucoup'.

Away on retreat, looking out of the window, the windowsill is my shore. On the other side, waves of sounds pass: an aeroplane flying low; a motorcycle; a siren; the rustle of leaves. Centre stage, stands the little hawthorn tree, in the middle of the landscape, on a slope down to a small river. Grand old trees delineate their boundaries—a great willow, copper beech, an oak. But there, standing proud and messy, and all of itself, the hawthorn. Trees know when to stop growing, when they've reached their own unique line that defines them from the endless space of the universe around it. The oak has a crown, says Manley Hopkins. And this little hawthorn, a favourite of mine, does its own thing—no line, no crown and yet somehow defined. It could only be a hawthorn and nothing else. Suddenly I know. Something inside me says, 'See?' All this time I've not seen, or understood, my own shape. I look at it, and I look at it, and I love it.

Death is not the end of life. Only of the me. Rose has taught me this. I know what I know from experience. Maybe what

I mean is that instead of thinking my feelings and thoughts, I experience them. Isn't that what Virginia Woolf meant with her remark that 'we experience afterwards?' I read about Stephen Hawking and his change of mind towards matter entering a Black Hole—that the material does not *totally disintegrate*. He stunned the scientific world with his statement which came after some twenty years of thought and experiment. Now he considered that, yes, matter disintegrated in the Black Hole, but *the information remains*. To me, this means in death our shell disintegrates, but what we have made of life remains. We don't know where energy comes from, nor where it is going. The poets know this, purely from deep observation. Shakespeare says it, "What is done cannot be undone."

My cousin Jas called. Her mother, Tata, now eighty-six years old, was in hospital, an emergency operation. Two days later, we spoke. Tata Leïla's voice was heavy, thick, underground.

"Tata, I will come in the Spring. In April. I'll read you my book." As I spoke the words, I wondered how on earth I was going to accomplish that.

She sounded pleased. Her voice light again.

Autumn passed, winter passed. Leïla recovered from the operation. I continued to write my book, increasingly aware of the approaching month of April.

*

Mid-march, another call from Jas. "This time it's bad," she said. The diagnosis was cancer and it was terminal. A tumour in the brain. It was beginning to show in her face, Jas said. Two weeks later I arrived in Geneva. My book was nowhere finished, but I might get away with reading her a few extracts.

"Mais non, ma Poussinette. Tu commences, et tu termines. Je veux tout savoir. Vas-y. Je t'écoute."

During the three days of my visit, I would arrive at her apartment in time for a late lunch snack, and afterwards, Leïla retired to lie on her bed. As always, she was surrounded by a thousand and one cushions, twiddling a strand of hair, eyes semi-closed, head back on a pillow, listening as I read into the afternoon. I would return to my hotel two streets away, walk a little, arrive back at the apartment for supper, and afterwards, resume reading. Now and then I'd look up to see if my aunt was awake.

At times she seemed in another world.

"Keep going," she said, "Je suis là. J'aime."

I thought she had dozed off.

"Pas du tout. Continues."

She knew the story, of course. Even the times when she wasn't there. My aunt had been part of my life since the beginning of time. I was the first, as she put it—her brother's firstborn, her first niece (she was barely thirteen years old), her mother's first grandchild. I always knew that she was there. I could take it for granted, even when I was living with my uncle and aunt in Strasbourg. Maybe the same went for my father who felt present to me even when he was not. But not my mother, who even in person was absent.

The nature of Tata's mood changed. I asked if she was in

pain.

She replied, "No, not pain. Very uncomfortable."

I appreciated that the difference did not mean 'better'. It was things like this, such shared moments, that were the gifts of a mother to a daughter. I needed them so much and they would bring me comfort when my turn came to face the unknowable and the uncomfortable, and the passing on to my children.

Her voice belligerent now, she asked, "What took you so long. Why didn't you come before?"

"Tata—I'm here, and by the way, this is my fourth trip. I've been driving across France to Geneva from London to come and be with you." I stomped my foot on the ground. "Et puis, je t'aime et puis on fait ce qu'on peut."

"Ah, oui. C'est vrai." And she laughed, eyes going back to a dreaminess, returning to her cushions.

I asked her about her memories. She'd once said to me that she had no memories, none whatsoever before the age of nine. There were other gaps, long empty spaces of time in teenage years. In fact, life as she remembered it, began at puberty—soon after she married (aged sixteen or was it seventeen?) an officer in the Brazilian army. The olive skin was a strong attraction for her. She said it was 'l'étranger' that attracted her, so much older than her and who, in my view, so much resembled her father.

I recognised something of what she said, a blankness surrounding her like a moat—an emptiness not of mind, not of the artistic, not of the intellect, but that deeper void in the soul. I thought of my untold experience in Strasbourg, of the black hole that came at night, the terror of it when it threatened to break through into my daytime. I thought of my grandfather (her father), and his silence. A silence that echoed emptiness, a darkness that threatened to steal your soul.

I continued with the reading.

"You know, your mother *did* love you." I was getting to the end of the part about Thea dying, perhaps her spirit sending me a message at the florist's stand. Tata's words went straight into my unprepared heart.

More reading.

"You know, it is the daughter who must forgive the mother. C'est comme ça. Il faut lacher. Et attendre."

"Balayé—oublié… Avec mes souvenirs… j'allume le feu…" we sang, a little off-key, paraphrasing Edith Piaf.

Leïla closed her eyes, and quoted, "*L'acte d'observation est une tendresse.*"

Tata would surprise me with favourite quotes from the great French writers of the seventeenth century. She loved Madame de Sévigné who, without formal philosophical instruction, wrote the most beautiful and brilliant epistles to her daughter, and friends. There was, in my aunt, the frustration of an undeveloped intellect, unrealised potential. I recognised and appreciated this all the more, given that I found in myself the excitement of putting my mind to work—I didn't know I had a mind---training to become a Jungian analyst. Having neither credentials nor degrees to my name, the odds were against me succeeding in such an endeavour. Each time I wanted to give up, though, I would remind myself that I'd walked across France, all the way, on my own two feet. It would turn into an education of the heart and the discovery of faith without a name.

Christmas

A big table laid up for twenty-two of us. We were at Jas's sister's house, Aysha. She has her mother's easy, lion grace and welcomed us all. Three generations in attendance—grandparents, children, grandchildren, nieces and nephews. Tata wore a gold cracker paper hat in the shape of a crown, which she would push down trying to cover the horrible swollen red thing that pulled her face in all directions.

"Je veux me cacher," she said. We told her we loved her as she was.

"Vous êtes sûrs?" she asked, with a smile both vulnerable and doubting.

Afterwards, I drove home to London, my fifth back-and-forth trip of that year. No more aeroplanes. The sensation of terror when up there in the air—triggered by even the slightest turbulence—cost me more than I had the resources for.

Leïla died two weeks later. I drove back across France one more time, thankful for being on the road, focusing on it like a mantra: time behind, time ahead, my body at one with the car. I daydreamed of a beach in Brazil, with meringue and batucada music, and red-lizard high heel shoes dancing off the clock. What is time to he who sits under the tree? What's left to believe in? Who will I speak to in two, three, four languages? Who will understand me when I mix them all up into a language of its own? Who will recognise what's happening to my face and know what is going on inside? Who remembers me when I was born? When I was one, two, three, four, five, six, seven and fourteen, fifteen, sixteen, eighteen (when my best friend Christine killed herself by not pulling the string of her parachute)? Then nineteen, twenty, twenty-one, twenty-two, when she came for my marriage to Bobby, sending a telegram: J'ARRIVE. All the way to seventy-two when she is gone and my liver is sick.

After the funeral, back in London, feeling strange, I took myself to the doctor who told me I was very ill, and should go home and rest. A blood test revealed my liver count had gone from 4.5 to 142, whatever that means.

"An evil virus has got to your liver," the doctor said. For weeks I didn't eat, didn't drink, didn't think, and I lost seven kilos. I took to lying on the floor, the only place I could feel that flesh and bone would hold me together. I lay supine, looking up at the skeleton of my flat—the rafters and beams in my sitting room on the top floor of an old building, an attic space—staring at nothing. That's when it happened. Scenes of my life, all of them like a pack of cards, fanned out through the air. The pictures had no meaning—I understood this—except for three of them. They stood out like three paintings, each spreading out in space, complete—there and then gone. It was like a dream, as soon as I focused, trying to remember, all faded even more. It was one of those visionary moments that remind one to keep going. The memory of such experience continues to teach me what matters, what to let go of.

*

An artist friend came to visit during this time. I told her about my drives across France, the disfigurement of my aunt's beautiful Syrian face, her dignity and difficulty and witchery, her way of not hiding her body, once so beautiful, but now so large and cumbersome. I spoke of the torment inside me while sitting there for hours, every day, reading my book to her; and how, as we talked, I looked upon her near-unrecognisable features—the weeping eye, the swollen cheek, the ugly redness of the tumour that looked like it would burst at any moment.

Consuelo, my friend, listening to all this, said, "So now you've seen your mother, now you have mourned her on all those drives across France, now you can say goodbye."

I didn't understand. I broke down after she'd gone as it became clear to me what she was saying. It was almost twenty years since my mother had died and all the lights in the house went out. She'd always hidden her face, never shared her pain the way Tata did. Thea died aged sixty-eight. Tata eighty-six.

Ah, Tata. My Tata. Leïla—I never called her by her name until she was old and the difference of age between us, for so long unnoticeable, became a grand canyon. Tata, my father's younger sister. My Tata, pour toujours. Tata in Mallorca, Tata in Greece—in Patmos with the patterned stone beach, or Paxos, or Mykonos, where we slept on the roof. Tata, ideal aunt, not so ideal mother, travelling with cases of Coca Cola, cartons of cigarettes, her cushions and blankets, bottles of bubble bath, straw hats, flippers in all sizes for her four children, and her six nephews and nieces, and even once her little MG sports car. And not to forget the two domestiques—one for cooking and cleaning, one for carrying and protecting. Tata on holiday was tribal. Direct family and closest friends only—Russian, Brazilian, French, Middle-Eastern, Italian—a duke or two. The sounds and rhythms of a macaronic conversation.

"A quoi ça sert plus de temps for pain?" she keeps saying. "Basta. Light me a cigarette. Et un Coca avec ice and lemon, ma chérie."

The nurse says, "Madame, on ne fume pas ici."

"Ah, oui," Leïla says, stubbing out her cigarette. Then, "Vous m'apportez un Coca s'il vous plait, mademoiselle," with a vague look on her face and dismissive gesture of the hands lights a cigarette.

Tata is enormous as a Buddha, legs crossed in her own version of the Lotus position—a kind of figure of eight— one knee up, elegant foot firmly on seat of chair, other leg across, foot drawing circles one way, then the other. Tata is fat and ugly and cross, while her manner of speech is royal.

"Et puis je suis trop vieille," she acknowledges. "J'en ai assez."

Jung

Sometime in the late nineties, when I was in my fifties, I made a third attempt at applying for the training to be a Jungian analyst. My first two approaches were declined, though the second time it was suggested it might be possible if I obtained a degree which could be in almost anything, enough to show I was capable of concentrating, studying, and applying the necessary discipline. The odds were against me—I had no degree and my family and my marriage were in distress. But I had tenacity and that was in my favour. My interviewer asked if I had other interests. I told him that writing, and the arts, were vital to me. It would turn out that this, too, was in my favour.

"Psychology isn't everything," he added. In his view, analysts had a tendency to lose themselves in their practice, and in the psyche of others, resulting in exhaustion and a kind of one-track mindedness. The healing process of both analyst and patient suffered. If I could write a four-page paper on my history, family background and working life, and my paper were approved, I would be given what he called an 'equivalency degree' and accepted for the training. And so it happened.

The following September, my work began. I was invited to attend a three-day workshop on the *Word Association Experiment* which, as devised by C. G. Jung in 1907, was to reveal who, or what, was really doing the driving in our lives. On the first day, we were given theory and details on how to work the 'experiment' and what to watch out for. We'd been asked to bring a large sheet of graph paper on which to mark the results, along with a stopwatch, drawing paper, coloured pencils. On the second day, we had to find a partner and take it in turn to read out our list of 100 words and write down the number of seconds we'd taken to respond—along with changes of expression, tone of voice, and so on. We were to do this twice. Each time took an hour and a half.

Finally, on the third day, our seminar leader said, "Okay, now you write a fairy tale using at least thirty of your skyscraper words," that is, the complex indicator words. The number of seconds it took for the response to a word was counted on the graph paper and each little square filled in accordingly. In this way, the page ended up with a Manhattan-like skyline of towers. We were to start with four drawings, and our tale was to begin with the words 'Once upon a time'. There was to be a heroine and a hero and an introduction with a statement of the problem, the ups and downs, and an ending with a climax (or, in analytical language, a lysis). The tale was not to exceed three pages.

The years passed. I forgot about the fairy tale, though I often wondered about my top skyscraper word—a verb, so simple: *Sing*. My practice evolved in both languages, French and English and, you could say, brought together the space between the two very different selves that dwelled in each language. The French language is more direct than English, and I am more direct when I am in the French context. The English language meanders and is elastic, with more than double the vocabulary. In English, I am more quiet (until I was forty-ish I didn't like to speak), more introverted, indirect, complicated. And I was not molested in French, an analyst remarked.

One day the urge to write returned. I wrote fables, short stories, bits of this and that, playing with words, and began what would turn into the book you are reading. My editor asked if I had anything short. I went through notes, forgotten journals, unfinished stories and something I didn't recognise—a fairy tale. I read it out loud to myself, filled with goosefleshy delight. The secret alchemy of literature was happening. An architecture of image and sound stood in the silence of a sentence. Sing,' my top skyscraper complex word said. And I did. Fairy tale turned into fable. Heartbreak and the love of life together. Amor Fati.

Mektoub.

The nightingale sang all night long

No Name
To Be A Witch Is Not A Willed Thing

Once upon a time, on the seafloor of an afternoon when the rivers ran wild and the oceans were full of fish, in a time between cities and countries, there lived a King and a Queen in a castle high up on a hill. They had one child, a girl, who was six years old. Life was good, or so they said. So long as the witch down the road let it be. But the truth is, such all-too-easy times were getting on the witch's nerves. She was more than restless. She'd lost her broom and this left her hard on the ground.

"Why, when things go on pretending to be happy for too long, it just isn't good," the witch mumbled, passing by the twelve toads meditating on her doorstep. She brushed off a tidy pile of dead flies with the tip of her red lizard-skin shoe and clapping her hands at the skies, the clouds replied with a burst of heavy rain. The clouds lowered themselves, lower and lower, until their woolly and ghostly forms solidified and, reaching the ground, turned into an army of men in suits of steel, with helmets of shiny black plastic and dark glasses made of mirrors. The army trooped across the mountains and across the plains, crushing in their path weeds and roses, all.

And there was war.

"That's better," the witch said to her denizens. "Now King and Queen will wail and weep and have a breakdown and things will change." Why, K & Q, always so terribly busy and

hurried, hadn't taken the time to give their daughter a name. Soon, as they'd felt the ground tremble under their velvet slippers announcing thundering armies, they had taken off in the royal ship and disappeared over the horizon quicker than smoke forgetting, in their rude hurry, their unnamed child.

A sickly atmosphere, manifesting in a mustardy yellow, wafted throughout the castle, making its ancient walls ooze and sweat. She without name, barely able to breathe in the poisoned air, gathered necessities and left the castle. There were no thoughts in her head. No need for thought when you have limbs that know what to do and where to go. She had a lamp—magic because it provided its own light when touched in a certain manner—and a book. The lamp cast a glow, encircling her in a gentle, pale moonlight warmth. The book, made of pictures and letters—some of which gathered themselves into the making of a word or two, depending on how you looked at them— informed her of many things. Things people couldn't or wouldn't speak of.

In the woods, where she was heading, there lived, and had lived for a very long time in fairy tale time, give or take a century, a young-ish bear. His name was Mishka. When he saw No Name trotting along inside a circle of a mysterious pale light, he followed. After a while, as day slipped away in its usual invisible way, and night took its place, No Name put her book down, rested her small head, empty of words, but full of everything else, and soon fell into good sleep—something she did well, trusting the falling. The secret is to let go, drop down to where there is no bottom, to where you just float on the ocean of sweet sculpted air.

Mishka the bear, really a prince from centuries past, had been cast into a spell by the eternally restless, witchy flux of his own nature. It was in this moment out of time that he understood two things. One, that there is no justice in the forest. Two, that Chance happens. He was being brought, if not sent, a friend. A she-friend no less, who might even help turn him back into the human being he once almost was but for his rather rough, if not to say unevolved, uncivilised, manner. Although he had no idea how such transformation might take place, he thought he might start by taking she who was nameless back to his den. And wait. And see. None of this was to do with kindness, it was just that the bear sensed there was something in it for him which he badly needed, even if he didn't know what that was, yet. He did give thought to how he might turn into the Prince he was truly meant to be. And even that it was up to him to reach through a misty memory, past the bitter root of existence, to some curse being laid down upon him—or inherited from his animal ancestry—so very long ago.

In this way, the bear knew his bewitched animal side could be set free, no doubt at some cost to his pride which, if willingly broken down, might then allow him to emerge into personhood. By instinct, he also knew that the curse would lift only if a child without name sang him a song true to the sorrows of bone and flesh. This was conditional, as most of life is, on the child singing from the heart in the way of the small bird, the wren, its tiny chest quivering with a lion-hearted songsound.

What Mishka did not know is that the little girl, in her fright, had left her voice behind, somewhere up in the castle on the hill, along with sensations yet to sound themselves into language.

Time, in such spaces as cities and countries, has a way of flying past and, before you know it, you are a hundred and one years old, and it's too late to wake up. But this child without name did wake up, if some years later, when the war that changed everything was over (just for now). Things were trying to grow again. The king and queen had returned, old and tired and sad, their hearts arid without a child to whom they might bequeath the sweet and sour of their kingdom come. Why, they'd even lost their capital letters to lower case. The stars they had once been in the firmament of No Name's sky had lost their shine, as stars do when night gives way to the truth of a day without love and care.

As night and day passed through the forest, trees listening and bending respectfully to the winds of change, there came to be, against the odds, a single young rose. Though growing in the deep shade of her forest-home made her a little leggy, the effort of it taught the rose how to stretch beyond her reach for those brief (so precious), slanted moments of sun rays.

No Name was turning into a lovely young woman and, though still not yet named, she was about to be the bride of the bear she had taken shelter with—or perhaps had been abducted by—she could never quite know, nor, of course, say.

But time spent with Mishka the bear, listening to his thoughts and wishes and the way he shared his (many) views on life, made her fond of him, and curious about the world he spoke of. While thoughts of her own, of the heart-centred kind, were rising in her, she could feel their different shapes and sizes jostling for space.

And so there was this nagging problem of finding the precious words that held the key to the closed heart of the woman-child without name. The much-needed words were fast asleep inside the book under the lamp, still not ready to slip off the pages and up into her sky-mind, like little fishes coming up for air. It was as if the words knew that the descent to the underworld is not so rare. The wisdom is that it may even be a necessity. The true struggle lies in the retracing of steps, the climb back to the upper air; there the labour lies.

Animals being more patient than men, Mishka as bear was quite content to remain a bear, gathering honey, rolling up the lazy bones inside his fur coat, remaining in the embrace of the cave during the long cold winters. On the other hand, the princely self within him was less contented and, if truth be known, the silence of the very slow-to-open rosebud was getting on his nerves. The witch was needed to stir things up again. After all, Mishka the bear did rather enjoy a good conversation and was lonely without it, more and more fantasizing about the rose-girl's name, wanting to ask 'Come here'. But, 'come here' who?

The much needed words tucked inside the book, detached from whatever they might once have belonged to, were words that appeared to be positioned on top of towers, all drawn in different heights. The first letter of each word stood up high, such as Voice, and Love. And then in a sort of cluster, a city skyline with words Fish, Bird, Forest, Bear. A few pages later, all by itself, sitting on the top of the highest tower of all, in a scribble, almost invisible, as if to remain silent—the word Sing.

Now the witch, when at home, suffering ennui, and more than a little morose for being a witch without a broom, sat on her chair made of bone and gristle and seashells and bendy willow branches—these last brought in by Mishka who was learning to befriend the forest witcheryness. She wore a long robe made of thick linen the colour of moody sky with scudding clouds, on the left breast was embroidered a large red strawberry with a tuft of green at the top. At her feet sat a grey cat, twitching its striped black and white tail, and beside the cat there lay one large, not quite smiling fish, gasping for air. Oh, it prayed, for just one drop of its mother ocean.

You may not know that to be a witch is not a willed thing.

When it happens to you, it hurts, a lot. Pain travels through people for centuries and nobody listens to what it says to them until the witch, her nature exhausted, lets go and weeps. Pain is her proof of life.

One full tear, the size of a pebble, rolled down the witch's hollow cheeks. The fish swallowed this one saline drop of life, shaped as the letter O, with true gratitude. "One more, please," asked the fish. It was then that out of its O–shaped mouth, rolled a ring, rolling all the way to the bear's den. And there, inscribed in the ring, was a name.

Mishka could propose.

In parenthesis: How was it that in this unexpected, still-as-night moment, the witch's broom had materialised? What could this have to do with love, she wondered, deciding to treasure the thought to herself.

When the young rose of a girl heard the sound of her existence—a name!—her heart broke open into a thousand and one pieces.

It was like the sea, a big wave rising and spilling out of her eyes, typhooning, whirlpooling, the wheeling the tumble the up-the-staircase roaring through her eerie shells.

The time had come.
Sing!

With each song note the bear raised himself up and then, in the stillness of that moment, animal skin and rawhide and coarseness of fur slipped away, revealing the splendour of him, and of his soul.

Half entailed
She rolls out
Of the wave of his thought
and then the curl, her hair
is foam, is wave, the crest, the spume
a wave, she is the wave
and like a mermaid she rides
the waves the swirl
and up the seashell's spiral stair
she lifts, she rises
whirlpool typhooning
across the sea
to land
a mermaid tossed onto the sand
as if a rose in his hand.

"Oh, Mishka," she said.

Endnotes

My book's story begins this way: it was when meeting an older woman publishing her first novel. The media seemed very excited that a 70 year old woman could write about life, sex, death in such a direct way. It was 1983. Her name was Mary Wesley and her book title was *Jumping The Queue*.

Mary lived in Totnes, Devon and had nowhere to stay for the launch of her book. I was separated (for the first time), in my forties, living with my daughters in Fulham. I invited her to stay. Kitchen and sitting room were open plan. On the first morning, I watched as she floated down the stairs. The scent of pineapple and strawberries filled the air as she descended in her pearl grey satin dressing gown. A cartoon balloon popped up in my mind. It said, "That's when you're going to write your book. In your 70s." I waved the balloon-thought away. I had by then ventured into the writing world and published an article in *Harpers Bazaar*, a short story in *The Literary Review* and was working on my story cookbook for Chatto&Windus. I considered myself to be well on the path of being a writer. But soon after I remarried my husband I embarked on the training as a Jungian Analyst and for this I had to put down my pen. It was not until almost thirty years later, divorced and living alone, that my writing spirit returned. I began to write my book in my late sixties and on into my seventies. Now to be published in a few months in my eighty first year.

Acknowledgements

To my (ex) husband for being there at the best and worst of times, together and apart; and to my daughter, beloved first born.

Analysts — it wasn't one but six Jungian analysts that I worked with over a period of more than twenty years, once or twice a week (including the five and a half training years. Appreciation and affection goes to all of them, as to my patients. Together, we learned about healing.

To Jan and Rowan Fortune at Leaf by Leaf, imprint of the publishers Cinnamon Press, for their endless patience and support and unprejudiced welcome, grateful thanks.

Thanks beyond words to Peter Watson, veteran journalist and author, for his reading of my manuscript in its growing up stage of life. He gave me his time, several pages of constructive editorial straight shooting. I treasure those pages.

Also to Consuelo Child-Villiers for the gift of the cover of Life&Fable. And photographer Ekaterina Kuzminova for the beautiful quality of her work.

Immense gratitude to Louise Doughty, novelist and screenwriter, Noonie Zand Goodarzi, journalist and author, Rose Billington at The Literary Consultancy, and Gillian Slovo whose group I participated in through Faber Academy.

Then there is C G Jung whose image and undying spirit appeared to me in dreams, whose thoughts and writings give me the ground I stand on; a life.